THE
Information
Establishment

Our Government and the Media

by
CHARLES S. STEINBERG

COMMUNICATION ARTS BOOKS

HASTINGS HOUSE, PUBLISHERS
New York 10016

Library of Congress Cataloging in Publication Data

Steinberg, Charles Side, 1913–1978
    The information establishment.

    (Communication arts books)
    Bibliography: p.
    Includes index.
    1. Government information—United States.   2. Press
law—United States.   3. Freedom of information—United
States.   I. Title.
KF5753.S75   342'.73'085   79-16275
ISBN 0-8038-3424-1
ISBN 0-8038-3426-8 pbk.

Published simultaneously in Canada by
Saunders of Toronto, Ltd., Don Mills, Ontario
Designed by Al Lichtenberg
Printed in the United States of America

Contents

Preface

A free press can of course be good or bad, but most certainly without freedom it can never be anything but bad.

—Albert Camus

THIS BOOK DEALS with the structure and function of a free press in three related and interlocking areas: the government informational bureaucracy, the liaison between the mass media and the vast federal information apparatus, and the responsibilities and obligations of both the government and the media to each other and to the people.

This is a time of enormous absorption in, and criticism of, the ever-proliferating phenomenon of information processing (news, public relations, advertising, information storage and retrieval). Mass communications media—newspapers, news magazines, radio and television—have made information available to the public with a speed and pervasiveness that could not have been anticipated by those who wrote the First Amendment. Yet, then as now, the fundamental philosophical issues are identical. They concern the integrity of government, the freedom of the press and the right of the public to know.

Now, however, there is a difference. Modern technology is

highly sophisticated and complex. The government information and communication effort is large, complicated and duplicatory. It is also highly competitive. And the mass media have assumed an overriding significance as conduits of news and as surrogates of the public. Above all, there have arisen new and complex issues of free press and fair trial, shield laws, problems relating to privacy and to freedom of information and "gag" rules against the press. The performance of both the media and the government has come into critical evaluation.

These issues are examined (along with a description of the informational apparatus of the White House, the Congress, the Supreme Court and the various federal branches and agencies) against the curiously adversarial and yet symbiotic relationship between the government and the mass media.

The author is indebted to many sources, both in the government and in the media. In particular, the public affairs offices of the following branches, departments and agencies were helpful and cooperative in supplying various materials: The White House Press Office; the Supreme Court of the United States; the Departments of State, Treasury, Defense, Justice, Health, Education and Welfare, Commerce, Agriculture and Labor; the Environmental Protection Agency; National Science Foundation; Federal Communications Commission. Acknowledgment is also due to Benjamin West, Superintendent, Press Gallery, House of Representatives; Mike Michaelson, Superintendent, Radio-Television Gallery, House of Representatives; Max M. Barber, Superintendent, Radio and Television Gallery, U.S. Senate; Ned Schnurman, Associate Director, National News Council; Robert Johnson, the Associated Press; Fred Ferguson, United Press International.

The offices of the following members of the Congress graciously supplied press releases and other materials: Senators Birch Bayh (D. Ind.), Clifford Case (R. N.J.), Frank Church (R. Idaho), Mike Gravel (D. Alaska), Jacob K. Javits (R. N.Y.), Warren G. Magnuson (D. Wash.), Edmund S. Muskie (D. Maine), Charles S. Percy (R. Ill.), Abraham Ribicoff (D. Conn.), Walter L. Scott (R. Va.) and Rep. Lionel Van Deerlin (D. Cal. and Chairman of the House Sub-Committee on Communications). The author found the Congressional

Directory and, particularly, the *U.S. Government Manual* valuable for source material on the Congress, the Galleries and the various agencies.

A special note of acknowledgment is due to Ms. Roberta Hadley of the CBS News Reference Library for her cooperation in obtaining many documents essential to the manuscript.

Finally, a note of gratitude to my wife, Hortense R. Steinberg, for her invaluable assistance and support in the preparation and completion of the book.

CHARLES S. STEINBERG

New York, 1978

THE GOVERNMENT OF THE UNITED STATES

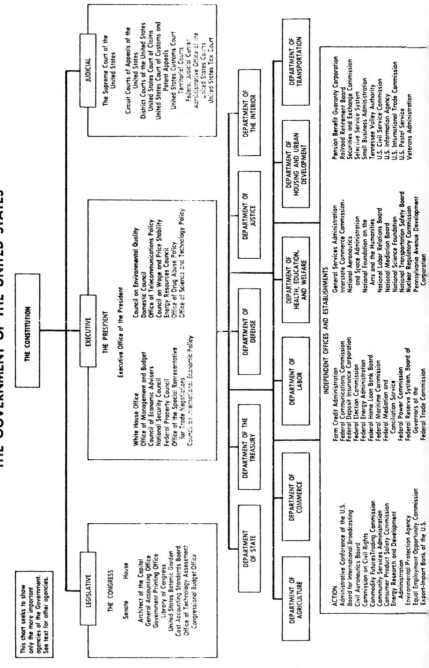

This chart seeks to show only the more important agencies of the Government. See text for other agencies.

THE CONSTITUTION

LEGISLATIVE

THE CONGRESS

Senate   House

Architect of the Capitol
General Accounting Office
Government Printing Office
Library of Congress
United States Botanic Garden
Cost Accounting Standards Board
Office of Technology Assessment
Congressional Budget Office

EXECUTIVE

THE PRESIDENT

Executive Office of the President

White House Office
Office of Management and Budget
Council of Economic Advisers
National Security Council
Federal Property Council
Office of the Special Representative for Trade Negotiations
Council on International Economic Policy

Council on Environmental Quality
Domestic Council
Office of Telecommunications Policy
Council on Wage and Price Stability
Energy Resources Council
Office of Drug Abuse Policy
Office of Science and Technology Policy

JUDICIAL

The Supreme Court of the United States

Circuit Courts of Appeals of the United States
District Courts of the United States
United States Court of Claims
United States Court of Customs and Patent Appeals
United States Customs Court
Territorial Courts
Federal Judicial Center
Administrative Office of the United States Courts
United States Tax Court

DEPARTMENT OF AGRICULTURE

DEPARTMENT OF COMMERCE

DEPARTMENT OF STATE

DEPARTMENT OF THE TREASURY

DEPARTMENT OF LABOR

DEPARTMENT OF DEFENSE

DEPARTMENT OF HEALTH, EDUCATION, AND WELFARE

DEPARTMENT OF JUSTICE

DEPARTMENT OF HOUSING AND URBAN DEVELOPMENT

DEPARTMENT OF THE INTERIOR

DEPARTMENT OF TRANSPORTATION

INDEPENDENT OFFICES AND ESTABLISHMENTS

ACTION
Administrative Conference of the U.S.
Board for International Broadcasting
Civil Aeronautics Board
Commission on Civil Rights
Commodity Futures Trading Commission
Community Services Administration
Consumer Product Safety Commission
Energy Research and Development Administration
Environmental Protection Agency
Equal Employment Opportunity Commission
Export-Import Bank of the U.S.

Farm Credit Administration
Federal Communications Commission
Federal Deposit Insurance Corporation
Federal Election Commission
Federal Energy Administration
Federal Home Loan Bank Board
Federal Maritime Commission
Federal Mediation and Conciliation Service
Federal Power Commission
Federal Reserve System, Board of Governors of the
Federal Trade Commission

General Services Administration
Interstate Commerce Commission
National Aeronautics and Space Administration
National Foundation on the Arts and the Humanities
National Labor Relations Board
National Mediation Board
National Science Foundation
National Transportation Safety Board
Nuclear Regulatory Commission
Pennsylvania Avenue Development Corporation

Pension Benefit Guaranty Corporation
Railroad Retirement Board
Securities and Exchange Commission
Selective Service System
Small Business Administration
Tennessee Valley Authority
U.S. Civil Service Commission
U.S. Information Agency
U.S. International Trade Commission
U.S. Postal Service
Veterans Administration

1

Freedom of Communication: An Historical Overview

SIX HUNDRED YEARS AGO, a talented individual by the name of Johannes Gutenberg began experimenting with an unusual device which was to become the printing press. The result of his labors was the Gutenberg *Bible,* considered to be the first book printed by means of movable type. Thus was the technology of printing by machine introduced to a society which was ready for an explosion of knowledge and scientific experimentation and achievement. The printing press, as is well known, created a new kind of society—literate, questioning, ultimately demanding of the advantages of democratic participation in the process of government. For the first time, information could be available to the masses, even though the majority were not as yet prepared for democratic government.

In the seventeenth and eighteenth centuries, a new and exciting political philosophy was expounded, largely by John Locke. This new politics called for government by consent of those who were governed. It emphasized both the expansion of freedom and the protection of property rights and, however implicitly and indirectly, maintained that the press was to function in a libertarian manner, free to write and publish without restraint. Unfortunately, no responsible safeguards were introduced other than a "self-righting" process, whereby the

I

falsehoods and errors would be corrected in a natural way, without any political intervention. The significant fact, however, was that a spirit of freedom pervaded society, despite some unfortunate limitations. Democracy was becoming a powerful concept.

A century ago, the world witnessed a most profound and far-reaching phenomenon, a series of developments that effected cataclysmic changes in the political, economic, cultural and social life of this nation. The Industrial Revolution of the nineteenth century has been compared to the transformations wrought by the earlier invention of the printing press. Many of the changes resulting from the harnessing of steam for the purpose of generating the power of the machine were considered economically sound and socially progressive. Many were not, particularly the evils attendant on the inevitable urbanization of society, the schism between capital and labor, the rise of the wealthy "robber barons," the disappearance of the once proud artisan and individual entrepreneur. What was evolving was the presence of a new, mass society.

The technological developments were both astonishing from a scientific aspect and far-reaching in their social impact and significance. The telephone was created and became an utterly indispensable instrument of communication. Who could—or would—do without it? The typewriter changed the function of journalism. The wireless and transatlantic cable provided speedy and miraculous transmission of messages between points that were once separated by days and even months. The Industrial Revolution created changes that were momentous.

The Communications Revolution

The technical revolution of the last 100 years or so has been eclipsed by the fruits it bore in the twentieth century. There is no era in world history even remotely comparable to the events of the past 75 years, and particularly to those of the past three decades. This century is the period of man's most astonishing scientific achievements. Despite the prescience of the writers Jules Verne and H.G. Wells, they could only react with disbelief to the scientific innovations of this era. Not only have the astronauts surmounted the formidable obstacle of space and been seen walking on the surface of the moon, but science has provided instantaneous communications by successfully using the new technology that has come out of the laboratories. In the twentieth century all things are possible. There will be instantaneous phonevision, providing communication by both sight and sound between sender and receiver. Large screen television receivers will encompass an entire wall space. Cable television will offer unparalleled opportunity for public access to a multiplicity of channels, as well as for business transactions, education, information and entertainment. Recording of programs and news events for subsequent replay will be within affordable reach of the public. Laser beams will provide speedier and more accurate transmission of information. The prospects of the technological revolution are limitless.

Communication—mass communication—is the seminal phenomenon, the scientific marvel of the twentieth century. This is, above all, the period of instantaneous, simultaneous mass communication. Courses in media history, criticism of the press, broadcasting, and information processing, storage and retrieval continue to proliferate in the colleges and universities. The still-controversial practices of advertising and public relations, by-products of the communications revolution, are attracting an increasing number of well-trained specialists. Research experts are devising new and more sophisticated and accurate ways of measuring public opinion.

The rapidly developing modalities of mass communication have been accompanied by a recognition of the prime purpose of mass media, which is not only to entertain but to provide *information,* so that a well-informed public can make intelligent value judgments and decisions. This recognition has led, in turn, to an encouraging awareness by those who purvey information in the form of communication content that media are important and, indeed, vital channels by which the public can receive messages. As a result, the process of communication as information has become professionalized and institutionalized both by the private sector and by the government. The press, itself a gigantic institution, is seen as a necessary adjunct to those whose function and purpose is to provide information. As the media have grown in importance, they have become conduits of information, unwitting sources of government propaganda, surrogates of the people and, increasingly of late, recipients of criticism from government officials, special interest groups, scholars and the public itself—both readers and viewers.

Government and Media

In no area is the role of media more significant than in its relationship to the government. In the Washington of the 1970s, few, if any, of the official agencies are without a public information officer, public affairs director or press officer. Through these offices a curious relationship has evolved with the press and other media. The involvement is, in a sense, symbiotic. Both the government and the press function independently, yet each needs and draws a kind of sustenance from the other. Government information could not reach the people without the press. And the press could not report to the people without the cooperation of the government. There have been times when the relationship has been parasitical. The government bureauracy has not hesitated to foist its public image on a sometimes willing press, and the media have used the government's handouts as a lazy mechanism for failure to do their own reportorial digging. Fortunately for public policy, this scandalous situation does not occur often and, when it does, it frequently results in either the government or the press getting burned.

The absorption by the press in government operations is total in this country. The national and local papers carry daily news of the activities and affairs of the bureaucracy—national, state and city. The national magazines have regular and lengthy coverage of government affairs. The broadcast media are unflagging in their zeal to include coverage of government in both network and local news programs. On the other hand, the information apparatus of the government is an ever-proliferating phenomenon, beginning with the executive branch and extending downward to every single agency of the official Washington hierarchy. There is not a department that doesn't boast of a public information section. In addition to the corps of information specialists, there are scores of unofficial communications and public relations advisers penetrating every aspect of the bureaucracy. Functioning somewhere between the official government and press agencies and the corps of unofficial advisers are public relations representatives of special interest organizations, press surveillance groups, consumer advocates, scholarly research organizations and lobbyists. Publicists are not required to register. Lobbyists must register as such, and many also perform a public relations function in addition to advocacy of their cause before the legislative bodies.

Historical Perspective

The point has been persistently reiterated that the relationship between media and government is not so much symbiotic as adversarial, although the two are not necessarily mutually exclusive. In fact, the relationship varies from harmonious cooperation to an adversarial stance that can become, on occasion, highly acrimonious—as in the deteriorating relationship between the White House and the press during the administration of President Nixon. In the main, however, the government needs the media as an outlet, and the media rely on the government as a source.

Historically, however, the press has not come by its prerogatives and privileges lightly. It has often had to battle every inch of the way in order to perform its obligations in a free society. The nature of the political infrastructure has been, in part, responsible for the development of the concept of freedom of information in this country. The vocal expression of the opinions of the public also has contributed to a climate of free expression. The press, itself a major business institution operating to make a profit, has generally resisted restrictions on its freedom to function, even while a good part of it has taken a "conservative" stand on the legislation offered by various presidents, notably Franklin D. Roosevelt. Beyond each of these influences, however, is the firm and lasting legacy of the Founding Fathers, which remains an unshakable bulwark of freedom of communication.

Despite the admitted fact that this country, even with valid criticism of media performance, boasts of the most open and free press in the civilized world, the struggle to achieve this position was not an easy one and the achievement is never a final one. If eternal vigilance is, indeed, the price of freedom, the press must heed that aphorism above all other institutions. Press freedom, as so many instances of restriction and repression reveal, is the result of a continuing effort on the part of the media. A communications system that does not value its freedom, respect its responsibilities and honor its obligations can soon lose its rights and privileges. The First Amendment is not entirely immune to erosion. There are always those who would inhibit the prerogatives of the press.

The first settlers did not enjoy freedom of communication. The British Crown, sensitive to the power of information and to the dissemination of news, saw to it that colonial newspapers were licensed and printed by authority. This privilege was closely guarded by the Postmaster, who represented the Crown and was, in effect, a press censor. It has often been noted that the writer whose work accomplished so much to free the colonial newspapers from the shackles of authority did not carry much weight with his own countrymen so far as the press was concerned. But John Milton's tract, *Areopagitica,* despite Milton's penchant for a dour Puritanism, was a signal influence in the creation of a climate of free expression in this country. Milton's argument is as fresh and relevant in the seventh decade of this present century as it was in the seventeenth century. Beware the censor who kills a publication, he stated, for this act "kills reason itself." In *Areopagitica,* the case against licensing is put forth clearly— to know vice is necessary "to the constituting of human virtue." Recognition of error leads to the confirmation of truth. Above all—a point highly relevant in the climate of the 1970s—Milton pointed out that the regulation of printing would lead inevitably to the regulation of all other activities and recreations. With most of the world's press consistently strangulated by government control, it is not difficult to find vindication of Milton's warning in countries throughout the world.

The establishment of an autonomous republic and the brilliance of the founders—notably Jefferson and Madison—gave a firm setting for the establishment of freedom of expression. The result of a compromise between Hamilton and Jefferson, the First Amendment became the basis for a free press in the United States. But it has not prevailed without challenge. The Alien and Sedition Acts of 1798 were clearly an attack upon, and an overt effort to exert control over, those journalists who represented the political group known as the Anti-Federalists. The Acts made it a crime to print "false, scandalous and malicious writing" about the government. They included a fine and imprisonment as punishment. Never withdrawn, the Sedition Acts simply faded away after 1800, but their significance was the revelation that a free press was not inviolate, despite the First Amendment. In an analogous way, the Peter Zenger case had earlier, in 1735, put a necessary restriction on the right of the authorities to censor the newspaper or to attack editors in the carrying out of their duties. Although Zenger agreed to edit a paper that would convey the point of view of a particular commercial group, that was not the point. The heart of the matter was that Governor William Cosby of New York objected to Zenger's criticism of his administration and charged the editor with sedition. The outcome of the case is well known. Represented by the aging Andrew Hamilton, the Zenger defense convinced the jury that although Zenger did indeed print matter deemed to be offensive to the administration, that was not the issue at stake. The basic issue was that what Zenger printed was justifiable truth. The words themselves could not be proven to be libelous. Zenger was acquitted.

These two incidents reveal that in the past as in the present, freedom of expression may be guaranteed but that the guarantee does not always work out in practice. Nevertheless, after the fortunate demise of the Alien and Sedition Acts, relative freedom of the press prevailed until the period of tension that preceded the Civil War. In this period, however, the press may have been free, but it could not be considered responsible. A highly partisan journalism, and a vituperative one, existed without much challenge. Most cases taken against the press were concerned with libel and were on the state level. The press, in the main, was irresponsible and often defamatory.

In the decade prior to the outbreak of the Civil War, there were a number of instances of government restrictions on freedom of information. Major verbal and physical assaults were directed against the antislavery editor William L. Garrison. One newspaper editor, Elijah Lovejoy, of the *St. Louis Observer,* an abolitionist publication, was killed by a rampaging mob which gathered to destroy his press. The Southern attitude was that if the press were theoretically free to publish, those who disagreed with this position were equally free to suppress expression if it were considered dangerous and inflamatory. Southern rebels were successful in mounting an effective campaign against the anti-slavery press in the Northern states while exerting total, repressive control over Southern newspapers. In the North, however, there were relatively few restraints on the excesses of the Copperhead papers, largely because President Lincoln was protective of the free flow of information until it became necessary for him to take punitive action as the result of increasingly vituperative attacks on him. Finally, he shut down newspapers and jailed recalcitrant editors.

The War between the States provided the first major test of press freedom against the government's need to impose censorship. In general, the correspondents covered battles freely—too freely, it appeared, because newspaper information became a source of intelligence to Southern commanders.

The period following the war again saw a return to the principle of a free press, and for many years freedom of communication prevailed, despite the fact that a partisan spirit was again manifested in the newspapers, which tended to express vehement support of politicians and parties without much exercise of either journalistic responsibility or independence of judgment.

The New Century

National crises and the attendant problems of security were not, however, the only phenomena that brought government pressures against the press. Owing largely to the dour efforts of Anthony Comstock, strong, repressive measures were taken for alleged instances of obscenity in print. And, although there was no causal relationship with repression because of obscenity, other restrictions were leveled against print journalism. In the case of *Toledo v. the U.S.* in 1918, the Supreme Court agreed that the courts had the right to bring judgment against material of a critical nature which appeared in the press. Indeed, in the opening years of the twentieth century, the spirit of government repression was evident in the formulation of the Immigration Act, which demanded deportation of those who advocated the violent overthrow of the government. Not since 1800 had a comparable spirit of repression of expression been manifested.

In 1918, the atmosphere of national tension generated by World War I resulted in the Espionage Act, which made it an official offense to obstruct recruiting or to denigrate the war effort. Under the Espionage Act, the Post Office, which carried out this legislation, effectively and dramatically brought repressive measures to bear on printed material which, in its judgment, was disloyal—a clear-cut case of government censorship of the press. The classic case of the period was that of *Schenck v. the U.S.,* in which Mr. Justice Holmes asserted the landmark doctrine that has been repeatedly cited and debated in cases involving freedom of communication—whether words are used in such fashion "as to create a clear and present danger that they will bring about the substantive evils that Congress has a right to prevent." Still another landmark decision was the highest court's ruling in the case of *Gitlow v. New York,* which extended the "liberty" and "due process" concepts expressed in the Fourteenth Amendment to the States and included the freedom of speech guaranteed in the First Amendment.

There were, of course, notable dissents to government restrictions on press freedom, such as those voiced by Justices Holmes and Brandeis; such dissents were similar to—though not as vigorous as—those of Justices Black and Douglas in the fifties and sixties on analogous issues. The unique aspect of the concept of freedom of information in this country, however, is that there has invariably developed a spirit of adamant resistance by the media to assaults by government or special private interests. In the *Ulysses* decision, for example, Federal Judge Woolsey stated that a printed work must be evaluated in its entirety, as a whole, not by a dissection of its parts. In the same way, the attempt by the Post Office to repress the distribution of *Esquire* magazine was rescinded by the Supreme Court. Above all, a cardinal principle of press freedom was enumerated by the highest court in the case of *Near v. Minnesota* in 1925. The State of Minnesota had leveled a "gag" rule against an infamous publication called *The Saturday Press* for printing material that was judged to be inflamatory and malignant. But the Supreme Court, perhaps surprisingly, held that the Minnesota decision was an example of prior restraint on print and therefore unconstitutional. Rendered by Chief Justice Hughes, the decision was based on the philosophy that the exercise of prior restraint constituted a greater danger to freedom of expression than the defamatory material in the publication. There was always, it noted, recourse to a libel suit.

Despite instances of censorship, the press remained largely a libertarian one. Such organizations as the Commission of Freedom of the Press set about to make recommendations on the exercise of responsibility, although this effort received little support from the newspaper publishers. In its report "A Free and Responsible Press," published in 1947, the Commission called for a spirit of social responsibility by the media and outlined specific steps to achieve that objective. A few years later, however, social upheavals brought about a temporary, but devastating, return of efforts at prior restraint in the climate of fear generated by the "cold war" period of the 1950s. The McCarran Act (Internal Security Act) called for members of the Communist Party to register with the Attorney General. Despite President Truman's veto of the Act as jeopardizing a free press, Congress passed it. Under demagogic pressure from Senator Joseph McCarthy, before the Senate's repudiation of "McCarthyism"—as a result of Edward R. Murrow's broadcast and the remarkable presentation by Joseph Welch in the televised Army-McCarthy hearings—journalists were hauled before the McCarthy Committee on Un-American Activities and subjected to unrelenting pressure and abuse. The press was acutely aware of the dangers of McCarthy's demagoguery and many papers fought it in print, but the fact is that McCarthy, whose wild accusations were ultimately shown to be utterly false, made news and generated enormous publicity.

The pendulum again swung away from repression with the decisions of the Warren Court, although many of these decisions have since been rejected by the Burger Court. The offensive McCarran Act was revoked as unconstitutional under the Fifth Amendment's provisions against self-incrimination. By 1960, the media had regained a unique degree of freedom and, in the case of *The New York Times v. Sullivan,* the Supreme Court gave further protection to freedom of expression by deciding that to be defamatory (libelous), that which was published must be shown to be malicious and to reveal a reckless disregard for truth. This definition has now been extended to public figures and to many individuals.

It was approximately at this juncture that the press and many special interest groups began to demand that the government open its files to public access and that the claim of "top secret," which was absurdly stamped on the most innocuous of documents, be discarded. Under the chairmanship of Senator Frank Moss (D. Utah), a committee drew up the first version of the Freedom of Information Act in 1966. The media assumed an important role in urging the Congress to promulgate this legislation. Two versions of the Act were passed by the Congress. Nevertheless, the current posture of the courts on instances involving the First Amendment and the increasing strictures against newsmen who try to protect the confidentiality of their sources certainly demand that every possible effort be made by the media to protect and advance their constitutional freedom to function as surrogates of the public.

Heeding the demands of the press for more access to documents summarily marked "secret," President Nixon, in March 1972, issued an executive order designed to lift the aura of secrecy from government documents. More recently, in July 1978, President Carter also issued an executive order liberalizing the procedures governing the classification of documents, but went a step further and created an oversight agency to deal with any bureaucratic efforts to circumvent the liberalized procedures.

2

Freedom of Information

THE UNITED STATES is the only country in the world that has enacted federal legislation relating to the free flow of information, legislation that gives both the press and the people the right to examine public documents. The Congress has also passed a Sunshine Law, opening many government agency meetings to the public. Many of the states, in addition, give protection to the newspapermen through shield laws, which permit the press to maintain confidential sources of information. No other government has passed such freedom of information legislation, for the impetus in much of the world seems to be moving away from the idea of a free or libertarian press to total control—either by fiat or government ownership—of the media of mass communication.

The fact remains, however, that it was found necessary in this country to enact an FOI Act, as well as the Sunshine Law—indicating that despite constitutional guarantees of freedom of expression, freedom of information is hard to come by and is, indeed, obstructed by representatives of the government bureaucracy. For decades, newsmen have decried the flamboyant and irresponsible labeling of even the most innocuous documents as ''top secret.'' The protective barrier of ''national security'' has been invoked, variously, to take lazy department bureaucrats off the hook, to protect their flanks and, in some cases, simply out of an arrogant disregard of the right of the press and the public to receive information relevant to their function and their interest. Consequently, in the 1960s a movement toward the structuring of a freedom of information law gained momentum. The media supported it. Public interest organizations urged such legislation. And members of the Congress notably Representatives John E. Moss and William Moorhead, were its strong advocates in the government.

Executive Privilege

Throughout history, the emphasis has been on the right of the media to perform their task without censorship or repression by government as guaranteed by the First Amendment. Inevitably, the concept of the right to know became a paramount concern and the media's need to have access to heretofore privileged information became a major issue.

Sporadic efforts to secure information in the past had not been successful. The shibboleth of "national security" was used effectively to maintain official silence and secrecy and to refuse to open even the most innocent files to the press. The government in explaining surveillance and classification has claimed that certain information has been held to be secure since our first president. Furthermore, President Eisenhower had expressed the doctrine of "executive privilege" so categorically as to make any relaxation of security almost impossible. The Eisenhower doctrine, though, was hardly new. George Washington had maintained that certain materials relating to the Presidency were privileged and must so remain. But the matter had not been brought to a head in those 200 years. President Eisenhower asserted executive privilege in a way that made significant areas of information completely off limits to both press and public.

Eisenhower's doctrine may have been paved with good intentions. He affirmed the right of the media to seek out and obtain information as a surrogate of the public. Also affirmed, however, was the right of the Chief Executive to refuse to divulge or release information which was subsumed under the category of executive privilege. In a letter to the Secretary of Defense dated May 17, 1954, Eisenhower set an important precedent. The letter directed the Secretary of Defense to order the Secretary of the Army to refuse information to a Senate committee investigating the altercation between the Army and Senator Joseph McCarthy. Eisenhower stated explicitly that while the Congress should achieve its legislative purpose by receiving information relating to any matter within the jurisdiction of the (Congressional) Committee, "throughout our history the President has withheld information whenever he found that what was sought was confidential or its disclosure would be incompatible with the public interest or jeopardize the safety of the nation."

Thus was President Washington's doctrine, expressed in a different period and under different circumstances, reaffirmed in a new light. Eisenhower held that the release of certain "conversations and communications" was not in the public interest. To some extent both Presidents Kennedy and Johnson made use of the doctrine of executive privilege, but it was Richard M. Nixon who attempted to solidify and extend executive privilege with every resource at his command, even while his administration purported, in Nixon's own words, to be an "open" one.

The major problem, however, was not merely the insistence upon executive privilege by the White House but the fact that lower strata of the government bureaucracy took it upon themselves to extrapolate the doctrine to the classification of information where no sound reason could be shown to justify such secrecy. Additional justification could be derived from a 1789 law known as the Housekeeping Act, which gave each agency control over its records and official papers. Thus the stamping of information as "classified" had been a long-standing prerogative of the government bureaucrat.

Despite complaints from the press, the government agencies remained obdurate. The argument against capricious classification was clearly enunciated. The quintessence of democracy is the expression of the will of the people. Judgment and action depend upon access to adequate information. Critical attitudes and a healthy skepticism are necessary to the function of a responsible press. Citizen attitudes and opinions and intelligent decisions evolve from an evaluation of accessible information. The media, above all, cannot function as surrogates of the people if information is controlled and arbitrarily classified as secret. What recourse, for example, does the citizen have against the use of sophisticated technology involving illegal wiretapping, methods of secret surveillance and other means of implicit harassment? The very size and ponderousness of the government information infrastructure, the keeping of records on the computer by business and educational institutions, the growth of special interest political organizations—all create overlapping of function and a self-perpetuating and unmanageable informational bureaucracy. As an inevitable result, the government rationalizes its tendency to control, manipulate and direct the news media. The immensity of big government makes it relatively easy to conceal, to classify and to set up barriers to a free flow of information.

Against this official penchant toward obstructionism, the press and the public fought a consistent battle to liberalize the sources of information. The public, in the first place, relies upon the integrity of the news media. The media, in turn, demand freedom to obtain information, unless it clearly can be shown to contravene the national interest. Access to sources of information gives the media an opportunity to determine that government decisions are in the public interest. It was primarily the confidence of the press in its own responsibilities and integrity that resulted in the disclosure of secret surveillance by the military, by industry, by the FBI, by the CIA. The work of intrepid investigative reporters also revealed the misuse of private information by the Internal Revenue Service and other agencies.

Although the press fought the absurdities of unjustified classification, it was to some extent not without fault. Timid or lazy reporters were too easily influenced by government officials. Some correspondents desisted in being critical and agreed to work with the agencies on a *quid pro quo* basis, an unwritten gentlemen's agreement. Others simply did not exercise the vigilance necessary to a free press or were less than scrupulous in digging for information. On the other hand, the press' hands can also be tied without legislative support from the Congress and, until 1966, this support was not expressed in legislative action. In addition, some press officers—notably Nixon's press secretary, Ron Ziegler—took apparent pleasure in "stonewalling" the reporters. Others, such as Arthur Sylvester and Jerry

Friedham at the Pentagon, showed an apparent disregard of the need to give reporters truthful information. All these factors contributed to a less than free flow of information.

If the print media had difficulties, electronic journalism also had to face the fact that it is a medium licensed and regulated by the federal government and is, theoretically, under the jurisdiction of a federal agency, the Federal Communications Commission. The Commission can exercise control by allocation of frequencies, by its power to approve or revoke station licenses, by its legal authority to issue "cease and desist" orders. The Justice Department also entered the regulatory picture by leveling an anti-trust action against the commercial networks. Additionally, the Federal Trade Commission has the authority to scrutinize broadcast advertising messages. The government can also exert indirect controls by its ability to establish or withhold lucrative contracts from companies that work on technological developments. In the Nixon Administration, it was not unusual for the White House to put pressure on the news departments of the networks and to work assiduously at fomenting antagonism between the networks and their affiliated stations.

Viewed from the perspective of these various restraints, some direct, others implicit, the need for some method of providing for a more free flow of government information was apparent to the press and ultimately to the Congress. If there were a precedent for executive privilege, there were both precedent and need for a liberalization of the channels of government information. George Washington may have felt justified in restricting information, but such figures as Jefferson and Madison, even while excoriating the press for dishonesty and partisanship, stoutly maintained a strong dedication to a free press.

The First FOI Act

The tension between media and government has prevailed throughout the history of the nation. But the idea of an official legislative act confirming freedom of information and access to such information by press and public was not formulated until the 1950s and 1960s. The basic premise that buttressed the idea of free flow of information was expressed by Kent Cooper as Managing Editor of the Associated Press. It was the notion that the people had, in Cooper's words, a "right to know," a phrase that has become the basic philosophy of a free and responsible press. The persistent complaint of the mass media was the obdurate and secretive posture of the various federal agencies, their absurd and irritating insistence on labeling all data as "top secret" or "classified" or as a threat to "national security."

In 1955, the House of Representatives established a Sub-Committee on Government Information. The prime mover was John E. Moss (D. Cal.), the committee chairman and the main motivating influence behind the passage of the 1966 Freedom of Information Act. Representative Moss had the support of large segments of both print and electronic journalism, which now reasserted their function as surrogates of the public and reaffirmed their right to access to information. The press also reiterated its claim that there was far too much unnecessary secrecy in government that had no relevance to the security of the nation.

The bureaucracy, in the decades prior to the passage of the Freedom of Information Act, had cited the "housekeeping" rule as substantial reason for withholding information. But a codicil was added to the rule, as the Moss Committee was getting underway, which was designed to prevent agencies from classifying certain data. The change was largely disregarded, particularly in view of President Eisenhower's insistence on the strict observance of "executive privilege." Throughout the 1960s the media sought to convince the Congress of the need to declassify hitherto top secret documents. In 1966, changes were made in the Administrative Procedures Act which were calculated to provide guarantees of more open access to government information. This was the passage of the 1966 Freedom of Information Act, which, unfortunately, was without any real power because of certain provisions and exceptions that gave federal agencies a ready excuse for continuing to classify information. The first FOI Act provided that

1. Each agency must make available information to the public.
2. Each agency must describe its organization and set forth methods by which the public could obtain information.
3. Each agency may delete material that constitutes an "invasion of personal privacy" but must justify and explain the reason for the deletion.

These are three of the salient points made in the first FOI Act. But the Congress, in passing the Act, made a grievous error. It included nine exemptions where the provisions of the Freedom of Information Act did not apply and thus provided the federal agencies with convenient loopholes to avoid making information available. The nine exempted matters were

1. Classified data on national defense or on foreign policy.
2. Data relating to the internal personnel rules and practices of the agency.
3. Data exempted from disclosure by statute.
4. Trade secrets or financial information obtained from an individual on a confidential basis.
5. Data which would be considered privileged information in a civil action.
6. Personnel and medical files which would constitute an invasion of privacy.
7. Investigatory files compiled for purposes of law enforcement.
8. Data relating to use by an agency responsible for the regulation of financial institutions (i.e., banks).
9. Data concerning the geology and geography of oil wells.

These nine exempt areas were speedily seized upon by the agencies as a basis for continuing to withhold information. In terms of the nine loopholes, it should be noted that there was an explicit provision in the Act giving a litigant or seeker of information the right of taking the case to the courts, which would then make a determination *"de novo* and the burden shall be upon the agency to sustain its *situ."* But this procedure failed to alleviate the difficulty the press encountered in prying information from recalcitrant bureaucrats who continue to sidestep the FOI Act.

Amended FOI Act

As a result, further hearings were begun in 1972 by the Moorhead Committee, officially known as the House Government Information and Foreign Operations Committee, under Representative William Moorhead (D. Pa.). The hearings substantiated the conviction that the government branches and agencies were obstructing, instead of implementing, the 1966 Freedom of Information Act. In 1973, the Supreme Court ruled on the case of *Mink v. EPA*, a case which directly involved freedom of information by the very agencies that were supposed to be responsive to the provisions of the FOI Act. Legal action was brought to receive federal agency reports on underground nuclear tests in Alaska. But the Court, following the bureaucracy, upheld the secrecy on the basis of the first exemption (i.e., matters of defense or national policy). Thus, it was abundantly clear that a revision of the 1966 Act was necessary. In 1973, Representative Moorhead proposed certain amendments.

1. That the federal bureaucracy must respond to reasonable requests for information.
2. That responses must be forthcoming within 10 working days of receipt of such requests.
3. That appeals must be decided within 20 working days.

The basis for these and other amendments was clearly that much of the information requested by the media was not of a classified or sensitive nature and that to refuse was both arbitrary and absurd. The revisions in the 1966 Act were also urged by Senator Edward Kennedy (D. Mass.), while Elliot Richardson, then the Attorney General, also suggested that historical researchers, as well as the press, be given access to informational material. Thus, despite pressure from the federal agencies, Congress amended the Freedom of Information Act in 1974 by the unusual vote of 383–8. Even at this point, however, the amendments were not promulgated easily. Surprisingly, President Gerald Ford vetoed the revised Act, but the Congress passed it overwhelmingly over the veto.

Has the revised Act proved to be successful? The evidence is ambiguous. Some agencies have responded reluctantly. Others have engaged in deliberate footdragging, claiming both lack of funds and personnel to implement the amendments. It is safe to conjecture that the bureaucracy will continue to seek ways to circumvent the Act unless the press mounts unrelenting pressure, which it has not seen fit to do. Yet, after February 1975, when the Act officially went into effect, there was a spate of requests for data from various agencies, which quickly complained that they could not process material in the time allowed for reply. Although the Congress discovered that the revised Act was costly to implement, advocates pointed out that it was still considerably cheaper than maintaining a large and unwieldly corps of assorted press representatives and information specialists.

In effect, most of the requests for information from the government have not come from the media but from corporations and their lobbyists—largely for reasons of competitive advantage. Representative Moorhead noted that he was astonished to discover "that the reporters, editors and broadcasters whose job it is to inform the American people have made little use of the (1966) FOI Act. They were the major supporters of those in Congress who created the law." Apparently, the media have not done much better on the amended version. This has operated to the advantage of the government and to the detriment of the press. Because the securing of information is time-consuming, the deadline-oriented press simply cannot wait even for brief periods to obtain information. It must be both speedy and accurate if the gathering of the day's intelligence is to proceed. Furthermore, editors and publishers have neither the time nor the inclination to go to the courts when information is not forthcoming on demand. This has also given government agencies an opportunity to practice delaying tactics.

Yet, despite these limitations, the important fact is that it was the media that were responsible for the passing of both versions of the FOI Act. There have still been many thousands of public requests for information. *The New York Times* reported that of all the agencies, the best record for speedy reply appeared to be that of the Pentagon. The Justice Department, on the other hand, was accused of a lethargic response because it apparently noted that the requests for material were, as the courts put it, "directory, not mandatory." Ralph Nader, in particular, was reported to have accused the FBI of "frustration and delay" in releasing requested information.

Despite difficulties, the revised FOI Act has been generally successful. For the first time, the *Times* noted, there was a positive effort by the press to gain information about the CIA's long-standing procedures in using mind-controlling drugs as well as information on the exchange of data between the FBI and the ACLU. In 1976, a survey showed that several thousand requests for information had been received. Few of these, however, reached a point where the media engaged in litigation to force the release of data.

The Sunshine Law

Analogous to the FOI Act is the recently passed Sunshine Law, which opens certain meetings that heretofore had been closed to press and public. The proposal for such a public law was first made by Senator Lawton Chiles (D. Fla.) in 1972 and was referred to the Senate Committee on Government Operations. A similar bill was proposed in the House of Representatives by Representative Dante Fascell (D. Fla.).

The basic philosophy was that of the Freedom of Communications Act. The proposal offered was that all meetings and hearings of government agencies where official action is being contemplated be open to the public. Exemptions would include meetings concerned with matters of national security, internal management questions, situations where an individual's reputation might be affected and matters which were confidential under statutory authority. Also to be open to the public were the proceedings of congressional committees.

The Sunshine Act was slow in coming to fruition. No action was taken by the 92nd Congress. Representative Fascell reintroduced the legislation in January, 1973. The bill was ultimately referred to the Senate Committee on Government Operations and assigned to the Sub-Committee on Reorganization, Research and International Organizations, of which Senator Abraham Ribicoff (D. Conn.) was the chairman. In 1974, this committee queried public and legal figures, scholars and public interest organizations, as well as journalists, asking for their opinions and comments. These were compiled in a report to the Senate and House.

The bill was again introduced in the 94th Congress in 1975 by Senator Chiles. Later, Representative Bella Abzug (D. N.Y.) introduced a revised version of the Fascell proposal. The revision was taken into consideration by the Sub-Committee on Government Information and Individual Rights (of the Committee on Government Operations) of which Representative Abzug was chairwoman. Finally, the Sunshine Act was passed and signed by the President in September, 1976. It was now an official document, sanctioned by law.

The law, known as a Public Law of the 94th Congress, was officially known as the "Government in the Sunshine Act." Under a Declaration of Policy, the following was affirmed:

> It is hereby declared to be the policy of the United States that the public is entitled to the fullest practicable information regarding the decision making processes of the Federal Government. It is the purpose of this Act to provide the public with such information while protecting the rights of individuals and the ability of the Government to carry out its responsibilities.

Under the provisions of the Sunshine Act, meetings of government agencies and of congressional committees were to be opened to the public. The feeling in the Congress was that the bill would "help increase the public's faith in the integrity of government, enable the public to better understand the decisions reached by the government, and better acquaint the public with the process by which agency decisions are reached."

Has the Act proven to be successful? Opinions on that question vary. Proponents claim it has provided for more open and accessible government. Opponents say that openness in government has not been achieved. The chief complaints against the Sunshine Act are that like the FOI Act, it is ignored by many agencies that continue to find reasons to maintain closed meetings. The public apparently is not aware of the Sunshine Act, and the government publicists have not encouraged attendance at meetings, which have been visited largely by special interest organizations and lobbyists. The government agencies also have been quick to take advantage of the exemptions in the Act. For example, the President's cabinet departments and other vital agencies are excluded from the obligation to hold open meetings. The exemptions also give the so-called open agencies a reason to hold private meetings. One example cited is the Interstate Commerce Commission.

On the other hand, those who support the Sunshine Act believe that the mere fact that such legislation exists has exerted a salutary influence in the direction of open information. The Act has also had a positive influence on those agencies which do hold open meetings and has increased their sense of responsibility to the public. The Washington bureaucracy, it is felt, is more responsive to the public interest and to the concept of the people's right to know. The FOI Act, the Sunshine law and the recently devised Privacy Law (whereby individuals cannot be denied access to records held about them) are all results of a long-standing effort to pry open the secrecy lid that has been tightly clamped by the government.

These laws have limitations and they have been circumvented by many of the federal agencies, but because of their passage, the need for a free flow of information has been underscored for both the media and the public.

Fundamentally, the demand for what eventually became the Freedom of Information Act was the result of both congressional and media dissatisfaction with increasing government secrecy. In summary, the basic representation by the press and by special interest groups representing the public was that

1. An informed public opinion is utterly essential to the proper and successful functioning of a political democracy.
2. Withholding of information does not cohere with the tenets of a free press system.
3. Government should function by consent of the governed, not by prior restraint or by arbitrary pocket vetoes over the flow of information.
4. The press is truly a surrogate of the people and, therefore, is constitutionally entitled to information from the government.

The hearings by the House Committee on Government Operations and the Sub-Committee on Government Information were based on these assumptions as part of our traditional political philosophy. It was as a result of these hearings that the FOI Act came into being. The press was a powerful advocate, but the role of the media has always stressed access to information. Walter Lippmann contended that the press does, indeed, represent the people and has a constitutional right to request and receive information from public servants. But he also believed in the value of the publicist, pointing out that the public relations officer is an important asset to the correspondent who cannot find all the news all the time without the cooperation of the (government) publicists as important catalysts.

The position of the federal bureaucracy persists, even after the passage of the Freedom of Information Act. It is not the role of the media, the government publicist claims, to be the sole determinant of what the people should or should not know. Responsible government officials who know more about the security needs of the country than media representatives are in a better position to make judgments on the release of government information. Furthermore, it is a primary obligation of the federal agency to give information to the executive branch and, particularly, to the Congress, which also serves as a guardian of the right of the people to know—a sophistic argument, however, because it is the news media, not the Congress, that publishes and broadcasts to the readers and viewers.

That an enterprising reporter can ferret out salient information does not explain away the significant philosophical issue concerning the continuing function of the press as "surveillance of the environment." A comparison of the political news available in this country against what Professor John Tebbel has called a "strangulation" of the press in other countries underscores the point. Yet, even in the United States, prior to the FOI Act, government agencies and government information purveyors arbitrarily withheld information, although no need to do so could be shown, either in terms of national security or as presenting a danger to public opinion. Even when a reporter does succeed in prying information from a reluctant agency—and most reporters claim that a good newsman will not be denied—the "news" may turn out to be a half-truth or incomplete or information which is manipulated and managed by the federal information officer. The reason is that the publicist inevitably must serve the agency first and the press second.

The media insist not only that they receive information about the activities of the political establishment but that the news not be managed or manipulated. The social responsibility claim of the press is that it can function freely and responsibly under the First Amendment's protection. It is the prerogative of the reporter and other gatekeepers to determine what should be conveyed to the public about its government and in what form it is to be conveyed. High government officials, however, frequently object to the way they are treated in a print or television news account. Because the press can behave irresponsibly, they insist, the government must be cautious in the way it channels information to the media, which tend to emphasize scandal and excitement instead of sobriety.

In short, what the FOI Act has accomplished is to provide the media with support from the Congress, thereby achieving a needed goal for the media—mandating that information must be forthcoming on request. The FOI Act is, in essence, the result of an alliance between the press and the Congress. It goes a long way, but not far enough, in reconciling the irreconcilable differences between the government bureaucracy and the media over the burning issue of what the people should know.

3

Information and
the First Amendment

FOUR OF THE VARIOUS AMENDMENTS to the United States Constitution have singular relevance to freedom of information and to the prerogatives of a free and responsible press. These amendments are the first, fifth, sixth and fourteenth. The First Amendment, cited so often and read so little, states explicitly that "Congress shall make no law respecting an abridgment of religion, or prohibiting the free exercise thereof; or abridging the freedom of speech or of the press; or the right of the people peaceably to assemble, and to petition the Government for a redress of grievances."

The Fifth Amendment—best recalled for the phrase "take the Fifth" during the House Un-American Activities Committee hearings in the mid-fifties—protects the individual from being compelled to be a witness against himself in a criminal case and states that no one can be deprived of life, liberty or property "without due process of law."

The Sixth Amendment assures the accused of a fair and speedy trial. This amendment is the basis of the so-called free press–fair trial issue, which has been so profoundly disturbing and troublesome to both the media and the courts, as well as to the bar associations.

The Fourteenth Amendment prohibits the *states* from depriving an individual of life, liberty or property without due process of law. It was the extension of the guarantees of the First Amendment to the states by way of the Fourteenth Amendment that made a classic case of the *Gitlow v. New York* litigation.

It is the First Amendment, with its so-often-affirmed right of press freedom, that is most often invoked by the media. Although the government subscribes wholeheartedly to the language of the amendment, the fact is that the bureaucracy's interpretation of the First Amendment is not invariably literal or absolute. The Attorney General in the Nixon Administration, when confronted with the First Amendment as protestors were being incarcerated, was reported to have said that the First Amendment would have to wait! Nor have the courts always been purists in their reading of the amendment, and any ambiguous decision by the Supreme Court has merely encouraged the lower courts to circumvent the intent of the Constitution and invoke heavy penalties against journalists who refuse to reveal confidential sources of information.

The Bill of Rights

Those who framed the Constitution, however, were acutely aware of the need to put on paper a statement having to do with freedom of communication. Indeed, it was almost certain that the Constitution would not be ratified without mention of the right to free expression, and the Governor of Virginia, Edmund Randolph, early espoused the passage of a Bill of Rights. The matter went to committee and was the subject of considerable debate among the convention delegates. With the contribution of Madison and the wholehearted support of Jefferson, the First Amendment was ratified. Madison, in fact, had suggested that the states cannot abridge freedom of speech, but as ratified, the amendment reads that the Congress cannot make such an abridgment. The addition of the phrase ''the press'' was added before ratification. With or without the First Amendment, the commitment of Jefferson and Madison to freedom of the press was unambiguous, despite their disenchantment with the journalists of the period. Jefferson announced that he did not believe what he read in the press but affirmed the right of the newspaper to publish and to be distributed without repression or prior restraint. Madison echoed this viewpoint.

What was acutely clear to the founding fathers was the categorical need for a free flow of information, along with the absolute right of the press to print and without government restriction. Milton had put it pointedly in *Areopagitica:* The publication of a book, magazine or newspaper has a life beyond life. The effects of prior restraint or censorship, as Zechariah Chafee, Jr., was to show about two centuries later, go beyond the prohibition of destruction of what is written and published. And, as the recent attitude of the courts has shown, the rash of subpoenas of newsmen and the jailing of many of them can only exert a chilling effect on freedom of expression, despite reference to the inviolability of the First Amendment to the Constitution. Yet, the courts have not always circumvented the Bill of Rights and, in fact, have generally tended to uphold it. It is not the affirmations, however, that are significant, but those instances where the interpretations have seemed to go beyond the clear language expressed in the prohibition of the abridgment of freedom of the press. When the courts have come out squarely for the language of the First Amendment, the effect has been to solidify the spirit of a free press. The *Near v. Minnesota* decision showed that the freedom to print was more important than the scurrilous nature of what was printed. Opinions, even if inimical, should find expression in a democratic, pluralistic society. Only when publications are placed under prior restraint and journalists jailed or shackled does freedom of information suffer, to the ultimate erosion of the public's right to know.

Alexander Meikeljohn, a staunch defender of the right to information, called the First Amendment "an absolute" (*The Supreme Court Review,* 1961). From the language of the Constitution itself, certain basic principles emerge. The authority to govern the people rests squarely with the people, for "political freedom is not the absence of government. It is self-government." This principle is confirmation that those who are assigned the task of running the government derive their authority not from some higher law, but from the consent of the governed. Under the Constitution, no agency of the federal bureaucracy can take it upon itself to curtail the rights of the press or the public to assemble freely and to publish without restraint or repression. The basis for this philosophy is abundantly clear. The people cannot encompass and understand the fast-moving national and international issues that become daily grist to the gathering of journalistic intelligence. The journalist functions in the capacity of public surrogate and even, at times, of advocate. The journalist provides information in the form of news. But the freedom of the journalist to perform this function must be protected by the freedom of the press guaranteed in the First Amendment.

Limits on Free Speech

Unfortunately, the fact that the First Amendment cannot supply absolutely at all times and under all circumstances has been seized upon by those who would subvert or circumvent it. Freedom to speak, Mr. Justice Holmes had stated, does not give anyone the right to shout "fire" in a crowded theatre. Words that constitute a "clear and present" danger to society are not, and do not deserve, the protection of a Bill of Rights. Defamation with clear-cut malice or reckless disregard for truth does not warrant protection. These instances obviously emphasize the need for applying intelligent value judgments and the rule of reason. They should not, however, be construed as a way of interpreting the First Amendment in a manner calculated to abridge press freedom.

In the past several years, the courts have displayed a surprising ambivalence in interpreting and applying the principles of the First Amendment. Many decisions have severely curtailed the rights and privileges of reporters, regardless of claims that their First Amendment rights have been ignored. Reporters, such as Earl Caldwell of *The New York Times,* have gone to prison rather than accede to demands that they reveal confidential sources of information, claiming that the relationship of the correspondent to source is no different from the confidentiality that exists between doctor and patient or lawyer and client. In general, the press has discovered to its discomfiture that it cannot place too firm a reliance on the courts for protection either of sources or of rights under the Constitution. The Supreme Court decision in the case of the "Pentagon Papers" was divided and acrimonious, rather than a unanimous affirmation of the First Amendment. A House committee demanded that CBS deliver material that never appeared on the air (known as outtakes) in the Staggers Committee hearings on the program called *The Selling of the Pentagon*. In a case involving the Idaho Supreme Court, the U.S. highest court refused to review an Idaho decision that held that the First Amendment does not protect a journalist in a libel suit. The reporter of the *Lewiston Tribune* went to jail for refusal to reveal a source of information in a libel action against the newspaper. What was of great concern in this decision was the fear expressed by the Reporters' Committee for Freedom of the Press that such a decision might trigger a spate of similar actions from those whose purpose was simply to pry the source of information from a reporter.

Ambivalence and Ambiguity

What has confused the media has been the continuing lack of consistency of the courts on First Amendment issues. This uncertainty has become endemic and has inevitably eroded the press privileges indicated by the Constitution. Occasionally, a judge has rendered a decision which firmly embraces the spirit and letter of the First Amendment. For example, an encouraging sign was the decision by the U.S. Second Circuit Court of Appeals in New York that journalists cannot be forced to reveal how they go about the process of editorial decision-making. Their opinions and thought processes, said Chief Judge Irving R. Kaufman, are singularly their own and need not be revealed or published. The case involved a suit by former Lt. Col. Anthony B. Herbert, who launched a libel action against CBS, Barry Lando and Mike Wallace. Lando, although he submitted what Judge Kaufman called a "staggering" amount of documents, refused to reveal or divulge his beliefs or opinions which, he insisted, were protected by the First Amendment. In a concurring opinion with that of Judge Kaufman, Judge James Oakes stated that "as soon as facts are set in their context there is editorial selection; as soon as that process is subject to scrutiny, there is suppression effect; and as soon as there is such an effect, the freedom of the press has evaporated." However, in the Spring of 1979, this decision was set aside by the Supreme Court in a 6–3 ruling which allowed Lt. Col. Herbert to probe "into the thoughts, opinions and conclusions" of Mr. Lando and the producers of "60 Minutes" in order to prove that he was libeled by the show.

The unfortunate fact is that other courts, including the highest court, have not revealed a *consistent* commitment to the principles of the First Amendment in cases involving the freedom of the media. Floyd Abrams, an attorney who has specialized in First Amendment cases, has stated his belief that court opinions have been mixed and ambiguous. In cases involving editorial judgment (e.g., the *Miami Herald v. Tornillo* case, where the Supreme Court upheld the right of the paper to print a critical editorial without being forced to give Tornillo the right of reply), the Court on the whole has favored the press. In other actions where protection of a newsman's source is involved, the Court has generally been found to be antagonistic to the media. In these cases, the Supreme Court has often refused to grant review. Abrams, however, views with greatest alarm the question of laws governing privacy. This tendency he calls "an ominous development" which could jeopardize a free press in cases where the Court considered what the press printed to be too private a matter. This "ominous" trend embraces not only print but electronic journalism as well, and it is a matter on which the Supreme Court ruling, if and when it is made, will be noted with more than passing interest by the news media.

The press has rights under the First Amendment. That much is freely admitted. But whether these rights are to prevail under all circumstances and whether they are absolute are hotly debated matters. Justice Hugo Black and Justice William O. Douglas stated that every bit of the language of the Bill of Rights is to be taken literally. Freedom of the press is an absolute freedom, as stated in the First Amendment, and cannot be vitiated under *any* circumstances. This position, taken by two of the Supreme Court's most vehement defenders of free expression, raises questions, of course. What of Justice Holmes' comment on the use of words to incite a riot? What role, if any, should the Congress take in legislation that guarantees access to information by the news media, despite the reluctance of the agencies and the ambivalence of the courts? The questions multiply, but the answers are not easy to come by. The Ellsberg distribution of the "Pentagon Papers," which were printed after much agonizing by several major papers, may have been, in the opinion of some, a violation of the criminal code, which provides that a document pertaining to the national defense must be delivered to a government official. But the "Pentagon Papers" had received internal distribution and their contents, it developed, revealed no secrets which were unknown to any potential antagonist. If, however, material is to be labeled "confidential," what First Amendment checks can be made against arbitrary classification by government bureaucrats? At worst, such classification frequently has resulted in selective "leaks" from other government officials to the press, which has subsequently accepted and printed them because there is the alternative of printing the leaked material or nothing at all.

The problem reverts again to the spirit and intent of the First Amendment and its guarantee of freedom of the press. But, in the long run, it is the press itself—not the government or any special interest—whose responsibility it is to weigh the need for freedom of communication against other values and to make an editorial decision concerned solely with the right of the people to receive information, which is, after all, a form of knowledge and a guide to intelligent action. There are editors who share the view that the media should not be exempt from the criminal law. Most journalists would agree that not all government material should be released without discrimination. The newsmen would agree, too, that there are occasions when confidential or "deep background" information should not be printed, albeit this is usually a reluctant agreement. *The New York Times* admitted in retrospect that it erred in refraining from printing the plans for the Bay of Pigs invasion. The same newspaper, however, was adamant in its refusal to recall correspondent David Halberstan from Vietnam when the Kennedy White House urged his recall.

The government has a long advantage over the media. High level officials are not on the spot in the same way as are news correspondents. The press is, despite the First Amendment, more vulnerable than the government, and if the media can damage official egos, the bureaucracy can damage the press. There is always the matter of postal rates, of the regulation of broadcasting, of the media's dependence on the Congress for the passage of the Newspaper Preservation

Act and, finally, of that most feared of government procedures, the anti-trust action from the Department of Justice. "Secrecy," said Max Frankel, of *The New York Times,* "is warranted as long as you can get away with it." The government agency gets away with it, in the opinion of many editors, far more capriciously than is healthy for a free press in a democracy. The media should be able to secure information and they should feel free to print it if it is newsworthy or informative. Even with the Freedom of Information Act, there is still a need for the Congress to take even more specific procedures toward the establishment of ground rules on declassification of documents.

The Congress, as well as the judiciary, can take a fresh look and issue a further affirmation of the rights of the press under the Constitution and, in particular, the right to keep sources of information confidential. Indeed, the government should encourage the media to protect confidentiality of sources. The government agencies should not, under most circumstances, hold the news correspondent criminally liable for performing his expected investigative function in the interest of bringing intelligence to a free society. Not all critics of the press agree, however, on the First Amendment rights question. The courts recently have held that *all* must testify on receipt of Grand Jury or Congressional subpoenas, that the demand for testimony is not harassment of the media and that the press is not a sacrosanct institution. But the press and its supporters believe that it performs a unique function in this society and that democratic government demands a free press protected by the First Amendment. To still other observers of the media the answer to freedom of information is not absolute privilege for the press, but rather responsible behavior by the judiciary. There is no question, however, that the increasing application of the subpoena power and the generally negative attitude of the courts have increased the need for a form of shield law, since the First Amendment provisions have not proved to be convincing in many court cases involving the press and the use of confidential information. The late Professor Alexander Bickel of Yale University believed that reporters are not exempt from criminal law but that their function ought to merit protective legislation.

A free press cannot be protected if neither the courts nor the

Congress demand that the prosecution, in cases involving the media, be forced to show a categorical need for the revelation of sources of confidential information and, further, to demonstrate that this information can be obtained only by subpoena of the journalist. It should be shown conclusively that justice can only be served by placing this additional burden on the press. Even these measures, many believe, are subversive of the spirit and letter of the First Amendment. The editorial function cannot be construed, journalists maintain, in such a fashion as to weaken and demoralize the prerogatives of the media. The journalist claims a right to gather and print information under the protection of the Constitution. The ethical journalist prints the news, even when the intelligence is of such a nature as to be contrary to his own interests and convictions. And the newsman has a right to demand that the government official cooperate by making information available as part of the obligation of a public servant. One way to assure that these responsibilities are carried out is by legislation, but this procedure would be selfdefeating and contrary to the First Amendment. It would be paradoxical to expect the government to regulate the media in the interest of preserving the intent of the First Amendment. The government bureaucracy cannot take action to enforce or to restrict publication. It can only exert a positive influence on the press by its own observance of the Bill of Rights.

Richard Jencks, a former CBS executive and an attorney, has called the First Amendment more than a legal document. In an age of mass media, the First Amendment expresses "communications policy," a *modus operandi* whereby print and electronic journalism can operate freely in the interest of a democratic society. This is particularly relevant in terms of the pervasiveness of the media and the constant flow of communications content. From both newspapers and television there pours forth, said *The New York Times'* James Reston, the greatest possible flow of information and "the loudest clash of divergent opinion ever inflicted on a long-suffering people in the history of the written and spoken word." Precisely because of this plethora of information, however, the public must have an opportunity to sift facts, make value judgments, arrive at intelligent decisions. This task can only be accomplished by the freedom of the media to do their job responsibly under the guarantees of the First Amendment. At issue is not so much the rights of the media, but both the need and the right of the people to receive and to evaluate information. Any restriction by the government of this need is subversive of the First Amendment.

Shield Laws

The negative decision of the courts in many cases involving subpoenas issued to reporters has raised the question of an acute need for federal shield laws which would protect a journalist from revealing his confidential sources. Many states have passed such shield legislation, but the Congress has not acted as yet. The debate on the efficacy of shield laws is acrimonious, even among the representatives of the media. Proponents believe that a totally free press is essential to democratic government. If newsmen cannot protect sources, the First Amendment would lose much of its unique value to a free press. But the courts do not always agree, demanding that journalists turn over their data and reveal their sources of information to grand juries under penalty of imprisonment. Several reporters have been jailed for refusal to conform.

Opponents of a shield law claim that such legislation would violate the Constitution because it would regulate the performance of the media. It would give the government an entry into the editorial process and an opening wedge toward control of the communications media. The pure purpose of shield legislation would be self-defeating and a free press would suffer the consequences.

Only one branch can pass shield legislation, and that is the Congress. The Federal Public Records Law (Freedom of Information Act) does not provide for shield law protection of the mass media; it can only be achieved by federal legislation giving the journalist absolute—not merely qualified—privilege. Although the media gave wholehearted support to the Moss Sub-Committee on Government Information (which constructed the FOI Act) and to the Moorhead Committee (which amended the FOI Act), the legislature apparently has been reluctant to pass a federal shield law protecting the right of the journalist to maintain confidential sources of information. Some editors, nevertheless, have expressed the opinion that it is not the function of the media to intrude upon, or participate in, the legislative process. What the media did accomplish in their support of the Moss Committee, however, was the creation of a climate of awareness in the Congress, so that legislation could be enacted that would attempt to put an end to the tendency of the federal bureaucracy to withhold information.

The increasing perception of the need for shield laws has come about as a result of the several court decisions against the press on matters relating to confidential information. To the media, the judicial signals are not encouraging. The Earl Caldwell case (a *New York Times* reporter who was jailed for refusing to reveal confidential sources of data relevant to an account about the Black Panther movement) was a discouraging decision to the media and, unhappily, set a precedent for other similar actions against reporters. The claim of the courts is that journalists have no rights that supersede those of any other citizens—a rationale that seems valid until one examines the peculiar role of the press as a surrogate of the public. By refusing to recognize the social responsibility of the media, the courts have shown a disregard for the special informational function of mass communications in a free society. As articulated by Mr. Justice White, the opinion of the Supreme Court appears to be that there is to be no recognition of the confidential nature of the relationship between the journalist and his source. Apart from the dubious effect of this opinion on the First Amendment, there is the inevitable drying up of news sources. If this occurs, the loss will be the public's.

The Supreme Court has implicitly challenged the Congress to come to some decision regarding the necessity of a federal shield law, for only this legislative body can now determine whether absolute privilege for the journalist is necessary or desirable. Despite the introduction of a number of bills, the Congress has yet to pass such legislation. To be resolved is the question of whether shield laws should protect only the media or be extended to embrace other information gatherers, such as historians, novelists, researchers and professors. What groups, if any, should be exempted from shield legislation? Or, should the law not go beyond the right of the journalist to keep sources of information confidential? From the reporter's viewpoint, a continuance of the present situation will inevitably result in the drying up of important sources of news. Therefore, despite the fact that 18 states have passed such laws, a federal law is necessary in order to provide national and uniform protection for the media. A federal shield law would mean added affirmation of the intent of the First Amendment.

Many in the Congress believe that there are valid reasons for not passing federal shield legislation and that such a law would pose serious problems for press and public. There is the danger that it would enhance the possibility of government control and lead to some forms of prior restraint. Shield laws would defeat their purpose by giving the public and the press more government by intrusion. At issue is not merely the need of the press to protect sources, but the clear danger of government intervention in the news process. Many journalists, for this reason, do not believe a shield law would be beneficial to a free press. They are convinced that the current procedure offers satisfactory protection, even in the light of recent court decisions against the media. A shield law could conceivably give the federal bureaucracy powers of implicit control which it does not, and should not, possess. Some editors even tend to agree with Mr. Justice White that the reporter should have no privileges or immunities that differ from those of other citizens.

These opinions raise the question of a suitable alternative. What course can the media take to preserve their information-gathering function? One way that has been suggested is for the media to mount and maintain its own editorial campaign, to use its own natural resources to fight decisions like Caldwell and, therefore, to reach and enlist the support of the people and of organizations designed to protect the public interest. It is doubtful, however, that the Supreme Court can be persuaded to bow to the pressure of public opinion. Historically, it has not.

The major concern seems to be that of the Congress passing legislation governing the behavior of the press. Thus, it is claimed, a shield law could become a two-edged sword, and the ultimate result might thwart the purpose for which it was passed and prove inimical to a free and responsible press. Those who maintain this opinion, however, might be reminded that a similar threat could be construed to be implicit in the First Amendment, which has managed to survive in a reasonably healthy state for 200 years.

4

The Information Establishment

THE WASHINGTON INFORMATION establishment is a large, sprawling, unwieldy phenomenon comprised of official directors of public information (or similar identification), unofficial public relations advisers and government department heads who practice their own unilateral brand of publicity, often without the knowledge of their own public information personnel. In addition, sub-department heads speak to the press, either by direct and official contact, by private and confidential "leaks," by backgrounders, not for attribution or quotation, or by what is known as "deep background" briefing.

Supplementing and working variously in either a cooperative or adversarial relationship with the federal public information officials are the huge Washington corps of correspondents. These news people represent wire services or press associations (foreign and domestic), national daily newspapers, local and regional daily newspapers, weeklies, assorted magazines (particularly news and business publications), newsletters, polling representatives and radio and television broadcasting correspondents.

Washington, it is said, is a publicity-oriented community, a city where secrets are constantly being confided and never kept in confidence. The General Accounting Office reported in 1977 that there were 3,366 federal employees engaged in public relations activities at an annual cost of $65 million. Just how this figure was arrived at is a mystery, however, since both the GAO and OMB (Office of Management and Budget) claimed to have no way of verifying the figures. At the same time, Senator William Scott (R. Va.) disputed the report of the General Accounting Office. Senator Scott stated that there are 3,390 P.R. personnel in the government at an annual cost of $93 million.

Oddly enough, despite the thousands of press releases that are distributed by the federal branches and agencies and that literally inundate the media, genuine, newsworthy information about the government is exceedingly difficult to obtain, by either the media or the public. Prior to the passage of the Freedom of Information Act, it was virtually impossible to receive the most innocent of documents. What is available are hundreds—indeed thousands—of booklets, brochures, reports and surveys that are well laid out, handsome to look at, but contain little in the way of genuine news. All are basically promotion pieces, many intended as reports to the Congress. Many are calculated to do little more than serve as an illustrated paean of praise for the institution that produced them. A few carry genuine information about the government agency and its activities.

Government Publications

The main repository and source of informational materials in Washington is the U.S. Government Printing Office, which also has branches in principal cities, where thousands of materials, ranging from large volumes to pamphlets, can be purchased. The Government Printing Office, housed in a massive square-block building, is the largest printing establishment in this country, and probably in the world. Its official publication is the *United States Government Manual,* a volume running to almost 900 pages and sold as the official handbook of the federal government. Each major agency of the government is covered in terms of its purpose and various programs, along with those of the quasi-official agencies and international organizations. It does not, however, include information about the internal information structure of the agencies.

The *Federal Register* is a daily publication that publishes—for the information of both press and public—various agency regulations, as well as documents of the executive branch. The system of records maintained by the agencies and the methods of obtaining information under the Privacy Act of 1974 (affirming the right to privacy and providing safeguards to prevent misuse of personal information held by the federal government) is also published by the office of the *Federal Register*. Workshops are held by the office in order to explain how interested parties can use the *Register* to keep abreast of federal regulations. Annually, the cumulative total of agency regulations is compiled in the *Code of Federal Regulations*. Freedom of Information Act regulations are contained in the *Code*. The *Weekly Compilation of Presidential Documents* includes transcripts of presidential press conferences, public speeches and other executive documents. Information about family history and genealogy is maintained by the National Archives.

The information available from the Government Printing Office, literally ranging from pamphlets on accident prevention to zoology, is not intended primarily for the media, but for the public. Government documents, books and pamphlets run to almost 25,000 publications each year and the available titles are offered to the potential reader in two monthly indexes. Publications issued under the imprimatur of various agencies and departments are listed in a compendium of government periodicals. Publications of the various departments vary widely. Agriculture lists 23 pamphlets; the Civil Service Commission offers 8; the Commerce Department as many as 41; the Congress, 11; the Department of Defense, 53; the Executive Office of the President, 4; the Department of Health, Education and Welfare, 36; the Department of the Interior, 11; the Judiciary, 5; the Justice Department, 5; the Labor Department, 12; the State Department, 9; and the Treasury Department, 12. In addition to these publications, descriptive literature and annual reports to the Congress by various departments may be obtained without charge directly from the public information office of the departments and agencies. Occasionally, a research-minded reporter can come across an interesting lead for a story by a careful reading and follow-up of information contained in an annual report, such as that issued, for example, by the United States Information Agency.

News Services

The activities of the federal branches, agencies and quasi-agencies are covered by a vast corps of varied correspondents. Some are "regulars," well known, reputable and respected. Others are part-time news people, stringers, correspondents who purvey news to a series of regional papers. This country has no so-called national newspaper, a situation that prevails in many countries abroad. The closest to a national press is probably *The New York Times*. But other large daily papers in major cities maintain Washington bureaus with regular correspondents (*The New York Daily News, The Los Angeles Times* and other papers in most metropolitan areas). Local papers occasionally have a Washington-based correspondent but are more likely to depend on three sources for news: a regional correspondent; handouts from the press office of the area Congressman; and, above all, the wire services, which, combined, reach virtually every one of the 1,750 daily newspapers published in the United States. Each of the two wire services, the Associated Press and the United Press International, has fully-staffed Washington bureaus with reporters covering all agencies of the federal government. The major news magazines (*Time, Newsweek, U.S. News and World Report*) maintain large and exceedingly able correspondents and researchers. And the radio and television network news divisions also have fully staffed Washington news bureaus.

Thus, the only so-called "national" newspapers distributed in this country are presently *The New York Times* and the seven regional editions of the daily *Wall Street Journal*. In other countries, particularly England and Japan, cities like London and Tokyo produce newspapers of a national character. In the United States, to a great extent because of the market configuration of both print and broadcast journalism, localism has become an important news staple. National news, especially in papers without Washington correspondents, is not particularly covered in depth, and the papers rely largely on the wire services. There is a far greater emphasis on local government news in this country than elsewhere, and the total news "mix" in general is a unique combination of national and local information, owing largely to broadcast news and to the press (wire) services. Wherever possible, both print and electronic media tend to try to give national news a local "slant." The daily phenomena of the newspaper and the split-second timing of the news broadcasts are gigantic technological achievements. News and informational flow now comes from various sources and is distributed by a highly sophisticated technology, including the use of domestic and international satellite communications, national, local and regional press services (as well as international services such as Reuters, Agence France Presse and Tass) and facsimiles. The news flow is also affected indirectly by the growth of newspaper chains and conglomerates and cross-channel affiliation of newspapers and broadcast properties.

Some observers of American journalism believe that this country offers a confusing variety of news, an informational glut which, rather than enlightening, tends to be mind-numbing. Debated vigorously is the moot question of whether there ought to be a national newspaper, or even a newspaper issued officially by the government. Such a paper would be a most unusual—and unwelcome—publication in the United States. In the first decade of the nineteenth century, one Samuel Harrison Smith began publishing *The National Intelligencer* in Washington, a paper which became a kind of quasi-official publication of the administration. Later, in the period of Andrew Jackson's presidency, a Washington paper called the *United States Telegraph* served as an administration publication. A Jackson aide, Francis P. Blair, also published a pro-administration newspaper in 1830 called the *Washington Globe*. But this country never has produced—and probably never will—a newspaper controlled and edited by the government along the line of *Pravda* or *Izvestia* in the Soviet Union. The free press would not sit still for it, the public would reject it, the Constitution would prohibit it.

The only so-called "national" news publications distributed in this country, other than the *The New York Times* and the *Wall Street Journal*, are the news magazines *Time* and *Newsweek*. Still, the

United States boasts of more newspapers—despite attrition over the last 20 years—than any other country, even though countries abroad have national newspapers. A mixture of localism and nationalism in our media is rooted in our tradition and in the system of mass communication that prevails in this society. The early newspapers in New England carried essentially news from abroad for the benefit of local merchants. Controlled by the Postmaster and printed only by authority, the press was highly restricted in its freedom of action. But the emphasis on a free press by Madison, Jefferson and others, the enormous pressure for States' rights from the Jefferson followers and the expansion of the West all combined to contribute to a strong incentive toward a local press system. With all of the contemporary emphasis on the "global village," our current broadcasting system is a combination of national (network) and local (independent or affiliated stations) news. Despite a growing internationalism in news, owing to satellites and world press associations, the public has not given up its felt need for local information about its own communities.

Wire Services

Five major press associations provide a daily service of worldwide news: The Associated Press and United Press International in the United States; Agence France Presse in France; Reuters in Great Britain; Tass in the Soviet Union. There are a multiplicity of smaller services, but these five offer an unprecedented news service in their speed and accuracy, timeliness and professionalism.

In the United States, news from Washington reaches most newspapers by way of AP or UPI. Very few papers, except the large metropolitan dailies, can afford a group of correspondents large enough to cover the sprawling federal agencies. As a result, the wires provide daily intelligence from Washington to more than a thousand newspapers. They also service news from other cities around the world, offering speedy reproductions of pictures and data from local and state government by means of their regional wires. Each press association supplies broadcasting networks and stations with news on the radio wires, although the three television networks maintain large Washington bureaus. At one time, the AP refused to permit radio stations to receive wire service news and, as a result, William S. Paley, Board Chairman of CBS, established one of the great news divisions of the world. Today, radio and television news are lucrative services of the press associations.

Despite criticism of the press associations for stereotyped, "inverted pyramid" writing, lack of originality and interpretive journalism, the fact is that both AP and UPI provide an indispensable service to almost all the newspapers in this country. The news about national politics and the federal government that reaches the reader is largely due to the expert staffs of the two major press associations in Washington. AP and UPI reporters, because of the wire services they provide, are usually in the vanguard of the press corps in covering trips by the President. They manage to report developments of virtually all of the branches and agencies of the government for their member papers. The Associated Press is a cooperative organization of member papers, each making news available to the other members. The United Press (now United Press International, having taken over Hearst's defunct International News Service) sells its news to member papers and is not, therefore, a cooperative venture. Both services are intensely competitive and offer a unique brand of timely and speedy journalism which utilizes the most modern and sophisticated of technologies.

Over the past decades, wire service staffs in Washington have increased from a total of about 20 reporters to 100 or more expertly trained and professionally skilled correspondents. Even the press associations, which have had to maintain a fairly set style because of the number of papers serviced, have engaged in greater interpretive reporting of government affairs. The wire service reporters also probe and dig for stories because of the demand for news from Washington from local papers, three-fourths of which do not maintain bureaus or reporters in the nation's capital. The combined impact of national, international and local political news is skillfully distilled by AP and UPI into a daily résumé of political information. Many local newspapers receive one or both services, and it is standard procedure to indicate on a story that the source is the Associated Press or United Press International. The newspaper chains, such as the Newhouse papers and others, rely almost exclusively on the wires for news out of Washington.

Thus, the press associations' telegraphic services exert enormous social control over Washington-based information and, indeed, are the chief source of national political news for most readers. It is now possible for wire copy to be sent directly to the composing room for typesetting and printing. The national and regional wires are, in a sense, the news centers of information about government activities and are relied upon by a large segment of both the press and the public—although most readers are not aware of the source of their news. The services make an effort not only to give local relevance to stories but also to be responsive to inquiries from their local papers. The major asset of wire service reporting is speed and accuracy of news flow, along with the use of computerization and automation.

The fundamental problem, however, is not technological but social and political in that there is inevitable control of news at the source. The reader misses diversity because of the necessity for standardization of political information. The very style of wire service copy implicitly influences news content, and many critics deplore the lack of innovative reporting. Critics also believe that even two highly competitive services do not provide sufficient diversity in Washington news. They believe that other sources of information should be developed. The need to meet the demands of so many papers unfortunately results in uniformity of product. On the other hand, there is the undeniable fact that the AP and UPI are highly competitive, and the speed and reliability of the service compensate for the limitations. Their Washington bureaus can boast a corps of seasoned, veteran reporters who are quite capable of separating news from political propaganda. Unfortunately—and despite a high degree of responsibility—the wire services must supply the kind of news that papers want and readers demand—news that tends to be sensational or exciting. In this way, important information on cultural and economic matters tends to be submerged, while news of scandals or disputes preempt the pages of the newspapers.

Local Coverage

The regional and local newspapers of the country are interested primarily in bringing to their readers news from Washington that has relevance to them. Of primary interest and concern are the activities of those in the government who represent particular cities and states—Senators and Congressmen, as well as other government officials from the home town. While the wire service reports on Congressional leaders are significant, the newspapers are inclined to seek out the opinions of those who represent the state and to try and discover local news relevance. The impact of legislation on gasoline pricing and the whole question of the energy crisis may be a national problem, but news out of Washington on these matters is peculiarly germane to the so-called oil-producing areas. Since most papers cannot afford to maintain correspondents in Washington, the wire services are supplemented frequently by the employment of a regional correspondent by several papers in the area. The basic assignment is to discover and relay Washington news with an orientation toward its local impact and significance. It is not unusual for one correspondent, in an area like the Pacific Northwest, to represent the interests of eight or ten papers in the region. These correspondents, familiar with local needs and problems, provide a valuable supplement to the wires, which cannot hope to encompass local needs fully.

Washington news of local significance involves primarily an account of the political and social behavior of local representatives in the national government. It explicates the position of elected officials on national issues in terms of their relevance to local problems and needs. Attendance at sessions, membership on committees, opinions on pending legislation, comments on executive decisions and on the progress of federal funding of projects in the area—all provide significant information to the local press for its readers. Altogether, at least 500 newspapers have arrangements for coverage on these issues, either by bureaus or, more likely, by special arrangements with correspondents. By this method, the local readers are provided with effective political communication in a way that contributes to their ability to make value judgments and more intelligent political decisions. Both the democratic process and the function of a free and responsible press are encouraged. An informed public opinion is more likely to result from direct information. And, although the presence of locally oriented reporters cannot fail to have some effect on the legislative activities of officials, that is not the prime purpose. The correspondent's function is to convey an accurate account of the work of local representatives in Washington and the relevance of that work to the area.

A most effective way of servicing the local press and its readers with news about Washington politics is the national syndicate. Hundreds of newspapers, metropolitan as well as local, rely on the syndicated political columnist for news—and opinion—about the government and its officials. Newspaper syndicates distribute news services, as well as cartoons, medical columns and advice of various kinds to the newspapers that contract to buy these services. Indeed, there is no more powerful group of journalists than the Washington-based political pundits. In the past decades, these have included Jack Anderson, the Alsops, Evans and Novak, Peter Edson, among others. Variously, these columnists cover social, political and cultural aspects of the "Washington Merry-Go-Round"—along with the political exposé and exclusive, occasionally with a touch of sensationalism. Their columns are sold to papers which subscribe to the various syndicates—Newspaper Enterprise Association, Bell Syndicate and many others. The more papers that take the service, the more lucrative the venture. The syndicated political writers, along with the Op Ed columnists for *The New York Times* and the *Washington Post,* comprise the so-called journalistic elite. Their columns are not only read widely but have significant effect on other journalists, as well as on the officials of the federal establishment.

News Magazines

Publications such as *Time, Newsweek* and *U.S. News and World Report* are eclectic news magazines, covering national and international affairs in the main part of the publication and various other subjects, such as science, the arts, education, religion and other areas in the sections known as the "back of the book." The main story is usually, although not invariably, political, dealing with an important breaking national or international news event of the past week. Even international affairs, however, are discussed, interpreted and appraised in terms of their significance to Washington and to the prevailing political atmosphere. Since the daily press and the broadcast media have already covered the basic news, the news magazines try to analyze problems in depth, to evaluate their effect on political decision-makers. Frequently the copy in the news publication contains an editorial slant, implicitly or explicitly expressed.

In addition to the weekly news magazines, the Periodical Press Gallery at the Capital has several hundred registered correspondents, representing a large variety of weekly and monthly publications, mainly magazines. None of these publications has the need to meet the rigors of a daily deadline, although *Time* and *Newsweek* do an unusually able job of putting out a magazine each week that offers fairly thorough coverage of what goes on in Washington and around the world. The emphasis of periodical publications, to a large extent, is on the thoughtful appraisal, the "think" piece, the speculation—based on present knowledge—about what might develop. Government events tend to be discussed in terms of broad public policy instead of hard news. This reportage demands that *Time* and *Newsweek* do considerable background research, including innumerable interviews with sources—some quoted directly, some noted without attribution. Each week, the major news magazines will usually select one major story and subject it to exhaustive discussion and analysis. Where and why, for example, do the President and the Congress differ on the question of natural gas deregulation? What special thinking or consideration went into a presidential proposal to the Congress? The purpose is not specific deadline data but rather an effort to probe a story from every conceivable perspective. This effort requires the seeking of opinion from a vast variety of sources. As a result, some of the news stories develop into major essay-type pieces on the state of national affairs—the energy crisis, Washington's role in the Middle East, the status of *détente* and so forth.

Time and *Newsweek* maintain large Washington bureaus, with about 25 or 30 on the staff. Smaller publications may have as few as two, three or four correspondents. The spade work for national news magazine pieces is done in Washington, although it appears that much of the writing and editing comes out of New York. Some observers have deplored the news publication pieces as writing by committee and have been critical of the degree of normative or judgmental values inherent in the stories. Clearly, however, the very nature of the publication implies a degree of subjectivity, since it does not attempt to convey straight, hard news. To be meaningful after the event, a degree of speculative writing is to be expected and should be appropriately evaluated by the reader. *Time* has stated that it "never claimed to be neutral . . . we do claim to be fair."

Newsletters

The newsletter is a unique phenomenon in Washington journalism. There is a wide and virtually endless variety of these publications, some of significance, others little more than "inside" gossip sheets. A few, such as the *Kiplinger Letter*, are respected and substantial and reach an influential group of subscribers. The newsletter is designed, like the news magazine, to go beyond the confines of conventional newspaper and broadcast journalism. The material purveyed by the newsletter is based on hard, long digging and research and is intended for specific publics such as the business executive, the educator, the government official, the public relations and managerial group and the labor leaders, among others. The purpose is not to relay news but rather information not available in the more conventional outlets. These newsletters base their evaluation of what might happen on what *has* happened. They are a guide to the formation of judgment and eventual action by the reader. Thus, they take on a great deal of seriously accepted responsibility to their subscribers.

Newsletters are as old as the Republic. One of the first was probably the *Boston News-Letter* in the eighteenth century. Then (as now) they were not large, voluminous publications. Today, the average newsletter runs from four to eight pages and there are about 1,600 newsletters published. The style is terse and brief. They do not seek a philosophical point of view but rather predictive information. One of the areas they try to avoid is a repetition of what has already been printed in the daily press or the weekly news magazines. They attempt a look down the road on what is likely to occur in the economy, in the professions, education, legislation. Kiplinger's credo is "look ahead." Newsletters generally avoid dogma and direction. They attempt to point out what might occur, what its significance might be, so that the reader can decide and act accordingly. Since they have no purpose in being on top of the news, they have none of the roles of the daily newspaper. One of the most respected, as aforesaid, and probably the oldest (it was established in 1923) is the *Kiplinger Letter*. This publication, as well as the others, reaches the subscriber directly by mail.

Newsletters usually do not attempt to influence public policy. Their function is not controversial, but informational. They have no goal to influence national politics or pending legislation. They are not special interest or advocacy publications. They provide information of value to the subscriber, so that he can make his own decisions on the issues discussed.

Sources of news and information to the public from Washington are various and complex and they frequently are duplicative. The government agencies, in particular, are inevitably competitive, because no newspaper could possibly print even a fraction of the releases that are distributed by the federal informational establishment. At the same time, no newspaper or service—not even the wires—could hope to cover all the activities of the bureaucracy. There is a flood of information available, most of it not newsworthy and most of it summarily rejected or ignored by the media. By a process of selectivity, the able correspondents try to separate genuine news from trivia and promotion and make an effort to surmount the barriers that often are set up to conceal genuine news. In short, there is no dearth of informational flow in political Washington. But most of it is not newsworthy. The vast information establishment grinds on, however, making this country the most news conscious in the world with—despite the roadblocks to genuine news—the best informed people in the world.

5

Government Publicists
and Newsmen

THOSE WHO REPRESENT the government as federal public information officers (known also as press officer, press secretary, public affairs director, assistant secretary for public information and so on) and those who function as reporters and columnists for the mass media perceive their roles as quite different from each other, although both concede that a necessary symbiotic relationship must exist if they are to function in a rational way.

Information to the people is a categorical necessity in a political democracy. But the press officer for the government is, overtly or implicitly, an apologist for the federal department or agency which he represents. The public, of course, has a right to know. It is entitled to intelligence about the federal bureaucracy which its taxes support, but the information officer contends that it must be disseminated only from the viewpoint of the sender. The media, on the other hand, perceive their function as more than a placid, cooperative recorder and expediter of public relations messages from the government to the readers, viewers and listeners. Those who have the assignment of reporting on the decisions and activities of the federal government want to dig beneath the surface, to probe, to ferret, investigate and explore. At this juncture, a point of resistance develops and the traditional adversarial relationship between the media and the federal bureauracy becomes operative. Fortunately, the adversary role of each is not exhaustive. Within this conflict of interest area, cooperation and accommodation must be developed. For reasons of sheer pragmatism, if for no other, the media and the federal bureauracy must work together—if not in the public interest, at least in their own. Both bear a heavy responsibility, not only to the public, but to their department heads, editors and publishers. Both are protective of their jobs and prerogatives, their reputation among superiors and their peer groups.

The government publicist functions as a persuasive communicator. His goal is to reach and influence opinion—in the Congress, in the mass media, in the agency itself and among the people. The media newsmen, as recipients, decide what to print and what to purvey on the air. The correspondents can be helpful or frustrating to the government's effort to persuade and to create consent. To the extent that the media serve as merely a conduit for government propaganda, without skepticism or questioning the source, they become unwitting tools of the federal public relations effort. It is not, however, the function of the media to participate in the informational process of the bureaucracy, which is why the reporter rarely accepts government news without wanting additional information in the way of interviews, further facts and relevant background data.

This healthy skepticism is the backbone of the media's function as public watchdog, and it was this probing tendency which so aroused the ire of the Nixon publicists, who claimed that the media ought to write "good" and not "bad" news about the administration. But news which interests the reader and viewer tends to be of the "bad" variety. Representative Wayne Hays would not have made the front pages of the nation's press if he had not been involved in an alleged scandal, because he would not have made news. Walter Lippmann pointed out a long time ago that the presence of an impending disaster is not news. It requires an overt incident to make a situation newsworthy.

Interaction and Communication

The joint endeavors of the public information official and the news correspondent—an interaction between sender and receiver in the process of public communication—are responsible for the daily flow of news on which public opinion and political action are predicated. Few, if any, countries have an analogous system of government–media news gathering and dissemination. In the United States, the public information process is an integral part of democratic government. When interaction between federal officials and the press is open and healthy, the public is the beneficiary. When the relationship deteriorates because of manipulative propaganda or withholding of news, the public is the loser. Veteran journalist I.F. Stone questioned ''if the government lies must the press fib?'' It is clearly not the function of the media to engage in publicity or apologetics on behalf of the government.

In recent years, there has been an increasing awareness of the presence and role of the government press official, particularly in such quarters as the White House, the Department of State and the Department of Defense. Some of these officials become widely known because they lie to the press, which, in turn, exposes those lies. Others are colorful for their cooperation with, or antagonism toward, the media, as in the respective cases of Pierre Salinger (the Kennedy Administration) and Ron Ziegler (the Nixon White House). Perhaps the Press Secretary with the greatest authority to speak to the media was James Hagerty in the Eisenhower Administration. On the other hand, J.F. ter Horst, who was newly appointed Press Secretary to President Ford, quietly resigned after giving wrong information to the press unwittingly and subsequently discovering he had been misinformed by his own White House. The mere fact that each of these officials was well known to the public is testimony to the increasing reliance of the government, particularly the White House, on the value of public information. All presidents since the administration of Franklin Delano Roosevelt have displayed an acute awareness of the power of the media.

The Washington press corps has two main functions. The first is to seek out the day's intelligence. The second is to convey this intelligence to the public by the technology of mass communication—in the press and on the air. Ideally, these dual purposes are best achieved when a cooperative atmosphere prevails between the reporter and the federal official. An informed public opinion is likely to result from this healthy accommodation and interaction of informational forces. Public issues which are implicitly controversial can be discussed and evaluated by means of the so-called "two-step flow," where news is filtered through opinion leaders to various groups, and a democratic consensus frequently results. The role of the media in this process is a seminal one. And the federal information apparatus cannot do its job without a nexus of agreement with the media. At the same time, many correspondents, particularly the elite columnists, have little traffic with government publicists other than an occasional request for routine material. To the major part of the press, however, the official is the primary source of information and the provider of press releases, interviews, conferences and the educated guesses out of which news will develop.

The rise in importance of the federal press official has been paralleled by a concomitant growth in numbers. Senator Scott's estimate of almost 4,000 government publicists is probably accurate (see Appendix for Scott statement on numbers and cost of government publicity). If it is, the ratio of public information officials to the press corps is about two to one. Such a vast and complex informational effort must inevitably result in duplication of effort, a waste of tonnage in paper for press releases and a fabrication of pseudo-events which becomes more exploitative than informative. It is an apparatus unique to the political climate of the nation's capital.

One of the first steps taken by new branch and agency heads is a look at the public information setup. Usually, changes are difficult because of the Civil Service tenure rights. But the awareness of the need for publicity inevitably results also in interagency competition and a jockeying for favorable position with the media. The competition increases the tension for self-aggrandizement on the part of some officials, although there are always a few federal bureaucrats who assign their public relations officer the task of keeping the press at arm's length. Ron Ziegler made it plain that President Nixon did not welcome the press and despised most of them, while President Lyndon Johnson—and to some extent John F. Kennedy—could make matters difficult for the Press Secretary by engaging in their own public relations with the media, often without the knowledge of the press officer.

Perceptions of Role

Several variables enter into the relationship that develops between the federal publicist and the media. Prime factors are the objectives and attitudes of the agency's management. A second consideration is the kind of administration in Washington, an "open" one or a closed door—a consideration which can affect the interaction of all government publicists with the news correspondents. These factors determine, in the last analysis, how an agency will function in the arena of press relations: whether it will attempt news management, whether it will attempt manipulation and propaganda or whether it will assume what the press would expect—a truthful and cooperative attitude. How these various attitudes evolve will ultimately determine how the press officer will operate. The most competent of information officers, some of them with previous newspaper or broadcast experience, see themselves as expediters for the media. Others try to control news by attempting to persuade the press to be no more than a channel to the public. Still others are so completely management-oriented that they see their function as primarily protective of the government agency's prerogatives.

Both the federal publicist and the correspondent, whatever the motivations and relationship that develop, influence the way in which political information is filtered to the public, although from different perspectives. Unfortunately, the federal bureaucracy operates in a way that often makes it virtually impossible to convey straight, uncolored, factual information to the media. Too many variables and internal situations intrude on the informational process. Institutional responsibilities, in particular, prevent the publicist from offering the news people the free and unfettered access to information which they seek as an ideal relationship between government and media. The newsman wants a clear explanation, without obfuscation, of government policy. The government official seeks as passive a reception as possible of what purports to pass as policy. Both claim to act in the public interest, but both, to a degree, are bound by self-serving considerations. The newsman seeks the excitement of a major story. The information officer seeks a favorable "image" for his institutional superior, as well as for his agency.

Unfortunately, too few government public relations officers have executive authority or status. A good part of the press cannot erase the opinion of them as government "flacks," mere messengers for the agency they represent. Part of this attitude may result from the fact that the agency head prefers to be his own public opinion strategist. In these instances, the press officer cannot function on a policy-making level and his perception of his role—as well as the perception which the media develop toward his role—is a negative one. Even under these restrictions, however, officials who deem a good relationship with the media imperative can provide useful services to reporters as guides to possible news, as aids in securing information, as instruments in finding answers to questions. Some government officials carry out these functions in spite of the fact that they must run an obstacle course within the bureaucracy itself. The basic conflict of all government publicists is inevitable—to reconcile the needs of protecting the agency with providing political information to the press. The reporter, despite publishers and gatekeepers, has no such divided responsibility. The elite, in particular, consider their sole obligation to be to the public. Professor John Merrill's view of the journalist is one of having no responsibility except a clear, libertarian responsibility to himself. The press is autonomous.

Another viewpoint of the journalist's function vis à vis the federal bureaucracy is that while the critical function of the press should not be abandoned, the correspondent also must look upon his work as demanding some sympathetic acceptance of what the government wants to see conveyed to the public. This view is expressed by Professor Ithiel de Sola Pool, who believes that the press, to some degree, *should* serve as a conduit for government information. Beyond the libertarianism of Merrill and the more empathetic viewpoint of de Sola Pool is the position of the "new" journalism, which insists that the reporter should not hesitate to probe, goad and speak out without reservation. But this action would destroy the necessary distinction among the divisions by which news is conveyed. "What happened" is an account of the breaking event. "Why it happened" is an interpretation or discussion of the implications of that event. But the question of whether it should have happened is generally reserved for the editorial page or the signed political columnist. In this way, the public can best distinguish between news and opinion. Since the inception of a national television service in 1952, the fact that this medium can now receive and convey "breaking" news more speedily than print necessarily has changed the style of newspaper coverage and has stimulated a greater tendency toward news analysis and interpretative journalism.

The Washington press is a mixed bag of a seasoned, respected elite—a group of "regulars" who cover various branches and agencies and a larger group of stringers, regional reporters and younger newsmen who are engaged in the struggle to make a place for themselves among the ever-growing corps of correspondents. Reporters function differently, depending on the agency they cover, the organization they represent and the place they hold in the hierarchy. The elite columnists are pretty much a law unto themselves. Most others work by assignment. Some reporters, particularly since the investigative fever generated by the Watergate and CIA exposés, devote their total effort to trying to develop a resounding front-page exclusive. In each of these situations, however, the perceptions of the federal official and the correspondent remain different. Rarely do their objectives reconcile. In essence, the difference in perception is that of what the public *should* know about the government and what the public has a *right* to know. Those press officers who can make determinations of public policy, as well as promulgate that policy as information, tend to be most respected and accepted by the media.

The Washington reporter quickly learns how useful a federal official will be to his purposes. The litmus tests are how often the press officer must check with superiors before acting, how quickly he can arrange interviews with agency executives and his ability to extrapolate on the information contained in official releases without resorting to a repeated "no comment" beyond what is printed. Thus, in government, even more vigorously than in industrial management, the information official who can make policy is the most effective media catalyst.

In Washington politics, more than in the corporate enterprise, the publicist's onerous task too often has a negative thrust—to obscure or refuse information to a frustrated press. When this occurs, the correspondent invariably seeks, and usually finds, other sources of news. Paradoxically, those sources may be in the same branch or agency as the public information officer. This, of course, further demeans the status of government publicists in the opinion of the reporters. Most correspondents, in fact, when asked to name their most forthcoming and profitable sources of news, do not cite the public information officer, but rather turn to superiors or middle-rank officials. The former is valuable for "deep background" material and the latter can usually talk without fear of being quoted because their names in print would have little meaning to the public. Only a strong press officer can resist these interferences with function. Most officials assert that they do not so much resent the fact that reporters talk to others in the agency, but that they are by-passed in the process. This is more the fault of agency management than it is of the press.

Sources of Information

The various sources of news in Washington politics vary and tend to be capricious and casual as well as formal. Beyond the official methods of press release, interview and press conference, a great deal of news that reaches the media out of Washington occurs by other routes. Some of it is fortuitous, a casual comment that leads to a news peg. Some of it comes from other agencies and branches. Some occurs at formal or informal lunches, cocktail parties or dinners. Some eventuates out of what seem to be routine and desultory hearings of various committees. Many reporters prefer all of these rather haphazard methods to formal outlets, because they are not controlled situations. But informal news of this kind is often the bane of existence of the government public information officer who, like it or not, is held responsible for whatever news appears that affects his agency. News of this kind can not only prove embarrassing internally but can also have a negative effect on the agency's relationships with the Congress.

The relationship, then, between government reporter and federal publicist is tenuous, despite mutual interests and needs. They see their responsibilities in different ways and perform their functions differently and toward different goals. The reporter is satisfied, at least in part, by developing sound news sources, receiving accurate and truthful information, an occasional "leak," access to executives at the source. The government publicist seeks little more than a favorable story, or frequently no story at all. A high-level assistant secretary for public affairs baldly stated that the government publicist performed a protective function, even if this meant "stonewalling" or subverting the truth. This behavior was justified, no less, by the astonishing statement that it ultimately served the public interest! The media, operating on a totally different set of assumptions, tends to make every conceivable effort to tear down these obstructive observations as being utterly contemptuous of the "right to know" concept. In Washington politics, above all, there are infinite opportunities for speculation and interpretation; there are a variety of sources of news. Nowhere is there a greater tendency to dig beneath the surface of a "no comment" or to demolish the bearer of a bald-faced lie.

It is fortunate that not many government publicists agree with the attitude of the aforementioned public affairs official. Most operate by the tested and effective methods of communication with the media. Among these are

1. The official press release.
2. The background explanation or "white paper."
3. The summary of an official speech.
4. The summary of proceedings at a hearing or committee meeting.
5. The press conference.
6. The personal and private interview.
7. The interview conducted for a few select press.
8. The off-the-record "leak" or the "backgrounder."
9. The official event.
10. The special forum, such as a television news interview or weekly news program.

The press release, of course, is the traditional and standard method of government information. It can be controlled at the source and is a matter of public record. But the press invariably goes beyond the information in a release and relies on a variety of the other methods of obtaining news. In Washington, particularly, a favorite method of communication between high officials and the media is the use of the "leak," the "trial balloon" and the story that is for "deep background" only.

Since the advent of TV, in particular, information by press conference has taken on considerable significance, but this form is restricted pretty much to the executive and, in some instances, to the Secretary of State and other cabinet officers. The print media have a mixed reaction to the televised press conference. It is claimed that it is a staged event and therefore not productive of genuine news. Ironically, too, some correspondents deplore the tendency of their peers to "ham" before the cameras. But the televised conference can—and often does—reveal the superficialities of the Washington informational apparatus far better than any other method of news dissemination. Even the news report on television, showing a press officer in the process of responding with a lame "no comment," is revealing of the nature of the federal informational bureaucracy.

News: As Information

What is the nature of the news that the information officers dispense? From the centrally located management viewpoint, news is what is distributed to the press, largely by means of the conventional release, even though what is released may be more self-serving to the government than informative to the press and the public. To the journalist, however, news is variously anything that is written or aired that will capture the attention and interest of the public. This is usually of the exciting or sensational variety. But this reliance and emphasis on what excites, interests or entertains the reader is a limited view of what the media should be conveying to the public. It does not cohere well with the principle of the right to know, the need of the people to be informed. It neglects issues that are significant, albeit neither sensational nor entertaining, and in which the public has a vested interest. More space is devoted to the scandalous affairs of a Senator than to relevant issues affecting vital public opinion. Genuine news, information which fulfills the requirements of what has been termed "news as a form of knowledge," meets certain basic criteria and answers certain questions.

1. Is the material conveyed truly informative, is it a "form of knowledge"?
2. Does it contribute to an informed public opinion?
3. Is it purveyed in a form which is comprehensible and intelligent to the reader and/or viewer?
4. Is it timely—does it cohere with other events of significance to public discussion and consensus?
5. Is there the possibility that it will result in overt feedback or public action? Will an exposé of government dereliction in certain areas, for example, result in a demand for change?

To meet some, or all of these criteria, the press in Washington manages to ride herd on the activities of virtually all the major branches of government, the official and regulatory bodies and agencies and the multiplicity of quasi-agencies. Some of these make news on a daily basis. Some have little to offer in the way of information, except on rare occasions. The White House commands constant attention. The Library of Congress does not. Altogether, the press corps covering Washington is the largest in the world, with upwards of 1,200 correspondents accredited to the House and Senate Press Galleries alone—and the number has grown by about one-third in the past decade. This constantly proliferating corps of newsmen seems to create a daily chaos, a cacophony of media voices that threaten to cancel each other out in the frenetic and bitterly competitive search for news. But, despite the milling and jockeying for position that goes on, political reporting from Washington at its best is generally accurate and highly knowledgeable—although it is often based on intangibles and is also subjective and ephemeral. A great deal of the copy that emanates from Washington is also based on the reporter's "gut" reaction to personalities and events. In no other area of informational services do personalities and personal relationships color the news as in the volatile political environment of the federal government. Each President makes his "friends" and his "enemies" among the press corps. Information officers have their favored reporters, and reporters have their favorite news sources. Ostensibly, each public information specialist must function to convey the news impartially and truthfully, since the very essence of the assignment is that of public service. But the facts are that information officers inevitably veer toward those reporters who are more amenable to uncritical acceptance of news than others and toward those who will desist from digging further when the bureaucracy puts a lid on the release of information. In such instances, it is the reporter who must make a value judgment, frequently on a personal interest level. Will printing the story dry up a good source of news or create antagonism that will be reflected in future behavior? Will the reader suffer by not having the information?

These questions were once relatively simple. But the competition for news, the pervasive influence of the press associations, the impact of broadcast journalism and the increasing numbers of both information officials and correspondents have created new and unforeseen problems for the media. The traditional methods of reporting political news are changing. In the new climate of journalism, five trends are apparent.

1. A far greater need for and emphasis on investigative reporting.
2. A more critical attitude toward the media on the part of the public. Ironically, this has happened since the press exposure of Watergate, the CIA and the FBI.
3. A greater emphasis on news analysis and interpretation, particularly since television news became a national commodity.
4. The development of the controversial "new" journalism, a curious kind of libertarianism in which the reporter is as much participant and opinion-maker as objective journalist.
5. An ever-greater reliance on wire services and press syndicates.

Of these, the strongest emphasis appears to be on interpretative political reporting, so much so that critics have deplored the amount of speculation coming out of Washington as confusing to the formation of intelligent public opinion. The reason for this phenomenon, however, is the growing need for well-educated and trained journalists who are capable of interpreting for the public the increasingly complex issues that are being discussed in the Congress and elsewhere—the gas deregulation bill, ecological problems, the health and welfare tangle, the complexities of taxation and inflation. Clearly, as political issues, these present certain dangers and challenges to the media. Facts tend to be ignored by many pundits in favor of speculative meandering and even vague editorializing. The reporter unwittingly may become a participant in the legislative process—a step clearly beyond the journalist's domain. The careful interpretative columnists try to narrow their discussions to "why" or "how" a problem developed, to be tentative and searching rather than dogmatic.

News analysis is not an innovation in twentieth-century Washington. Correspondents in the earlier days of the Republic couched letter-style analysis as well as opinion and considerable idle political gossip in their reports. Nor is the opening-of-the-Pandora's-Box style new to Watergate. The short-lived, but powerful, muckraking movement saw such trenchant reporters as Ida M. Tarbell, Lincoln Steffens and Upton Sinclair use various media modalities to launch a vitriolic attack on the various evils of the "robber baron" era. The growth of the government bureaucracy, however, and the duplication and competition between agencies has created an ever-increasing need for the reporter who can not only garner the facts but sort them out in a sensible and coherent fashion. Complex issues demand skilled interpreters, a new breed of newsmen who are better educated and trained than the average reporter. No single general reporter, for example, is equipped to handle with certainty such diverse information as a Supreme Court decision on busing, an issue involving the First and Sixth Amendments on free press and fair trial, a presidential message on defense spending or complicated information involving changes in the tax structure. Some newspapers, despite their opposition to anything resembling the television Fairness Doctrine, have begun to include columns by syndicated writers with widely divergent points of view on the political spectrum. Other newspapers, like *The New York Times*, make certain to label interpretative reporting as "News Analysis."

Interpretative reporting, although it is not editorial opinion, does move beyond the boundaries of straight news or information. It is a difficult assignment and calls for extraordinary skill on the part of the correspondent to refrain from editorializing and to stick to an analysis of the "why" of what happened. At its best, written by wise and seasoned correspondents, it is another useful device in the arsenal of sound journalism. To preserve a democratic system, to maintain the philosophy of government by consent of the governed, Walter Lippmann asserted that the public must make decisions based primarily on knowledge gleaned from the news media. This surrogate function of the media is "no mean calling."

What Influences Media Content?

The informational grist that comes to the readers and viewers from the vast reportorial nexus of Washington political happenings is inevitably influenced by the social, economic, cultural and political climate. Would Senator McCarthy be as powerful a demagogic force in the 1970s as in the 1950s? Would Watergate have happened in the presidency of Dwight D. Eisenhower? Moot questions, of course, but the point is that events and the way they are reported—media content—are influenced by political and social currents, and they both influence and are influenced by prevailing public opinion. What affects media content and information flow is not so much the federal bureaucracy or the media as the political, economic and social environment. In a secondary sense, media managers and the press do exert an influence on content, the former by control at the source and the latter by various gatekeeping procedures. Special interest groups can also influence news content, particularly in news relating to government. Thus, many variables affect media content: senders and receivers, the intrusion of adventitious circumstances ("what else happened that day"), social, economic, political and cultural conditions. But there is an inevitable dependence of the federal information official on the reporter and, to a lesser extent, a dependence of the reporter on the informational source. The newspaper chains also depend to a great degree on the wire services and syndicates for Washington news, largely for reasons of sheer economic necessity. With more than 300 syndicated services available in this country, there is no paucity of available political copy. This inter- and intra-dependency can also affect media content.

Economic Influences

Although smaller by far than other major industries and with less "hardware" (as in the case of television), the investment by publishers, broadcasters and other mass media management is still sizable. When successful, as in broadcasting, the profits are astronomical. The public itself, as well as the advertiser, invests in media, even though the public investment is not great. And this investment is as much for information as for entertainment. The public also expects, indeed demands, intelligence of the activities of the government from the media—a demand unheard of in so many countries with government-controlled news sources. In this country, the government regulates one medium (broadcasting) in a limited way and assists the media by preferred postal rates, allocations for public television and subsidies for books and library services. In effect, the public looks upon the electronic media as indispensable commodities, along with refrigerators and automobiles. And, during newspaper strikes, there is a genuine need for this daily news phenomenon. So great is the economic and cultural commitment to mass communications that some fear there may be a resultant glut, an informational overload in which the meaning and implication of the news are lost in the constant inundation of information. This observation is particularly true of the tons of informational releases that pour out of the federal bureaucracy.

From an economic point of view, there is no political information system comparable to that of the United States. The media constitute a large, institutionalized endeavor, often accused of being monopolistic, yet uniquely independent of government control. No other country boasts of a similar system, and even Great Britain, with its long tradition of libertarianism, has laws which are restrictive of the press. Our media system is managed by private entrepreneurs, supported by advertising revenues, generally resistant to government pressures and dedicated to serving the public interest, despite the fact that a small minority of newspaper publishers are not as independent in news judgment as they might be. The public is the recipient of information out of Washington and this information is almost invariably conveyed by a press independent of federal pressure. The press is, of course, an instrument of social control. And, as one-newspaper situations tend to increase and competition decreases, there is a serious question as to the ultimate effect of concentrated power. In more than 70 areas, for example, there is one-ownership of both broadcast and newspaper properties. Indeed, the three major problems of concentration concern the following types of ownership.

1. Cross-ownership: ownership by the same management of press and electronic media in the same community.
2. Chain ownership: one company controlling a large number of newspapers (e.g., Newhouse, Gannett, Knight-Ridder).
3. Ownership of media properties by companies which have conglomerate interests. The Justice Department a few years ago, for example, looked askance at a plan for IT & T to take over ABC.

Does this lack of economic competition jeopardize the way news is handled, particularly in the sensitive area of Washington political information? Many students of the problem think not. Some believe that one newspaper, without competition, increases the need for responsibility and objectivity. Thus, lack of competition may not mean superior service, but it does not necessarily mean poor or biased news service. Unlike most countries, which have media systems that operate either under direct government control or ownership or are quasi-private but subject to restraint by government, the United States media system operates independently. Yet, some of the more severe critics of this country's informational system believe that the media are accessible to manipulation by the federal government, that news itself is not objective, that media managers exercise self-censorship at the source, that business considerations supersede the public interest and, finally, that reliance on advertising is a generally corrosive influence.

Undoubtedly there is a concentration of economic power. A coalition of publishers can be a powerful influence on government policy, not always in the interest of the people. Cross-channel ownership does offer opportunity for control of two formidable informational conduits. The fact that more than 50% of the newspapers are owned by chains is not, on the face of it, a healthy situation. The Newspaper

Preservation Act, by which Congress permitted two newspaper organizations to use one printing plant for economic reasons, has also been cited as a further stimulus to monopoly and control. Yet, despite these facts, the media have managed to perform their responsibilities as surrogates of the people's "right to know" and have resisted government pressure on news flow and content.

The central issue is whether fewer owners and more concentrated ownership is necessarily deleterious to the public interest so far as the accuracy and completeness of political information is concerned. The prevailing opinion at present—albeit with some vocal dissenters—is that it does not, that the newspapers and radio and television stations now operative assure a pluralism of voices sufficient to meet the public's needs. The government itself has recently become active in the matter of ownership by instituting anti-trust action and by an effort to break up media cross-ownership situations.

Politics and the Press

As the quantity of political news out of Washington increases, there has been a concomitant sophistication in news content. The credibility gap, so much discussed during the Johnson and Nixon Administrations, and the successful investigative reporting by the *Washington Post* in the Watergate scandals have exacerbated the traditional adversarial relationship between press officers and reporters—to the extent that information officials now complain that perhaps investigative reporting is no longer a result of a healthy skepticism, but rather a competitive race on the part of the media to expose and to find the constantly sensational in the news. Katherine Graham, chairman of the board of the Washington Post Company, quickly pointed out that the emphasis on "disclosure . . . is doing harm—harm to the nation in general and to the nation's press in particular." In the case of Watergate, "the press became not just a party, but an aggrieved, self-conscious party to the case" and the role of the media, Mrs. Graham asserted, became distorted. There is no doubt that the aftermath of Watergate left its bitter taste in the mouth of the press, but there are critics who question whether the race to be first with a shattering revelation is a healthy journalistic objective. The purpose of the press is to investigate, but it is also to bring the countless more mundane items of pertinent information to the people. Not all political news is revelation; not all government officials are potential scoundrels. As a result of this tendency to expose, it is felt by some government information officers, as well as by thoughtful journalists, that such topics as inflation, health legislation and other matters of public interest do not receive adequate news coverage by the media.

By selective perception, the press prints what it believes will excite and interest the public. And by the two-step flow theory, news from the Washington correspondents reaches those opinion leaders who have a more than ordinary interest in political communication and who then become important factors in the formation of public opinion. The media themselves implicitly serve as opinion leaders and molders of public policy. Of the multitude of correspondents covering Washington news, however, the seasoned government information officers regularly seek out a minority for the filtering of information. This selective method of yielding information is calculated to offer at least some measure of control. It is a device that is as old as the country, for Washington himself cautioned the members of the Constitutional Convention to be highly selective in what they told the press in order to curb popular speculation. Yet, then as now, the awareness of the service rendered by the press was clearly articulated. "A government without popular information or the means of acquiring it," Madison stated, is either a farce or a tragedy. In this era, Douglas Cater referred to the press as a "fourth branch of government." At no time, then, have government officials failed to recognize the role of the media in the formulation and dissemination of public policy. From George Washington to Jimmy Carter, the press has been seen as sometimes helpful, sometimes dangerous, but always as an indispensable institution of social control. As a result, government officials try to release news selectively and cautiously.

One of the widely accepted cautious methods of servicing the media (because of its very nature, some call it "planting" news) is the "backgrounder," information given to the reporter with the understanding that the source will remain confidential and the material will be used on a not-for-attribution basis. In the political climate of Washington, this has been virtually standard operating procedure, particularly in those branches and agencies where the news tends to be of a sensitive nature. Most reporters object to this method as manipulative. But most reluctantly go along with it in order to obtain kernels of information that would not otherwise be forthcoming. The device of the political background story, however, has several limitations. It is not good journalism. There is no ethical way the reporter, if challenged, can yield his source. The healthy adversary relationship becomes clouded in an atmosphere of implicit collusion. The ideal method is for full attribution, but both reporters and information officers agree that this ideal goal is simply not possible of achievement, particularly at the White House or State or Defense Department levels. A serious objection to the use of the backgrounder by government officials is that efforts are made to use the media to convey messages which go beyond a legitimate journalistic function. The reporter who is aware of this manipulative pitfall must reject this device and refuse to channel the information without attribution, no matter how newsworthy the item may appear to be. Yet, reporters claim, if they did not accept background and unattributed news, sources would dry up and the enterprising newsman would find investigative reporting exceedingly difficult.

The not-for-attribution story raises the pertinent question of whether the correspondent has any responsibility to assist the government in the purveying of information—whether, indeed, the media have any obligation to be a conduit for the dissemination of government policy. The prevailing opinion seems to be that the government is entitled to a fair and even sympathetic hearing from the media, but that the media have no responsibility to the federal bureaucracy beyond fair and honest reporting. Some observers hold the conviction, however, that there are occasions when the press must support government policy, when sensitive news should be omitted in order to cooperate with government policy-makers. In such cases, the press must relinquish both its surveillance and critical functions, steps which it has occasionally taken, but usually to its ultimate regret. The press' obligation extends to reporting accurately on government policies and activities. It has no obligation to agree with or to further such policies.

The media have a positive obligation to report; their interpretation and editorial opinion of what is reported, however, does not have to reflect the government's viewpoint. Professor Ithiel de Sola Pool's position is that for society to function, the press must occasionally decide to support and affirm government action. An adversarial position carried to extremes would be disruptive and chaotic. Thus, in the tug and pull of media-government interaction, the rule of reason must prevail, with the media recognizing the limitations of government publicity and the government recognizing the needs of the media for an accurate and truthful account of public policy.

Information gathering is the quintessence of journalism. In the Washington arena, the reporters who manage to secure the most newsworthy data tend to be specialists, rather than generalists. But even the most highly specialized reporters frequently complain of what they term "distortion" of their story, not from the federal source, but from the gatekeepers who handle the copy prior to publication. Publishers are not often accused of interference, although inferentially most newsmen are aware of the publisher's policies in the political spectrum. But headline writers and other editors can unwittingly change the meaning of a story in ways that are subtle yet which deflect from the original intent of the correspondent. Publishers, at least since the days of William Randolph Hearst, have become less involved in the editorial and reportorial process as they have become more involved in the business and promotional side of journalism. Nevertheless, there are students of American journalism who claim that the publisher's political philosophy is clearly evident in many newspapers such as *the New York Post* or *the New York Daily News*. Yet, these papers—particularly the large-circulation *Daily News*—usually do not fail to render a complete and accurate account of the day's intelligence, and stories of merit are not sacrificed because they do not meet a political point of view.

The reporter who, by inference, tends to try to reflect what the publisher's position may be is not an independent journalist. As it is, the news flow comes from a welter of diverse sources—bureaus, wire services, special correspondents, columnists, editors, syndicated writers—and the one element that gives the press credibility and respectability is the exercise of independence and social responsibility to the reader. Even the business side of the paper (and the commercials on television) influence the news by determining and limiting the space and time available for information. In short, beyond the influence of the federal information specialist, various factors and variables influence the news flow. Not the least important, however, are the government public relations officers.

Polls and Politics

Few phenomena in recent decades have captured the public imagination more than the device for measuring opinion known as the public opinion poll. This procedure is now an important—indeed an essential—instrument of the government information apparatus. It was said of Lyndon Johnson that he carried the latest poll figures in his pocket and did not hesitate to show them to the press when they were favorable to the President or to the administration. Polls are an integral part of Washington's political atmosphere—constantly studied, cited and discussed, particularly with respect to the barometric pressure readings of presidential politics and popularity.

To the media, polls are important because they make news, and nowhere do they make news as strongly as on political issues. Major political decisions have been made on the basis of the results of opinion measurement, particularly when those results have received widespread coverage by the mass media. For polls have two main features: they offer information and frequently a good story lead for the journalist and they frequently supply—particularly if they are favorable—the material for a newsworthy release from the federal agency.

Reporters, like so many others, are ambivalent about polls. Few accept them uncritically, but all agree that they supply the grist for news. What the public opinion measurement experts claim to supply is basic information that can lead to intelligent action. Although a great deal depends on the structure and purpose of the poll, one complaint by critics is that the very publication of the results of a poll does not *inform* public opinion, but creates and directs opinion. As distinguished a public opinion specialist as George Gallup believes that polls are not directive or manipulative, that they do not tend to support the status quo, but simply function as "fact-finding" agencies and suppliers of relevant information. On the basis of this information, viable alternatives can be weighed and decisions arrived at in a rational way. Apparently both the media and the public accept the polling procedure as a valid one, because there are now more than 200 such organizations in this country and the number is still increasing. The best-known of the pollsters are often pundits whose surveys are carried by as many as 100 and more newspapers. With this kind of circulation, however, it is difficult to see how the results of a poll can be mere useful "information" without exerting some influence on media content and without influencing public opinion.

The most avid users of the poll are government officials, a fact which explains why the press inevitably becomes interested in the results of public opinion surveys. From the standpoint of such organizations as The American Institute of Public Opinion, the poll might be conceived of as a form of journalism. Certainly the use of the poll by Washington constitutes political journalism. But it may be questioned whether political polls are genuine news or information. Presumably, the poll reports on what people "think" about the problem or issue posed. But the press is also interested in reporting what people do, a more accurate journalistic device from the standpoint of the news. To the government official, however, polls can be blueprints for courses of public action, for what they purport to do is to foretell with considerable accuracy the possible outcome or consequences of a conceived action. Unfortunately, it is still not possible to divorce the information contained in the poll from the informational process which is called news.

Polls offer information. Critics of public opinion measurement, however, question whether, in the political process in particular, the poll does not—by accident or design—lead the government official, the media and the public to conclusions which may bear out a particular point of view. Polls can create as well as inform public opinion, despite the fact that those that measure opinion may be scrupulous, ethical and reliable. Most people, say the pollsters, do not lie. But students of public opinion claim to have discovered that people frequently give the answers they think are expected of them.

On the whole, however, opinion measurement in politics has been unusually accurate, which is one reason for their increasing popularity as a device for measuring political and other opinions. Gallup has published his results twice weekly in well over 100 newspapers. In the 1976 election campaign alone, about 250 companies were engaged in opinion measurement. Gallup sees the poll as a "new and exciting adventure in journalism." Whether polls are journalism or not, they have proved to be valuable to the government if only because they can predict possible public response to impending legislation. Used by the media in this context, they are, for better or worse, a valid and valuable source of news.

The Fourth Estate

In the nineteenth century, Macaulay referred to the press as the "fourth estate," a designation that has persisted until Douglas Cater's description of the media as still a "fourth branch" of government. These are meaty concepts of the role of media. Is the press truly a public policy-maker and adjudicator, along with the executive, legislative and judicial branches of government? Or is it a commentator and conveyor of the policies enumerated by these branches? Those who framed the Bill of Rights, particularly Jefferson and Madison, saw the press as a necessarily libertarian medium, a watchdog of government, a potential guarantor and preserver of "government by consent of the governed." These functions later became known as a "surveillance of the environment." The contemporary press, particularly the press that covers national politics, is a conveyor of information and intelligence in the form of news, an interpreter of official and unofficial attitudes and events, a critic of the government and an investigator of alleged or suspected misfeasance in the federal bureaucracy.

Not only the government official, but a large segment of the public has been wary of the media since Watergate. Public confidence in the press, radio and television is strong, but there is greater criticism of media performance. But this attitude is not new. In his spirited defense of a highly partisan and political press, Jefferson also plainly stated that those who do not read the falsehoods and errors purveyed by the newspaper may be better informed than those who do. The press, however, does sort out the plethora of informational messages that flow from government. It articulates for the reader salient differences of opinion on issues among the branches. For its own part, the bureaucracy cannot perform its function in today's media environment without taking the needs of the press into serious consideration. Perhaps, as some believe, this requirement tends to involve the media too deeply in the process of government, but to maintain a pluralistic and democratic society, the cooperation of a free and responsible press is essential to that government. Free inquiry can only prevail in a political climate that encourages and protects freedom of the media.

Washington Press Survey

One observation seems self-evident: the government can only justify such an immense and costly communications program by the amount of service it renders to the public, which in turn, through its taxes, supports the information bureaucracy. The cutting edge of this service is the effectiveness of liaison between the bureaucracy and the mass media. While the press is certainly not an infallible institution, its opinions and perceptions of the federal information program are certainly valid.

Clearly, if the press receives pertinent information, the public can only benefit in terms of its need to make intelligent choices and value judgments. The media, both directly and by means of the so-called "two-step" flow, are the main conduits from the government to the people. The integrity and effectiveness of information flow from the bureaucracy can be determined best not by peer groups or the public, but by the evaluation of government performance by the media correspondents.

In order to determine how the reporters evaluate the information services of the government, a random sampling was made of Washington correspondents who represent various media—newspapers, magazines, wire services and broadcasting. The reporters and editors who were queried are all accredited to the various galleries—press, periodical and radio-television, both in the House and in the Senate. A total of 60 correspondents received questionnaires, with the option of responding either anonymously or with attribution. Several of the respondents agreed to attribution, among them Roy E. Bode (Bureau Chief, *The Dallas Times Herald*), Robert E. Boyd (Knight-Ridder Newspapers), David Brinkley (NBC News), David S. Broder (*The Washington Post*), Grant Dillman (United Press International), Mel Elfin (Washington Bureau Chief, *Newsweek*), Tom Fiedler (*Miami Herald*), George Herman (CBS News), David Kraslow (Cox Newspapers), Mary McGrory (*Washington Star*), Loye Miller, Jr. (*Chicago Sun-Times*), Dean Read (Editor, Newhouse News Service), Hugh Sidey (Washington Bureau Chief, *Time*), Elizabeth Wharton (United Press International), James Wieghart (*New York Daily News*), Richard E. Zimmerman (*Cleveland Plain Dealer*).

These correspondents and others received a questionnaire embracing eight aspects of government information services. The correspondents were asked to express an opinion on each of eight respective questions. The questionnaire, with a tabulation of replies follows.

Questionnaire

Number distributed 60
Number of responses 29
Percentage 48%

I. Which of the following is usually the best source of information: information officers; top-level officials; middle level officials?

Category	Number	Percentage (%)
Information officers	0	0
Top-level officials	5	17.2
Middle-level officials	14	48.3
All three categories	3	10.3
Congress	1	3.5
Don't know	1	3.5
Top and middle level	5	17.2

II. Of the following, which is most productive of news: press releases; press conferences; personal interviews; confidential information?

Category	Number	Percentage (%)
Press releases	0	0
Press conferences	3	10.4
Personal interviews	9	31.0
Confidential information	7	24.1
Personal interview and confidential information	10	34.5

III. In your opinion, is there an effort to manipulate news flow by the government agencies?

Category	Number	Percentage (%)
Yes	21	72.4
No	3	10.4
Occasionally	5	17.2

IV. Are your sources of news in government generally—and truthfully—responsive to your questions?

Category	Number	Percentage (%)
Yes	19	65.5
Mostly	7	24.1
Occasionally	2	7.0
Don't know	1	3.4

V. In your opinion, has the Freedom of Information Act improved the flow of news to the press?

Category	Number	Percentage (%)
Yes	25	86.2
Somewhat	3	10.3
No	1	3.5

VI. In your opinion, are there too many federal publicists?

Category	Number	Percentage (%)
Yes	22	75.9
No	2	6.9
Perhaps	4	13.8
Don't know	1	3.4

VII. Do you find the brochures and annual reports put out by the government useful sources of news?

Category	Number	Percentage (%)
Yes	4	13.8
No	8	27.7
Occasionally	14	48.2
Rarely	2	6.9
Annual reports only	1	3.4

VIII. In your opinion, is there duplication of services among government departments?

Category	Number	Percentage (%)
Yes	18	62.1
No	1	3.4
Sometimes	1	3.4
Don't know	9	31.1

In most instances, the correspondents were categorical in their opinions. Almost half relied on middle-level officials as sources of news. There appears to be a basis for this phenomenon. Middle-level officials tend to be more anonymous and more insulated as sources of news and less subject to quotation or attribution. On the question of the most productive sources of news, there were some differences of opinion, with approximately one-third preferring personal interviews and an equal number selecting a combination of personal interview and confidential source information. There was no doubt, however, that the government agencies attempted to manipulate news. About three-fourths of the respondents replied in the affirmative. At the same time, about two-thirds felt that there was an effort to respond truthfully to press inquiries.

Surprisingly—since Washington information sources have been quoted as noting that relatively few media correspondents used the Freedom of Information Act in comparison to industry—four-fifths stated categorically that the FOI Act had improved the flow of news to the press. Three-fourths of the respondents believe that there are far too many federal publicists, an opinion which coheres with that of

Senator Scott. Most did not find government brochures helpful, but some used annual reports. Finally, there was agreement by two-thirds that there was duplication of services among the many government agencies.

Clearly, the media—despite criticism of the information bureaucracy for duplication of effort, unnecessary personnel and manipulation of the news—find government information officers useful, if not utterly essential. While most of the press prefer to deal directly with middle-level administrators, there is also a realization that public information personnel perform a function in making data available and in serving as channels of communication between the government institution as sources of news and the media correspondents, as receivers. Implicit in Senator Scott's criticism and in the opinion of the press, there is the conclusion that, useful as they may be on occasion, there are far too many government information personnel, at far too great a cost to the taxpayer, and offering too little in the way of a productive information flow, either to the media or to the public.

6

The Presidency
and the News Media

THE ONE CONSISTENT SOURCE of news from Washington is the President of the United States. Even when there is no "hard" news, when the Chief Executive does little more than spend a quiet weekend at Camp David, it is news and the reporters are there to cover it. Almost everything that the President does is news, and what the President does *not* do is also good for a story. Yet, White House reporters frequently lament their assignment as boring and unproductive, except on rare occasions. Many complain that they do not speak with the President often enough and that the Press Secretaries are not ordinarily productive of newsworthy information, even with two press briefings each day. Furthermore, covering the White House is an arduous task, demanding attention at odd hours, traveling on short notice and breaking news without sufficient warning. But covering the President is still a treasured assignment, one which most political reporters would not turn down, whatever the tribulations and limitations it imposes.

Historical Precedent

The press conference as a major device for communication between the Chief Executive and the media is not new, but it has grown in importance since the advent of television. Used as a fine art by

Franklin Delano Roosevelt, the news conference has been employed with various degrees of success by Truman, Eisenhower, Kennedy, Johnson and Carter. President Nixon held fewer press conferences than any other President of the century, but the press was anathema to Mr. Nixon, and his avoiding reporters became one of the hallmarks of his administration. President Carter has held regular twice-monthly meetings with media correspondents.

The relationship between various Presidents and the newspaper reporters has been a fascinating one, emphasizing at one and the same time the President's commitment to freedom of the press, while often filled with resentment because of the treatment given by various newspapers. The first President did not hold press meetings, nor did his successors. Indeed, the conference as an integral part of presidential–press relations did not become policy for more than a century. Washington, moreover, while committed to the principles of a free press, did not like or trust the newspapers, and with good reason. His press relations were less than exemplary. One Benjamin Franklin Bache, in a paper called *Aurora* accused Washington of having "debauched" the country. Other editors called him a "hypocrite." It is not surprising, then, that Washington would have little to do with newsmen and, although supporting the principle of a free press, the President was deeply concerned over the partisan misrepresentations in the newspapers. Washington was supported, however, by Hamilton's anti-Federalist newspaper, *The Gazette of the United States,* edited by John Fenno. Fenno's viciously partisan attacks against Jefferson troubled Washington, although Jefferson had strong support from the Federalist newspaper, *The National Gazette,* edited by the "poet of the revolution," Philip Freneau.

Washington was angered and discouraged by press criticism and attacks on him, and he even went so far as to accuse Jefferson of collaborating against him. He had little taste for engaging in a direct adversarial relationship but was sufficiently angered to give the first "exclusive" to a friendly paper; he offered an advance copy of his Farewell Address in 1796 to the *Pennsylvania Packet and Daily Advertiser*. Saddened and disillusioned by the partisan press, Washington nevertheless expressed his faith in the principle of press freedom.

John Adams, who succeeded Washington, also had little taste for a direct confrontation with editors, although he discussed the press in letters written at the close of his administration. His involvement with newspapers was not great. He did spend some time writing for the papers, however, and some of his comments appeared in *The Gazette of the United States.*

Adams' link to the press largely devolved around the passage of the first example of repression and prior restraint, the Alien and Sedition Acts in 1798—perhaps the most flagrant anti-press action ever taken in this country. While it is true that the excesses of the partisan press were scandalous, the Alien and Sedition Acts dealt with the newspapers' derelictions by a restraint which was clearly a violation of the Bill of Rights. The purpose of the Adams Administration was clear—to silence criticism by the press. But the Acts, fortunately, were unsuccessful and, while never formally rescinded, simply lapsed into disuse after 1800. Adams was sufficiently angered by the attacks upon him to suggest an official newspaper, but a quasi-official organ did not appear until the administration of Andrew Jackson. At the completion of his term, Adams finally undertook to rebut criticisms of himself by writing letters to various papers.

Of the first presidents, few were more concerned with the philosophy of a free press than Jefferson and Madison, both of whom were largely responsible for the ultimate passage of the First Amendment. Although critical of the press, Jefferson and Madison expressed a deep and abiding commitment to press freedom.

Jefferson's fundamental libertarianism overcame his feeling, often expressed, that he was victimized by the newspapers and that one could take little credence in what they printed. He was of the firm opinion that the press was mendacious and vitriolic but was himself involved with a partisan paper, *The National Gazette,* in its vendetta with Fenno's *Gazette of the United States.* Jefferson's ringing affirmation of press freedom has served throughout history as one of the major declarations of journalistic responsibility: ''And were it left to me to decide whether we should have a government without newspapers or newspapers without a government, I should not hesitate a moment to prefer the latter.'' Jefferson affirmed also that everyone should receive newspapers and be capable of reading them. The Jeffer-sonian philosophy of the press is best expressed in three convictions: First, the people need, and must be given, political information. Sec-ond, this information should be non-partisan and honestly conveyed. Third, it is essential, in a political democracy, that the people be able to read, that there be a literate public, capable of receiving and eval-uating information from the press. The consequence of these affirma-tions was a spirited effort by Jefferson and Madison to secure passage of the Bill of Rights and the First Amendment.

Jefferson's philosophy of the press was libertarianism, a belief not so much in social responsibility as in the ability of the people to right matters that were wrong. In questions of press freedom, he de-fended a venal and partisan editor's right to publish, while deploring what appeared in the newspaper. He totally supported Ben Lyon, the Vermont printer who was jailed under the Alien and Sedition Acts, and his opposition to the Acts persisted in the face of an abusive and offensive press. His faith in an ultimately less partisan press evolved from his conviction that the people could see the right and that the will of the people ultimately would prevail. Throughout a period of per-sonal and political criticism and abuse, Jefferson's belief in a free press never was vitiated, although he considered the attacks upon him by the Federalist press heinous. The ultimate remedy against press abuse, however, was always an enlightened people.

Jefferson's attitude toward freedom of communication was sup-plemented and implemented by that of James Madison, both prior to and during Madison's term in office. Active in the writing of the Fed-eralist papers, Madison became involved with Freneau in the establish-ment of the *National Gazette*. His Federalist essays were published in the *Independent Journal* and in the *Daily Advertiser*. He was, above all, a pivotal figure in the establishment of the Bill of Rights and sec-ond only to Jefferson as an ardent advocate of a free press and free-dom of expression. Any restriction on the free flow of information troubled Madison, and he vigorously opposed a delivery tax on news-papers as restrictive to freedom of information. The press, according to both Madison and Jefferson, was the linchpin of a democratic gov-ernment and a free society. Freedom to print was, to Madison, a necessary and vital aspect of public communication and information in a political democracy.

Although Madison at one juncture advocated the establishment of an official government newspaper as an antidote to the excesses of partisan journalism, it was not until the administration of Andrew Jackson that a quasi-federal paper was published. Jackson may be said to have been the first Chief Executive to develop and maintain an overt and fairly consistent liaison with the press. An individual without the strong libertarian intellectualism of Jefferson or Madison, President Jackson was convinced that the newspapers should serve his administration, both as organs of information and as a way of relaying the President's point of view to the people. He was the first President to appreciate the value of the press as an organ of political public relations. Fortunately, Jackson could avail himself of the talented services of Amos Kendall and Francis P. Blair, who might be called an early precursor of what was many years later to become the institution of the Press Secretary. For the first time, the President relied upon an aide to speak for him to the press. One newspaper of this period could be termed a kind of unofficial administration organ—the *U.S. Telegraph,* edited by one Duff Green.

Like his predecessors, Jackson was not immune from partisan attacks. As Jefferson's private life came under press vilification, so Jackson was flayed in the press for having enjoyed a less than moral personal life—hardly a subject to determine Jackson's political qualifications for high office. In combating both personal and political attacks, Jackson had excellent guidance from Blair and Kendall, who in a literal sense were the first bona fide presidential advisors. Both helped to place certain papers in a position to give powerful support to the President.

Andrew Jackson's relations with editors was more direct and vigorous than any of his predecessors. Not unlike current practice, he was criticized for appointing editors to government positions, as newsmen today often leave to become federal information officials in the Washington bureaucracy. For the first time, a President did not hesitate to use the resources of the press for fiercely partisan political purposes.

Abraham Lincoln's difficulties with the press were a result of vitriolic attacks leveled against him by editors who did not agree with him on the slavery question. Reluctantly, he eventually took punitive action against viciously partisan editors, but on the whole, Lincoln's relationships with the press were successful. He was clearly aware of the significance of the newspaper as an organ of public information and as a molder of public opinion. Unfortunately, the Lincoln–Douglas debates, as healthy a forum as they may have provided, once again stirred the embers of the fierce fires of partisan journalism. A good part of the press, including Horace Greeley's *Tribune,* threw its support largely to Douglas, although Greeley was capricious and unpredictable in his attitude toward Lincoln. Although press accounts of political issues were fairly factual and accurate, the editorials were full of fierce invective by both Democratic and Republican organs. The newspapers, however, were not unaware of Lincoln's remarkable qualities, particularly in their accounts of his speeches and debates, and this coverage served as a spur to his political career. Until obliged to take action against partisan editors, Lincoln tried to avoid confrontation with the opposition press, and he pointed out that little purpose would be served by exacerbating the national agony which the nation was experiencing.

Unlike Jackson, President Lincoln had no great instinct for political publicity. To this point, there was as yet no institutionalization of relations between Chief Executive and news media, and Lincoln's meetings with reporters were casual rather than either formal or contrived. In fact, formal relations with the press on a regular basis were not to occur until the accession of Franklin D. Roosevelt. Even during the years of the Civil War, Lincoln made no special effort to set up a structural pattern of disseminating information to the newspapers and, although troubled by the heavy military censorship, he did little about it. As President, Lincoln was rather uncertain and ambivalent toward prior restraint. He was, of course, the subject of bitter attacks by the Copperhead press and was finally brought to the decision to suspend publication of the *Chicago Times,* a move he later retracted. But other papers also underwent a brief suspension of publication as a result of increasingly heated and vituperative criticism of Lincoln.

On the whole, it was not until many years after his term in office that the press recognized the rhetorical eloquence and democratic genius of Abraham Lincoln. In a curious way, Lincoln—while not soliciting press support—was aware of the importance of the President to the newspaper. His very caution and reluctance indicated an understanding of the nature of news, of public opinion and of what might be called political public relations.

The first President Roosevelt, Theodore, was a flamboyant newsmaker, although he did not always consciously try to achieve personal publicity. But at the time of his presidency, the number of newspapers was increasing to meet the needs of a proliferating population and the resultant need for information. This was the period of the emerging twentieth century, a time of the growth of the United States as a world power. Teddy Roosevelt was a strong and colorful political figure. In terms of the criteria of the press, what he said and what he did made news. His strong and resolute attitudes extended to his dealings with the reporters and he expressed a firm belief in a free press. There was a fairly stable relationship between Roosevelt and the newsmen. His sense of timing intrigued them, and he accepted them uncritically if he felt that he was being dealt with fairly. He was certainly the first President to agree that the press had a right to cover the activities of the Chief Executive; he had a keen sense of what made news and was not reluctant to help the reporter develop a story.

Theodore Roosevelt was the first and only President, according to available evidence, to become involved in litigation with a newspaper. He sued Pulitzer's *New York World* for an editorial—part of Pulitzer's new, crusading journalism—written by editor Frank I. Cobb, calling for an official investigation of an alleged scandal concerning the acquisition of the Panama Canal. Roosevelt brought suit, but Cobb asserted that the President could not put a muzzle on the press. The Supreme Court decision was to uphold the press and determine that the President could not sue in a federal court. Roosevelt's contention had been that, apart from personal defamation, the government itself had been libeled.

Despite certain inconsistencies, Roosevelt was a persistent believer in freedom of communication and enjoyed a generally excellent rapport with the press. By means of direct interviews, colorful deeds, letters and public addresses, he received greater and more positive press coverage than any previous President.

A period of national crisis, engendered by a war, is never a healthy period for freedom of the press. Political as well as military information tends to dry up. The clamor for censorship is invariable and strong. Woodrow Wilson's term in office occurred during such a period—World War I. Normal press relations have never existed during wartime, and World War I saw the formalization, for the first time, of a method of dealing with information and intelligence. Shortly after the entry of the United States into the war, President Wilson set up a Committee on Public Information. Its function was the release of pertinent data pertaining to the conduct of the war. Wisely, Wilson selected a newspaperman, George Creel, to head the information program. Creel did what became a classic and brilliant job of wartime news dissemination, terming his effort a "publicity proposition," as well as an "enterprise in salesmanship, the world's greatest adventure in advertising." The contribution of Creel to a free press atmosphere was significant. He avoided censorship and restraint in favor of a policy of honesty and openness with the media, thereby gaining their respect and cooperation. No other similar organization performed its duties with a more scrupulous regard for the Bill of Rights than the Committee for Public Information under Wilson and Creel. At no time did the government more conscientiously fulfill its function of bringing information to the people.

Yet, Wilson's administration was still a wartime one. In 1917, the Espionage Act was passed and the inevitable repressiveness of crisis periods was instituted. Those who were suspected of not supporting the war effort suffered from criticism and suppression. Foreign language newspapers were denied mail privileges. Eventually a Censorship Board was established with control over communications.

The Espionage Act was also accompanied by the Sedition Act, the first such since 1798. Both of these acts caused considerable concern that First Amendment rights were being eroded, but they were upheld by the Supreme Court. The significant contribution of the Creel Committee was the regard it held for the First Amendment and the way it went about obtaining voluntary cooperation from the press without resorting to censorship, repression or prior restraint. The fact is, however, that the Sedition Act put a government sword of Damocles over the media.

President Wilson, a believer in civil liberties, was an inevitable victim of the wartime effort which he headed. In terms of the media, however, he had a keen awareness of the value of a supportive press. He did not set up any regular schedule of news meetings, but he managed to see members of the newspapers at fairly regular intervals. Of inestimable value to the President was Joseph P. Tumulty, perhaps the closest approximation of the kind of individual who was later to be known as a Press Secretary. Tumulty's knowledge of the ways of the press and a natural instinct for news made him a valuable asset to the more diffident Wilson, as well as a good source of news for the journalists. Unlike FDR, Wilson had no real taste for give-and-take encounters with the representatives of the press and tended to shy away from confrontation situations. Although he enjoyed a rather pleasant personal relationship with selected editors, Wilson apparently never had a nose for news, nor did he place full faith in the integrity of the press. He simply did not comprehend, as did Franklin D. Roosevelt and John F. Kennedy, the needs of the journalists nor the nature of what made news. If relations with the press were fairly stable, it was through Tumulty's efforts, not Wilson's. During the war years, Wilson had neither the time nor the inclination to see reporters and even suggested that it might be wise to have stories checked in advance of publication so as to avoid the unwitting violation of security. In general, Wilson did not have the charisma of some of his successors, nor did he have the interest, understanding or patience required for first-rate media relations. What he lacked was a sense of news as well as of public relations.

The Modern Era

Franklin D. Roosevelt had a sense of news and a superb flair for publicity. His inauguration as President ushered in the period of modern press–government relations, a totally new and refreshing concept of the interaction between the White House and the news media. Whether in a "fireside chat" on radio or at an informal press conference, Roosevelt made news. He used the channel of the radio superbly to convey his political philosophy and public policies to the public and, although he was anathema to many publishers because of his social and economic programs, the newspapers could not avoid covering his activities as no President had been covered before his period in office.

Roosevelt held regular press conferences, the first President to do so. He was neither diffident nor reclusive and clearly enjoyed the give-and-take and the sarcastic barbs which he did not hesitate to level at newsmen who asked questions he disliked or thought were silly. His criticism of the reporters could be embarrassing, but the press uncharacteristically stood still for the Roosevelt barrage. Thus, he had a continuing and generally healthy relationship with the media, as did Eleanor Roosevelt, who received almost as much publicity as the President, not all of it favorable.

If Wilson had his Tumulty, President Roosevelt had Steve Early, a former wire service man, who understood the needs of the press and played an important role in presidential press relations. Together, Roosevelt and Early laid down ground rules for the President's contact with the journalists—when and when not to quote, what and what not to attribute, what was and was not "off the record" news. Thoroughly aware of the antagonism of the newspaper owners and publishers, FDR nevertheless knew that he enjoyed a sound working relationship with the correspondents, primarily because the press respected a sound sense for news and Roosevelt conveyed that news sense, even to the point of subtle suggestions as to how a story might be handled. Despite his persuasiveness and public relations skills, however, Roosevelt affirmed to the journalists that the administration would make no effort to obstruct the free flow of political information.

Despite his rapport with reporters, Roosevelt had a most acrimonious relationship with publishers and business leaders in general. The business establishment was unalterably opposed to the principles and philosophy of the New Deal. Ultimately, the President alienated several of the Washington elite journalists, notably Walter Lippmann, who had been at one time a keen supporter. Unlike previous Presidents, FDR did not accept press criticism supinely, but rather launched his own attacks, which of course made news. At the same time, the President, during World War II, took pains to assure both press and public that there would be no withholding of information from the public, and he asked that the media agree to cooperate on a voluntary basis with the government in the interest of maintaining national security. During this wartime period, Byron Price assumed duties analogous to those of George Creel during World War I, while Elmer Davis headed the Office of War Information.

Franklin D. Roosevelt understood the needs of the journalists as had no previous President—and better than most of his successors. The journalists appreciated the President's understanding of their needs. The President understood the value of maintaining good press relations.

With the election of Harry Truman and of those who followed, a dramatic and extensive series of changes took place in Washington media relations. The advent of television climaxed the growth of mass communications. The press and wire services, as well as the electronic media, developed speedy, efficient and brilliantly conceived and executed new technologies. Public relations and publicity became an important part of the communications process. In the administrations of Truman, Eisenhower, Kennedy, Johnson, Nixon and Carter, the role of the Press Secretary became institutionalized. The whole spectrum of the government–media interaction was drastically changed.

Truman's relations with the media were feisty and direct. He saw the press on a regular basis and held conferences which were arranged by Press Secretary Charles G. Ross. Dwight D. Eisenhower, although liked by the press, was not a newsmaker and left much of his press liaison to James Hagerty, a Press Secretary who—to the delight of the reporters—spoke with the full support and authority of the President. John F. Kennedy enjoyed an excellent liaison with the media, although in retrospect the correspondents felt that efforts were made to manipulate them to some extent. When Kennedy asked *The New York Times* to recall correspondent David Halberstam from Vietnam, the paper was adamant in its refusal. Lyndon Johnson, a shrewd politician in the Congress, was probably too shrewd in his press relations. He played one newsman against others and could not accept press criticism with any degree of tolerance. Furthermore, his tendency to play favorites did not endear him to a good part of the press corps.

Richard Nixon's rejection of the media was total. He held few press conferences, although he used the medium of broadcasting more than any other recent President. His Press Secretary, Ron Ziegler, who had no background in journalism, further contributed to the alienation of the press and to the generally unpleasant atmosphere that prevailed between the White House and the media. Jimmy Carter has been generally available to the media and has maintained a schedule of regular press conferences.

The medium that wrought far-reaching changes in the way both the Federal information bureaucracy and the press functioned was television. Its first use in political communication was the coverage of the results of the Truman–Dewey election in 1948, and it has reported every election since that date. In recent years, sophisticated technology like the computer and the use of "vote profile analysis" have enabled the national news divisions to make early "calls" on election winners. The enormous power and influence of electronic journalism was emphasized in the Kennedy–Nixon "great Debates" of 1960. In order for these televised confrontations to take place, the Congress suspended Section 315 of the Communication Act, the rule which demanded that, if one bona fide candidate were given air time, all such candidates must receive "equal time." For the first time, millions of viewers heard and saw the candidates present their positions on political and other issues on the television screen. Nixon later was supposed to have claimed that it was his "image" as well as his effort to confront substantive issues which cost him the election. In 1968 and 1972, he made skillful use of television, not for debate, but for carefully prepared advertising and promotion "spots." In 1976, since Congress did not suspend Section 315, the clumsy device of having an outside organization arrange the Ford–Carter confrontations was resorted to. In this way, equal time provisions were by-passed because the networks covered a legitimate news event. It was unfortunate, however, that the news divisions were not permitted to arrange the Ford–Carter meetings as part of their legitimate journalistic function.

White House Press Corps

The press office of the White House is now thoroughly institutionalized. No longer is there an ad lib relationship between the President and a public relations-oriented adviser. The White House has its own Press Secretary and Deputy Press Secretaries, along with a support staff. The First Lady has press aides. The Vice-President has a press officer. Press relations are structured, regular meetings are held, presidential press conferences are the result of painstaking preparation.

The White House office of the Press Secretary is comprised basically of the Press Secretary to the President, two Deputy Press Secretaries, a Chief Speedwriter, a special assistant to the President for Media and Public Affairs, three Associate Press Secretaries, a Photographic Office and the Editor of the News Summary. This is a formidable array of information officers in itself, but the growth of the press corps, particularly since the televised press conferences and interviews, demands a staff large enough to cope with the increasing appreciation of the extreme importance of presidential media relations.

The White House Press Office, in response to a questionnaire sent to various key branches and agencies of the government, described itself simply as "White House Press Office." Forty-five people in this office are employed for the purpose of providing information. Included in this group are news summary preparers, press advance persons, special writers, photographers and media contacts. The Congressional Directory of the 95th Congress also notes that approximately 260 members of the White House News Photographers Association are listed to cover the White House.

Replies to the questionnaire provide both an insight into the workings of the office as well as its attitudes. Duties include issuance of approximately 25 press releases weekly. And if the President is interviewed by the press, a press officer will be present, although not with his aides. Answers regarding the media–White House Press Office relationship were less direct. In response to the question, "Do you feel that the media give accurate and knowledgeable information," the reply was "usually." No response was given to the question of how the press can improve its coverage. In answer to the question, "What in your opinion is the best way of getting information to the press,'' the reply was as follows: ''Depends entirely on many factors—timing, complexity, the medium (TV, newspapers, and such), news sources and many others.''

On the other side of the coin, coverage of the White House by the press includes the following breakdown: 10 wire service correspondents, 10 representatives from major metropolitan (large, national) daily newspapers, approximately 30 from local papers (although this number fluctuates), 50 from radio and television (including the technicians), and 30 magazine reporters. This large contingent of assorted newsmen are housed in the West Wing. This group includes the so-called regulars, whose exclusive assignment is to devote all of their time and energies to covering the President and the White House activities on a daily basis. Reporters, in addition to briefings, are provided with the usual armamentarium of the working journalist—telephones, typewriters and so forth. Normally, the Press Secretary is the major source of information. The difficulty with the job for many such officers, unfortunately, has been the President. J.F. ter Horst, President Ford's Press Secretary, resigned after a brief period in office because he unwittingly gave erroneous information to the press as a result of being misinformed by the White House. Frequently, the Press Secretary must fall back on ''no comment'' or on temporizing, because he does not have answers to questions. On occasion, the President may insist that certain inevitable, but sensitive, questions be avoided.

The press travels with the President on his trips though most do not achieve the status of riding on the presidential plane. A nucleus of wire service, broadcasting and one or two newspapermen usually are responsible for conveying breaking news to the bulk of correspondents who follow on another plane. Press conferences generally depend on the inclination of the individual President, although recent Presidents, with the exception of Richard M. Nixon, tend to schedule regular meetings with the media. The Press Office holds briefings twice a day, and more often when there is a breaking or running story.

The President has at least two major goals in dealing with the mass media. One is to convey policy, to offer direct information. The other is to develop and maintain a positive climate of opinion, a favorable ''image.'' The tone that develops in media relationships and the interaction between the White House and the mass media are extremely important to the opinion which the public—viewers and readers—have of the Chief Executive. Despite the fact that each President goes through a honeymoon period with the media, followed almost invariably by a period of criticism and disillusionment, the Office of the President carries a certain aura of respect and of charisma that transcends personalities. This is particularly emphasized in this age of television coverage. Even when the President is not on the screen, the setting of a network White House correspondent reporting from Washington against a background of the White House gives a credibility and patina that are of enormous significance to the public.

There are few White House correspondents who have failed to voice criticism of the President's press conferences. Hedrick Smith, of *The New York Times'* Washington bureau, looks upon these encounters with media representatives as a lethargic, pallid and synthetic ''ritual,'' particularly the conferences held during the Nixon Administration. Other Presidents have held regular and even lengthy meetings, but substantial news does not always result and hard questions are not often asked, particularly since the televising of the press conferences. Gerald Ford instituted a healthy innovation, the practice of permitting the reporters to ask follow-up questions, but if the President wants to avoid or beg a question, he can still do so. The President is in almost total control of the conference. He is in complete command of who asks what and, if he does not want to be responsive to difficult questions, he can avoid them without too much effort. Thus, criticism of the conduct of the press conferences is not lacking. Reporters themselves have accused their peers of asking ''easy'' questions, of laziness in accepting answers without challenge, of standing in awe of the presidential office. What viewer, in fact, has watched a press conference and not wondered at the lack of substance in the questions posed by the press? At a meeting of the Radio and Television News Directors in Houston during the midst of Watergate, the local station news correspondents were accused of asking President Nixon ''soft'' questions because most stations supported the administration. Smith has called the presidential press corps "lapdogs, instead of watchdogs, of government," a scathing critique of the calibre and quality of White House reporting. Yet, it is admitted that the press corps is not the British Parliament, facing the Prime Minister. The White House press is expected to show due regard and respect for the office of the presidency, making any genuine adversarial relationship in the give-and-take of a press conference difficult.

The reportorial group does agree somewhat on the fact that there might be more probing, tenacious and "in-depth," and that some method ought to be devised to prohibit the cutting off of questions before they are answered. Other recommendations include limiting the conference to one or two significant issues, not a tangled skein of varied topics, each with little relevance to the others, and the supplementing of the formal conference with informal meetings with the President. These recommendations reflect a certain negative attitude of the media toward the press conference atmosphere. For example, there is severe criticism of the way in which the meetings are televised, although no one has suggested ameliorative measures. The use of *TV*, it is felt, makes a theatrical special event of the meeting. The situation tends to be formal, there is a certain tension, time deadlines must be met. As one correspondent phrased it, the President is "on" and he is aware of it. As a consequence, the thrust is directed toward the viewer and is not a bona fide *press* conference. Yet, it is also recognized that television is in itself a powerful source of information which also offers insight into the President's character. The public, at least theoretically, is the better informed for it. One suggestion is for the President to alternate the *modus operandi* of the conference every two weeks by holding one for the correspondents alone and having the second covered by television. But the consensus seems to be that genuine hard news does not ensue from a "special" on television.

At its best, with or without the presence of the cameras, the presidential press meeting is essentially a carefully prepared showcase—or forum—for the President. It gives more often the appearance rather than the reality of producing genuine information. It is at its best when used for a dramatic announcement, such as that the President will make a whirlwind tour of eight countries around the world. It is important too because, symbolically at least, it presents a method of asking accountability of the Chief Executive and becomes a check on presidential power. It is a symbol of democracy in action, despite the superficiality of the questions and the artificiality of the setting.

The President does control the conference in many ways. He can consume time with a long-winded opening statement, and thus indirectly set the tone for questions. He can select certain reporters and ignore others. He can circumvent questions by unresponsive or ambiguous replies. He can change the subject abruptly. Even with these advantages though, the very real fact of the President facing the media does force a regard for public opinion and a need to address public policy.

Professor Lewis W. Wolfson, of the American University, in a Report on the State of the Presidential Press Conference has made certain recommendations for improvement of the press conference format.

1. That the conferences be held twice monthly, preferably on television.
2. That the press do its "homework," that it come better prepared.

The Times' Hedrick Smith suggested that certain steps be taken by the White House Correspondents Association.

1. That press conference questioning be limited to a single topic.
2. That each questioner be permitted at least one follow-up query. (Gerald Ford established this procedure).
3. That the basic purpose of the press conference—not achieved as yet—be to make the President accountable to the nation.

Clearly, both the White House and the press corps have come under critical fire for their interaction with each other. The reportorial peer group have accused the media of being too easily manipulated by the White House public relations apparatus, of considering themselves an untouchable journalistic elite, of avoiding major issues, of asking ridiculous questions and of accepting press office handouts uncritically. But those who cover the White House counter that when they do exercise their prerogatives, they are accused of being too tough and disrespectful of the Office of the President. Furthermore, they believe that the White House conference, particularly when televised, is not a productive situation for obtaining information. Beyond the press meetings, the press corps points out that they see little of the President, are dependent to a great degree on wire service and "pool" reporters and cannot gain ready access either to the President or his key aides.

Supplementing the White House Press Office is the Office of Media Liaison. This unit has issued a description of its function.

THE OFFICE OF MEDIA LIAISON
OF THE WHITE HOUSE PRESS OFFICE

The Office of Media Liaison is the special contact in the White House for non-Washington news media.

Its marching orders are to pay the same attention to the non-Washington media that the White House press corps traditionally has demanded and usually received.

The Office's work falls into three catagories:

MAILINGS: Periodically—averaging four to six times a month—the staff prepares and mails to editors, news directors and columnists materials which explain administration positions. Most of these reports cover major legislation. Others may include a random selection of quotes from President Carter capsulizing his views on various topics, or occasionally the full text of a speech, or other document.

BRIEFINGS: The staff, on request, will set up a briefing for associations of working journalists. These groups may range from 30 to 200 persons and the briefers will be from the White House staff or federal agencies and departments.

New with the Carter Administration is a series of editors' conferences, held about 20 times a year for groups of 30 editors, editorial writers and news directors invited by the staff. These day-long sessions—all on the record—feature four to six briefings, including a 30-minute press conference with the President.

PHONE QUERIES: The staff fields 80 to 100 phone calls daily from reporters and editors who want to know anything from "What is the administration really doing about unemployment?" to "What is the President's hat size?"

The staff tries to get back before the deadline—with an answer, word as to where to get it or an explanation, if for good reason the deadline can't be met.

The office is headed by Patricia Bario, associate press secretary, under the supervision of Walter Wurfel, deputy press secretary. It is staffed by seven professionals—with the usual assistance of two or three college interns.

The staff members also take their turns on the regular White House Press Office night and weekend duty rotation.

Politics and the Media

Most White House incumbents have recognized media problems, but few, if any, have tried to rectify them. Herb Klein, Director of Communications during the Nixon Administration, was—in retrospect —rather at odds with the negative philosophy of the Press Secretary, Ron Ziegler. Klein, a trained editor, appeared to believe in the Nixon promise of "open government." But the "open government" idea became public relations talk and was never implemented, although a great show was made of talking with such former White House press officers as Pierre Salinger, George Christian and Bill Moyers. In truth, Ziegler's performance in dealing with the media was disastrous. Klein, on the other hand, looked upon his own function as one of supervising and developing "information policies of the overall government." To put informational services on a policy level, Klein advocated that cabinet officers be given an opportunity to explain the policies of their departments to the public—an event which never occurred. Other than Henry Kissinger, virtually no cabinet-level official met with the media. Though Herb Klein's ideas were both sound and sensible, they were never implemented by the administration which he served.

The President has enormous advantages in his interaction with the media. He exerts a measure of control as the source of news. He can, and sometimes does, irritate and even antagonize the press, but what he says and does, as well as what he does not say and does not do, are newsworthy. In his relations with reporters, the President can subtly play favorites, he can offer discreet exclusives to sympathetic correspondents, he can direct his press office to show appropriate displeasure with reporters who are not in favor. These prerogatives stem from the increasingly disturbing concept of the "Imperial Presidency," which has just begun to receive a serious challenge from a restive and more assertive Congress.

But the President also has internal problems within the federal bureaucracy that affect his relations with the media correspondents. Contrary to popular belief, the Chief Executive cannot control the bureaucracy. In many agencies, fears, jealousies and uncertainties about executive programs trigger the development of other liaisons with the press. There is not a President who has not carefully planned the release of an announcement at a press conference, only to have the story "leaked" to the media by a potentially affected agency or bureaucrat. The media, of course, are faced with a value judgment in deciding whether to use the leak, but considerations of news value usually tip the scales in favor of publication. This is almost as unfortunate for the journalist as it is for the President, since it does little to cement White House liaison with the press, but it must be accepted as inevitable in the brutally competitive environment of Washington political journalism. The media representatives are convinced that news is legitimate, whatever the source. In the adversarial relationship with the government, the press seeks information which has genuine news content. The more exciting or intriguing, the more likely it is to draw a positive reader or viewer response. The more positive the response, the more papers are sold and the more people watch the news on television. Moreover, there is little the bureaucracy can do about this situation. With ever greater need for public support, the federal bureaucracy must rely on the cooperation of the media in its efforts to inform and to persuade opinion regarding public policy.

The point of conflict of interest arises when the press demands news but the White House seeks to withhold, manipulate or control the news flow. This conflict has been a part of presidential–press relations in every administration from George Washington to Jimmy Carter. There have been occasions when a delicate balance must be struck between the White House and the media—in instances such as the Bay of Pigs, the Glomar Explorer, the exposé of the CIA. In these cases, above all, the value judgment made by the media may make a fundamental difference in the conduct of the government and certainly a difference in public opinion. The media, in retrospect, have been both right and wrong in withholding or deciding to print and air certain information which may prove embarrassing to the White House. On at least one occasion, the White House later admitted it erred in asking a major newspaper to withhold a story, and the paper admitted it erred in not printing it. The incident was the Bay of Pigs, the President was Kennedy and the newspaper was *The New York Times*.

In the past two decades, some critics of American journalism claim that they discern a great improvement in the media coverage of the political environment. Ironically, this is due to the increasing number of better trained public information officials, most of whom have a background in mass communications and some of whom are former journalists. But the very increase in government P.R. officers and the increasing significance of media coverage of Washington also accentuate the problems. Too many public information officials make for bureaucratic competition and duplication. Too great an emphasis on competitive journalism breeds a race for news but does not provide motivation for thoughtful and reflective coverage of politics and government. James Madison believed that government by the people cannot exist without "information or the means of acquiring it." This statement is far more true today in a country of this size, but the very competition for information and the intense need to meet deadlines are not conducive to the most carefully thought-out coverage of the news. Furthermore, the need for news can exacerbate conflict between government and media. The government has a greater need to try to mold the news, and the press has an equal need to resist such manipulation.

In essence, despite its frequent tendency to complain about and berate the media, the White House is dependent on the press and radio and television for aid in channeling news to the public. In this sense, the media are instruments for political action and disseminators of public policy. That the President is not unaware of this role of the media is clearly evident in the increasing reliance on televised press conferences, the growth of the White House press staff and the timing of White House releases and activities to coincide not only with press deadlines and news formats but also with the demands of prime-time broadcast schedules. The relationship and interaction between President and media is predicated on mutual need. But despite the power of the media, the Chief Executive is still a strong controlling force.

7

The Congress:
Public Information

THE PRESIDENT'S PROBLEMS with the Washington press corps are dwarfed by the immensity and sensitivity of his liaison problems with the Congress. Although the media are powerful forces, the ultimate control of news flow rests fundamentally with the White House. That is one reason why the President and his press aides are so concerned about leaks from agencies which diminish and vitiate the degree of executive control over information. But the Congress can cause the President monumental problems in terms of his "image" by the impact of its acts on public opinion. It does not increase the President's credibility with the public to have Congress pass a bill over his veto, as was done with President Ford's veto of the Freedom of Information Act. The 95th Congress has persistently disregarded President Carter on gas deregulation, health and welfare services and other legislation which the President has recommended or formally proposed. All these congressional actions and reactions are duly recorded by the media and they affect the President's standing within the bureaucracy, with the press corps and with the people.

The Congress, since Watergate, has done finally what the political press has traditionally accused it of not doing. It is no longer a "do nothing" body, even though its actions and reactions may be negative.

The 95th Congress, in particular, has been more assertive of its prerogatives, has steadfastly refused to be amenable to White House pressure and, as a consequence, has given the media a rare opportunity to write about Congress–White House relations. Complaints by members of Congress that the President has not dealt with them properly and that the White House has overwhelmed them with impending legislation has made news of this adversarial relationship. Many in the Senate talk of asking the media for "equal time." And, in addition, the Republican "loyal opposition" in both Senate and House complain of presidential domination of the broadcasting channels. All of these new and more aggressive attitudes had their origin as early as the Gulf of Tonkin Resolution in the administration of Lyndon Johnson, and they became increasingly powerful in the aftermath of Watergate. The result has been that the President now confronts two relationships that are fundamentally, although differently, adversarial: a more aggressive Congress and more investigative reporters.

The President's obligation to the media is to be responsible and responsive to the needs and will of the people by information given to press, radio and television. His obligation to the Congress, apart from the intangible relationships that are so important, is to report to the Senate and House by a State of the Union Message, a submission of the budget and by proposed legislation. In all of this, he has the advantage of being the President, a natural newsmaker. As a result of the pervasiveness and power of the news media, critics of the White House claim that the President casts messages not in terms of the Congress and its possible reaction, but in terms of how the media will respond. This is still another bone of contention between the leaders and the Chief Executive; the press and public opinion are pre-empting the Congress in importance. Congressional leaders also resent the fact that they rarely appear on the nightly network news where information out of Washington is dominated by the President. There is, moreover, little that the Congress can do about the situation. Only a national crisis, such as the hearings on the impeachment of President Nixon, can catapult heretofore little-known members of Congress to national prominence by their appearance on the television screen.

Coverage of the activities of the President is usually glamorous, exciting and charismatic. By contrast, what the Congress does is mundane and unexciting. Former Senator William Fulbright complained that the only news about the Senate that was purveyed by the media was "bad" news. Scandal makes the front pages, but the serious and deliberative side of the Senate is ignored by the news media. Fulbright, during his tenure in Washington, was a staunch advocate for giving the Senate greater visibility to counter the propaganda and informational advantages of the White House press apparatus. Unfortunately, the development of media technology has tended to increase the visibility of the President and decrease that of Congress. As a result it has been proposed that a regular "equal time" arrangement be made for the "loyal opposition." The media have also been taken to task for ignoring the Senate and House, unless a provocative scandal story developed. Fulbright claimed that the polls show a dire need for greater congressional access to the media, so that the Congress can have an opportunity to address the people on national political and social issues.

The Congressional Galleries

Few members of the Senate, and fewer in the House, are known to the public outside of their own states or districts, with the exception of a few key figures in each house. In general, the chairmen of various committees tend to make news, particularly when the meetings are covered by the press. In addition, an invariably successful method of achieving press coverage is through the establishment of newsmaking hearings and official investigations. These events have an aura of excitement that attracts the media and, in addition, they are apt to be accusatory and acrimonious. The appearance of Bert Lance, President Carter's Budget Director, before a Senate Committee, for example, became a nationally covered event, both by the print and electronic media. But the Congress cannot schedule repeated special events for their publicity value, while the President's every move makes for a news item. The advantage is clearly with the White House.

The correspondents accredited to cover the Senate and the House of Representatives become members in good standing and entitled to admission to the various media galleries of the houses of Congress.

Each house maintains, respectively, a Press Gallery, a Press Photographers' Gallery, a Radio and Television Correspondents' Gallery and a Periodical Press Gallery. Rules governing the Galleries are set up by Standing Committees and approved by the Committee on Rules and Administration in the Congress. Together, the various Galleries have fairly accurate round figures of membership (as listed in the official Congressional Directory).

Press Galleries: Members of the Press Entitled to Admission: 1,200

Newspapers Represented in Press Galleries: 650

Press Photographers' Gallery: 190

Radio and Television Correspondents' Galleries: 700

Periodical Press Galleries: 810

The largest contingent of Press Gallery correspondents represents the Associated Press, which is listed as having 77 reporters and editors. The United Press International boasts a Washington bureau staff of 50. Apart from the large staff of the *Washington Post,* which covers local as well as national news, the Washington bureau of *The New York Times* is the largest of any daily metropolitan newspaper with a bureau staff of 43 correspondents. The Washington bureau of *The Wall Street Journal,* which is published in various regional editions, has 30 members. The *Los Angeles Times* bureau has 23; the *New York Daily News,* 13; the Gannett newspapers, 16. Other various daily metropolitan papers have bureau staffs ranging from three to seven members. The reliance on wire services for most of the political news from Washington is evident, since most papers simply cannot cover the multiplicity of branches, agencies and quasi-agencies that function in the federal government.

An excellent description of the background, structure and function of the House of Representatives Press Gallery, which may be taken as typical, is provided by the Gallery Superintendent, Benjamin C. West. This gallery is located, as are the others, in the Capitol. It was established by the Congress in 1857 so that newspapers could have access to and an opportunity to report on the actions and deliberations of the House. The Senate Gallery was created at about the same time. As members of the corps of correspondents grew, additional facilities and galleries were established by the Congress. Each of the Galleries contains all the equipment necessary for the operating activities of the working press, even to transmission by telegraph. Of the 1,200 correspondents who are accredited, representing some 600 daily newspapers, about 350 utilize the Galleries on a regular, full-time basis. Both the Senate and House Press Galleries are administered by the Standing Committee of Correspondents, subject to approval by the Speaker and the Senate Rules Administration Committee.

Newsmen are elected and accredited by the Standing Committee of Correspondents, which has established rules for membership. The major qualification is that the correspondent work actively at the task of relaying news on a daily basis to his newspaper. The Galleries are separately operated by superintendents, each with several assistants. Their functions are to process the daily batch of press releases and other informational items, to supervise press conferences and committee hearings, to keep a running log of floor proceedings and, in general to maintain the complex technology of modern communications. Correspondents look to the Gallery Superintendent for information regarding scheduled meetings and hearings and on the status of pending legislative matters.

Although the Congressional Directory lists about 680 members of the Radio-Television Correspondents Association who are accredited to the Senate Radio-Television Correspondents' Gallery, the Superintendent of the Gallery, Max M. Barber, notes that the current figure is approximately 750. Of these, some 20 or 25 cover Senate activities on a daily basis. This Gallery office issues no press releases but is a distribution point for Senators who disseminate releases to the press. Approximately 25 are received each day.

In the House Radio-Television Correspondents' Gallery, Superintendent Mike Michaelson describes the function as one of liaison between the House of Representatives and the broadcasters assigned to cover it. Anywhere from 40 to 100 reporters and technicians may use the Gallery at one time. The Gallery staff is available to provide information about the work of the House and its committees and about pending legislation. Through the Gallery, the House members distribute press information and releases, which can number from a few to as many as 30 on an active day. One of the functions of this Gallery is to arrange for broadcasting coverage of various committees, including arrangements for necessary technological equipment.

It will be of interest to the taxpayer to know that the cost of operating the Galleries is not defrayed by the media but by the Congress. And the cost is considerable for facilities that must be maintained constantly. But the Standing Committee of Correspondents will not pay for the Gallery upkeep, and there is a need for the Congress to maintain facilities for the media to receive information. Congress is keenly aware of the requirements of the press and makes every effort to meet this daily need. The Standing Committee, selected from the accredited correspondents, consists of five members, elected for a two-year term. The Committee examines applications for admission to the Galleries and serves as a kind of super-ego on the deportment of the members. For a period, the Standing Committee did not admit radio and television coverage of Senate and House.

Each of the Congressional Galleries publishes rules governing the function of the particular Gallery. Following are the rules, respectively, covering the Press, Press Photographers', Radio and Television Correspondents' and Periodical Press Galleries:

RULES GOVERNING PRESS GALLERIES

1. Administration of the press galleries shall be vested in a Standing Committee of Correspondents elected by accredited members of the galleries. The Committee shall consist of five persons elected to serve for terms of 2 years. Provided, however, that at the election in January 1951, the three candidates receiving the highest number of votes shall serve for 2 years and the remaining two for 1 year. Thereafter, three members shall be elected in odd-numbered years and two in even-numbered years. Elections shall be held in January. The Committee shall elect its own chairman and secretary. Vacancies on the Committee shall be filled by special election to be called by the Standing Committee.

2. Persons desiring admission to the press galleries of Congress shall make application in accordance with Rule 34 of the House of Representatives, subject to the direction and control of the Speaker and Rule 34 of the Senate, which rules shall be interpreted and administered by the Standing Committee of Correspondents, subject to the review and approval by the Senate Committee on Rules and Administration.

3. The Standing Committee of Correspondents shall limit membership in the press galleries to bona fide correspondents of repute in their profession, under such rules as the Standing Committee of Correspondents shall prescribe.

4. Provided, however, that the Standing Committee of Correspondents shall admit to the galleries no person who does not establish to the satisfaction of the Standing Committee all of the following:

(a) That his or her principal income is obtained from news correspondence intended for publication in newspapers entitled to second-class mailing privileges.

(b) That he or she is not engaged in paid publicity or promotion work or in prosecuting any claim before Congress or before any department of the government, and will not become so engaged while a member of the galleries.

(c) That he or she is not engaged in any lobbying activity and will not become so engaged while a member of the galleries.

5. Members of the families of correspondents are not entitled to the privileges of the galleries.

6. The Standing Committee of Correspondents shall propose no change or changes in these rules except upon petition in writing signed by not less than 100 accredited members of the galleries.

THOMAS P. O'NEILL, Jr.,
Speaker of the House of Representatives.

Approved by the Committee on Rules and Administration of the Senate.

HOWARD W. CANNON, *Chairman.*

RULES GOVERNING PRESS PHOTOGRAPHERS' GALLERY

1. (a) Administration of the Press Photographers' Gallery is vested in a Standing Committee of Press Photographers consisting of six persons elected by accredited members of the gallery. The Committee shall be composed of one member each from Associated Press Photos, United Press International Newspictures, magazine media, and local newspapers and two "at large" members. At large members may be, but need not be, selected from a media otherwise represented on the Committee.

(b) The term of office of a member of the Committee elected as the Associated Press Photos member, the local newspapers member, or one of the "at large" members shall expire on the day of the election held in the first odd-numbered year following the year in which he was elected, and the term of office of a member of the Committee elected as the United Press International Newspictures member, the magazine media member, or the remaining "at large" member shall expire on the day of the election held in the first even-numbered year following the year in which he was elected, except that a member elected to fill a vacancy occurring prior to the expiration of a term shall serve only for the unexpired portion of such term.

(c) Elections shall be held as early as practicable in each year, and in no case later than March 31. A vacancy in the membership of the Committee occurring prior to the expiration of a term shall be filled by special election called for that purpose by the Committee.

(d) The Standing Committee of the Press Photographers' Gallery shall propose no change or changes in these rules except upon petition in writing signed by not less than 25 accredited members of the gallery.

(e) Notwithstanding the provisions of subsection (b)—

(A) the term of office of the local newspapers member elected in the election held in 1968 shall expire in 1969.

(B) the term of office of the United Press International Newspictures member holding office on January 1, 1968, shall expire in 1969, and

(C) the term of office of the United Press International Newspictures member elected in 1969 shall expire in 1970.

2. Persons desiring admission to the Press Photographers' Gallery of the Senate shall make application in accordance with Rule 34 of the Senate, which

rule shall be interpreted and administered by the Standing Committee of Press Photographers subject to the review and approval of the Senate Committee on Rules and Administration.

3. The Standing Committee of Press Photographers shall limit membership in the photographers' gallery to bona fide news photographers of repute in their profession and to Heads of Photographic Bureaus under such rules as the Standing Committee of Press Photographers shall prescribe.

4. Provided, however, that the Standing Committee of Press Photographers shall admit to the gallery no person who does not establish to the satisfaction of the Committee all of the following:

(a) That any member is not engaged in paid publicity or promotion work or in prosecuting any claim before Congress or before any department of the Government, and will not become so engaged while a member of the gallery.

(b) That he or she is not engaged in any lobbying activity and will not become so engaged while a member of the gallery.

The above rules have been approved by the Committee on Rules and Administration.

HOWARD W. CANNON,
Chairman, Senate Committee on Rules and Administration.

RULES GOVERNING RADIO AND TELEVISION CORRESPONDENTS' GALLERIES

1. Persons desiring admission to the Radio and Television Galleries of Congress shall make application to the Speaker, as required by rule XXXIV of the House of Representatives, as amended, and to the Committee on Rules and Administration of the Senate, as required by rule XXXIV, as amended, for the regulation of Senate wing of the Capitol. Applicants shall state in writing the names of all radio stations, television stations, systems, or news-gathering organizations by which they are employed and what other occupation or employment they may have, if any. Applicants shall further declare that they are not engaged in the prosecution of claims or the promotion of legislation pending before Congress, the Departments, or the independent agencies, and that they will not become so employed without resigning from the galleries. They shall further declare that they are not employed in any legislative or executive department or independent agency of the Government, or by any foreign government or representative thereof; that they are not engaged in any lobbying activities; that they do not and will not, directly or indirectly, furnish special information to any organization, individual, or group of individuals for the influencing of prices on any commodity or stock exchange; that they will not do so during the time they retain membership in the galleries. Holders of visitors' cards who may be allowed temporary admission to the galleries must conform to all the restrictions of this paragraph.

2. It shall be prerequisite to membership that the radio station, television station, system, or news-gathering agency which the applicant represents shall certify in writing to the Radio and Television Correspondents' Galleries that the applicant conforms to the foregoing regulations.

3. The applications required by the above rule shall be authenticated in a manner that shall be satisfactory to the Executive Committee of the Radio and Television Correspondents' Galleries who shall see that the occupation of the galleries is confined to bona fide news gatherers and/or reporters of reputable standing in their business who represent radio stations, television stations, systems, or news-gathering agencies engaged primarily in serving radio stations, television stations, or systems. It shall be the duty of the Executive Committee of the Radio and Television Correspondents' Galleries to report, at its discretion, violation of the privileges of the galleries to the Speaker or to the Senate Committee on Rules and Administration, and, pending action thereon, the offending individual may be suspended.

4. Persons engaged in other occupations, whose chief attention is not given to—or more than one-half of their earned income is not derived from—the gathering or reporting of news for radio stations, television stations, systems, or newsgathering agencies primarily serving radio stations or systems, shall not be entitled to admission to the Radio and Television Galleries. The Radio and Television Correspondents' List in the CONGRESSIONAL DIRECTORY shall be a list only of persons whose chief attention is given to or more than one-half of their earned income is derived from the gathering and reporting of news for radio stations, television stations, and systems engaged in the daily dissemination of news, and of representatives of news-gathering agencies engaged in the daily service of news to such radio stations, television stations, or systems.

5. Members of the families of correspondents are not entitled to the privileges of the galleries.

6. The Radio and Television Galleries shall be under the control of the Executive Committee of the Radio and Television Correspondents' Galleries, subject to the approval and supervision of the Speaker of the House of Representatives and the Senate Committee on Rules and Administration.

Approved.

THOMAS P. O'NEILL, Jr.,
Speaker, House of Representatives.

HOWARD W. CANNON,
Chairman, Senate Committee on Rules and Administration.

RULES GOVERNING PERIODICAL PRESS GALLERIES

1. Persons desiring admission to the Periodical Press Galleries of Congress shall make application to the Speaker, as required by rule XXXIV of the House of Representatives, and to the Committee on Rules and Administration of the Senate, as required by rule VI for the regulation of the Senate wing of the Capitol; and shall state in writing the names of all newspapers or publications or news associations by which they are employed, and what other occupation or employment they may have, if any; and they shall further declare that they are not engaged in the prosecution of claims pending before Congress or the departments, and will not become so engaged while allowed admission to the galleries; that they are not employed in any legislative or executive department of the Government, or by any foreign government or any representative thereof; and that they are not employed, directly or indirectly, by any stock exchange, board of trade, or other organization, or member thereof, or brokerage house or broker, engaged in the buying and selling of any security or commodity, or by any person or corporation having legislation before Congress, and will not become so engaged while retaining membership in the galleries. Holders of visitor's cards who may be allowed temporary admission to the galleries must conform to the restrictions of this rule.

2. The applications required by rule 1 shall be authenticated in a manner that shall be satisfactory to the executive committee of the Periodical Correspondents' Gallery who shall see that the occupation of the galleries is confined to bona fide and accredited resident correspondents, newsgatherers, or reporters of reputable standing who represent one or more periodicals which regularly publish a substantial volume of news material of either general or of an economic, industrial, technical or trade character, published for profit and supported chiefly by advertising or by subscription, and owned and operated independently of any industry, business, association, or institution; and it shall be the duty of the executive committee at their discretion to report violation of the privileges of the galleries to the Speaker, or to the Senate Committee on Rules and Administration, and pending action thereon the offending correspondent may be suspended.

3. Persons engaged in other occupations whose chief attention is not given to the gathering or reporting of news for periodicals requiring such continuous

service shall not be entitled to admission to the Periodical Press Galleries. The Periodical Correspondents' list in the CONGRESSIONAL DIRECTORY shall be a list only of persons whose chief attention is given to such service for news periodicals, as described in rule 2, except that admission shall not be denied if his other work is such as to make him eligible to the Press Galleries or Radio Correspondents' Galleries.

4. Members of the families of correspondents are not entitled to the privileges of the galleries.

5. The Periodical Press Galleries shall be under the control of an executive committee elected by members of the Periodical Correspondents' Association, subject to the approval and supervision of the Speaker of the House of Representatives and the Senate Committee on Rules and Administration.

THOMAS P. O'NEILL, Jr.,
Speaker, House of Representatives.

HOWARD W. CANNON,
Chairman, Senate Committee on Rules and Administration.

Media Coverage of Congress

The Congress does not have the impact with the media that prevails in the White House or in the Departments of State or Defense. Nevertheless, it can on occasion be an excellent source of news, particularly during hearings and meetings of various committees where provocative items are discussed. Some members of the Senate and House have a distinct penchant for making news. Others are rarely heard from, except by occasional releases sent to the Galleries by their press aides. Inevitably, the Senate, by its structure and function, is a more productive source of news than the House of Representatives, although it is unfortunate that members of the House seem to dominate the news when they are involved in a scandal that the media expose. But in both houses of Congress, the amount and quality of media coverage depends on the incumbent's nose for news and his personal relations with the correspondents.

Unlike the White House and Cabinet departments, the Congress is dependent largely on local and regional media. Both the Senate and the House are covered by the wire services, though the former receives greater coverage by the Washington bureaus of the large metropolitan newspapers and by the national news magazines and network television news broadcasts. Relatively few Senators achieve national prominence despite this advantage in coverage, so all members of the Congress feel a genuine need to maintain a sound, ongoing interaction with correspondents from newspapers and broadcasting stations in their respective states and cities. Some of these outlets have media representatives in Washington. When they do not, the Senator or Representative—particularly the latter—arranges to communicate with constituents by a variety of devices: local press releases, weekly reports, direct mail to voters and the press, distribution of regular reports in the form of scripts, tapes or cassettes to local radio and television stations and copies of the *Congressional Record,* among other informational and promotional materials. The *Congressional Record,* in fact, is criticized for being used as a publicity tool by the Congress on behalf of various causes, groups and individuals. Members of Congress also make it a point to return to their home base for local press, radio and television interviews. When a newsworthy issue of great interest to the public arises, the media will cover it on a national basis, including exposure on the major network news interview programs such as *Issues and Answers, Face the Nation* and *Meet the Press.*

Colorful figures invariably make news. These tend to be the chairmen of various special investigating committees, the heads of regular committees and the more articulate critics of the administration. Members of the Congress are of particular value to the media when they either leak news of impending White House activities or choose to comment for the record on various proposals put forth by the President.

A number of activities tend to make news for members of the Congress.

1. Hearings that are open to the press.
2. Investigative committees.
3. Confrontations with presidential candidates for a high government post who seek approval.
4. Special events occurring out of a national crisis, such as the House Impeachment Committee meetings on Richard M. Nixon.
5. Statements of public policy by congressional leaders, such as Senator Robert C. Byrd's (D. West Va.) various published advisories to the President in the Senator's capacity as the Senate Majority Leader.

In general, the correspondents use the Galleries to pick up releases and obtain fundamental information. The grist for the news, though, comes more readily from meetings with Senators in the President's Room, which is located near the Senate lobby. At these casual encounters, members of the media have an opportunity to elicit comment and opinion from Senators about current and impending legislation and particularly to obtain intelligence about White House–Congress liaison. Thus, the relationship between the correspondents and the Congress tends to be more casual and less structured than that between the White House and the press. Reporters generally appear to be less constrained in their relations with the members of Congress than with the President or the Secretary of State or Attorney General. The Congress is, in the main, more readily accessible and more eager to cooperate. In fact, one of the criticisms leveled at the mutual friendship that exists among many correspondents, Senators and Representatives is that there may develop, perhaps unwittingly, a tendency on the part of the media to shape and suggest the news, as well as to report it. At times, the correspondent will come across, usually fortuitously, a genuinely newsworthy item about a member of the Congress. These items, however, are usually of the sensational variety and the Congress, as the activities of the Ethics Committee revealed, is reluctant to point an accusing finger at its own members. The reporters, on occasion, have been known to go along and studiously neglect to report items that might prove embarrassing to their regular sources of news. Influential and elite correspondents have fallen into this situation, not only in the Congress but also, in some instances, in the heady atmosphere of the White House. It is also not uncommon, on occasion, for a correspondent who has a good story, but needs a quote, to suggest a comment from a willing legislator.

In many ways, the Congress provides creature comforts for the media representatives—from special parking privileges to preferential treatment in the dining facilities. The technical facilities provided for the correspondents are far more complete and sophisticated than those at the Supreme Court, for example. Technical equipment, including studios, is superb and assistance is always available in the Galleries or the broadcast studios.

These amenities, however, did not always prevail. In the early years of the nation, the lawmakers were rather chary of the press, and with good reason, since, as Jefferson remarked, one would be hard pressed to place any credence in what appeared in the partisan press. Despite the belief in a free press, the newspapers simply antagonized and alienated the Congress by their partisanship and vituperation. As a result, the Senate originally did not admit reporters and editors to its deliberations, although the small, four-page news sheets of the period were serviced with a record of what took place in the Congress. One semi-official newspaper, *The National Intelligencer,* was permitted to report proceedings directly from the floors of the House and Senate. It served as a kind of recording organ for the activities of the Congress until 1834, when the *Congressional Globe,* which was the predecessor of the *Congressional Record* was established. Reporters were not allowed on the floor of the House until April 1789 and did not have access to the Senate until January 1802.

As public interest in news from Washington became greater and public demand for information about the government increased, figures such as James Gordon Bennett, the superbly professional publisher of the *New York Herald* demanded greater access. What was later to be called the "people's right to know" became an important concept in the development of news coverage from Washington. Bennett, in particular, fought the preferential treatment given to local Washington papers at the expense of other newspapers. As a result of increasing pressure, more space was made available for reporters. The number admitted was screened and the rules of behavior were stringent, for there was still considerable opposition to permitting coverage by a press which did not have an enviable reputation for integrity. The newspapers, in fact, were vicious in their attacks on those who argued against the admission of reporters to Congress. Bennett was in the vanguard of a developing journalism that was both enterprising and accurate, and his newspaper was the first to offer verbatim accounts of congressional proceedings. It was not until the beginning of this century, however, that the Congress began to take a serious interest in providing adequate facilities for press coverage.

One of the basic reasons for current congressional interest in the media is that they constitute a valuable counteracting force to the impact of the White House and certain Cabinet departments. At the same time, the relationship between the correspondents and the Congress is both ambiguous and ambivalent. The leaders speak of an open Congress, complain about White House secrecy and demand that their mandated function to "advise and consent" be recognized and respected. Yet, the Congress is as apt to "stonewall" the media as any other federal institution when it does not want its deliberations to be publicized. There are still, in spite of the Sunshine Law, too many secret sessions, too many embargoes on news releases, too many unnecessary security measures over the dissemination of information. The press has complained that very little positive action has resulted from the Legislative Reorganization Act of 1970. In the past decade, it is claimed, about 40% of the meetings have been closed to press and public, although the Legislative Reorganization Act called for open meetings. A majority vote in the House can still effectively close a meeting and can take advantage of legal loopholes in the Freedom of Information Act to preclude the media from securing information that the Congress does not want it to have. The Congress itself has been slow in promulgating the principles of the FOI Act. In recent years, most of the Education and Labor Committee meetings have been open to media coverage, but the House Armed Services Committee usually has met behind closed doors. The record of other committees has been spotty. In the Senate, too, the Armed Services Committee has not admitted the correspondents. Nor has the Finance Committee. Other meetings have been closed almost half of the time. Even with the Sunshine Law, the press does not enjoy easy access to official meetings.

Sources of News

Despite its "stonewalling" of the media, the Congress is keenly aware of the need for media support, particularly in its interaction with the White House. Publicity-conscious members know what makes news and attempt whenever possible to grasp opportunities for the development of special events such as hearings and official investigations. The most powerful public relations tool available is the use of the investigative power, and Congress is learning to use this authority in a most sophisticated and newsworthy manner. It is, as one member phrased it, the only way to counter the press coverage of the President cutting the first flower of spring in the White House rose garden. Investigation, however, can be a dangerous weapon, particularly when the media sense that it is being conducted, not for legitimate informational purposes, but for public relations. Hearings, if not properly prepared, can also backfire in the media. The hearings on Bert Lance, before he resigned as Director of the Office of Management and Budget, drew critical fire from the press because the committee seemed inadequately prepared. Since these hearings were televised, they did not contribute to a positive image of the Senate with either media or public.

On the whole, there is quite a disparity between the publicity achieved by the Senate and the House. The work of the House is not ordinarily glamorous or sensational and, therefore, it does not attract media coverage. The Senate works differently. It is a smaller, tighter body. Its members are better known nationally. Many are potential candidates for the Presidency. The Senate, further, is in a better position to create and question policy. The House is more concerned with local and regional matters and does not have as much concern as the Senate for a national constituency and for broad public consensus. Thus, the House looks to the wire services and local representatives for press coverage, while the Senate sets its goal on the national news media. The Senate is also thrust more directly into the maelstrom of national crises than the House. Both houses of Congress face analogous problems in securing adequate and favorable coverage. The reason is that both try to control and direct the flow of information to their respective advantage. The media, for their part, are guided primarily by a reportorial instinct for news, along with an assumption of what the public wants and their editors expect. Each correspondent maintains a perception of what constitutes news and each has firm ideas as to how a story should be developed. These perceptions do not always cohere with the goals of the Congress.

Each day a plethora of publicity handouts are placed in the Press Galleries by the public information aides in the Senate and the House.

Most of these are neglected by the media, for if all were printed, there would be little room for other news. And few reporters print releases without wanting to talk with the source, to expand the story or to get quotable material. Many of the press handouts are self-serving or simply for the record, and no one expects them to be used as bona fide news. But the press itself, to its discredit, has been known to help willing congressmen fabricate news on a dull day—a procedure which neither enhances journalistic ethics nor benefits the public. The local press, too, frequently is derelict in carrying information that the constituents ought to know about their elected representatives. As a result, the emphasis on wire service copy and on sensational items obscures legitimate information about the Congress—the background, record and political philosophy of the members, where they stand on issues, how they vote, what contribution they make or fail to make to the legislative and investigative functions of the Congress.

At the same time, the nationally syndicated columnists rarely offer serious and substantive comment on the deliberations of the Congress, except for coverage of a few leaders—and then mainly in terms of their relations with the White House. For many syndicated columnists the rule of thumb seems to be that if there is no sensational news, there is nothing to write about. It was only *after* an alleged scandal relating to the personal life of a member of the House was publicized that the columnists printed columns critical of his behavior as a congressman. Yet, this member had a reputation for high-handed and acrimonious dealings, both with his peers and with the media.

Public policy and publicity by way of the mass media inevitably interact. What appears in print or on the news broadcasts not only reflects but also influences policies in the federal bureaucracy. As a result, more information is demanded due to the opportunity available to evaluate, discuss and attempt to come to consensus. Because media content inevitably influences policy, the Congress uses the media for feedback and input which becomes valuable in the determination of action. Feedback mechanisms, particularly in the local media so far as members of the House are concerned, are an important determinant of official behavior. Thus, the media themselves are influential in reaching other influentials in government.

What appears in print and on the air concerning the activities of the Congress is determined to a great extent by several related factors: the ability of the member to make news, the perception of the correspondent of what kind of information constitutes news, the interest or disinterest of the public and the policy of the editor or publisher. A few correspondents rely on press aides for leads. Most do not. Some reporters spend time, much of it fruitful, in casual but productive visits to the President's Room or at private lunches with congressmen. Some rely on what appears in the *Congressional Record*. Basic determining factors in whether a story will be used are the person involved, the nature of the information released and the dramatic appeal of the material. Some reporters seek hard news, while others prefer to write interpretive pieces. Opinion magazines, such as the *Nation* and the *New Republic* tend to evaluate, criticize and suggest reforms. Unfortunately, relatively few members of Congress are cognizant of the needs of the media in terms of what constitutes news. The correspondents face a bewildering array of committee meetings, hearings and other events and appreciate help from either the member or the press aide in selecting what to cover. But too many press officers offer suggestions which turn out to be self-serving and ultimately alienate the press. The result is a tendency on the part of the reporters to seek out a few trusted informational sources and to follow up on leads offered them. Although primarily independent in their search for news, most correspondents find that they cannot cope with the bureaucracy without some reliance on sources they can trust.

In the last analysis, it is not the government official or the public which determines the news flow. The media inevitably define not only what will be considered news but also what major issues will be controversial enough to stimulate the development of public opinion and consensus. The media are a responsible determinant in the political information process by defining and delineating what is news. The bureaucracy can take steps that are potential news. But the press defines the news and, by selective perception, controls to some degree the flow of public information. This function, which the press abrogates to itself, has not escaped criticism. Despite the talk of social responsibility, the media are accused of neglect and irresponsibility in failing to report certain data and in emphasizing the exciting and the sensational. The media are accused of a supine acceptance of press releases and leaks without adequate follow-up and investigation—in other words, of lazy reporting. Some correspondents have been scored for developing ties with officials that become too personal and, as a result, the reporter becomes not a source of news but an unwitting publicist for the official. The media, however, cannot avoid shaping the news, and some believe that they should not try to achieve the ephemeral goal of "objectivity" because it is simply unattainable, particularly in political reporting. Influential and elite columnists influence public policy, whether they consciously try to or not. They exercise a profound effect on the Congress and can actually exert an influence on the course of legislation. Events are inevitably shaped and suggested by the media, and no one has yet devised a sound way to avoid this phenomenon.

Investigative Function

The one important lever for media coverage which is open to the Congress is its investigative power and its special hearings on various controversial issues. This is the single force that can be used effectively to combat the White House influence on news flow. But investigation can backfire as it did in the Bert Lance hearings. On occasion, these events can generate an exploitative atmosphere which some members of Congress have a tendency to develop. Parts of the hearings on the Daniel Schorr case, where the former CBS correspondent was alleged to have given a "secure" report to the *Village Voice,* did not reflect favorably on the Congress, either in the print media or on television. In February 1976, the House of Representatives discovered that a report on United States intelligence was in the hands of television reporter Daniel Schorr. Eventually, through a circuitous chain of events, the so-called "Schorr Report" was published in the *Village Voice,* which apparently agreed to pay for it in the form of a contribution to the Reporters' Committee for Freedom of the Press. This publication set off a furor that extended from the White House to the Congress and, although parts of the report were already common knowledge, the House Ethics Committee set out to investigate the source of the "leak." It was believed by many observers that the action of the House was simply to justify suppression, since the Report of the House Intelligence Committee under Representative Otis Pike (D. N.Y.) had been excerpted in *The New York Times*. Schorr made an appearance, cited his reportorial conscience as the moral reason for not divulging his source, and the investigation ended with a whimper. Schorr had honored the Congressional subpoena but had maintained the confidentiality of his source. Along the way, however, Schorr was accused of attempting to cast suspicion for the leak on his colleague at CBS News, Leslie Stahl. Although CBS gave him partial support, he was suspended and then resigned. Schorr justified his refusal to identify his source by telling *The New York Times* that the principle was "the people's right to know." The main issue, he said, concerned the reporter and his job. "If they can hold me in contempt, or have me charged with a crime, then they can get any reporter next week."

The investigation is a legitimate function of congressional committees and it serves a useful public purpose, provided that it is not developed merely as a device to achieve coverage by the media. The media, in covering hearings, have a dual function. Primarily, they operate to cover what is newsworthy. But they also, in their surveillance function, can inform the public of official behavior which goes beyond the legitimate investigative function of the Congress—intimidation, ill-prepared and offensive questions, expression of bias or personal antagonism.

Under optimum conditions, which seldom prevail, the public interest is best served when the Congress and the media cooperate responsibly with each other. In this way there is a joint recognition of the need to develop an informed public opinion. This interaction can be achieved only when the Congress recognizes its basic obligation to the people and the media do not deviate from their obligation to provide the public with vital political intelligence. This is not to suggest that the Congress not seek to develop good press relations. Those members who meet regularly with the correspondents serve not only the interests of press and public but their own as well. There is a decided personal advantage involved. The congressman's views tend to be solicited by the correspondents, enhancing the opportunities for a sound press "image." As a result, the member becomes a quoted authority in certain delimited areas.

One of the recurring points of conflict between the media and the Congress from achieving optimum cooperation is failure to lay out and follow ground rules. Each should have a clear-cut understanding of what is to be considered for quotation or for background only, what is on or off the record and what is not for attribution. In this need for liaison, the congressional press aide, if he is professional, can play an effective role of bringing a common understanding of the principles involved to both the correspondent and the member of the Congress. One way to avoid misunderstanding is for the Congress to avoid asking the correspondents to make suggestions on legislative matters, as well as to avoid soliciting advice on their personal public relations. Such a liaison is not productive of news and it operates against the best interest of both protagonists. On the other hand, the reporter can serve as an important feedback source to the Congress by sharing any information that may be legislatively useful or that may suggest an appropriate investigation. The public interest is served by this attitude and, in addition, the media may have the makings of a sound news story.

Broadcast Media and the Congress

For a long time, the Congress has been considering the admission of electronic journalism on the floors of the Senate and the House of Representatives. One bone of contention between the broadcasters and the congressional leaders is the question of control. The Congress wants to control the broadcast coverage procedure, while the television networks claim, legitimately many believe, that they cannot relinquish their independence as journalists and that the determination as to what to cover and how to cover it are their prerogative. At this time, the Congress has not reached a firm decision on permitting television coverage, but the controversial issue of control appears to present a knotty problem. In any event, the televising of the Congress in session inevitably will make a difference in the conduct of the meetings. On the positive side, the members will realize that the proceedings are being visually relayed to the public—a decisive factor in the conduct of the members. Negatively, there is the fear that the sessions will lose whatever spontaneity they had and become a television event or "special," to the detriment of orderly legislative process. The broadcasters remain convinced that television coverage of the Congress can only reflect favorably on the democratic political process. Technology, the media say, has now become so unobtrusive that it would have no effect on the proceedings on the floor.

While Congress has been keenly aware of the value of broadcast coverage, it has also been concerned about routine coverage. The cameras have been permitted at such special events as the Kefauver crime hearings, the deliberations on the impending impeachment of President Nixon and various investigative and "advise and consent" hearings. Reporters for the electronic media, while not admitted routinely, have covered, therefore, particular newsworthy occasions. The first radio broadcast from Congress took place in 1939, the same year that television was first tested from the New York World's Fair. In 1977, approximately 700 correspondents and technicians were listed for the Radio-Television Correspondents Gallery. But coverage in the chamber itself is still prohibited, as discussions continue as to whether coverage will be permitted and under what circumstances. In spite of restrictions, both networks and local stations continue to report on activities from the floor of the Capitol or the White House. In the continuing debate over access, CBS' Roger Mudd, Chairman of the Executive Committee of the Radio-Television Correspondents Galleries, had urged as far back as 1969 that two network pool cameras be admitted, along with regional and local stations. But there was resistance to pool coverage as generally unsatisfactory and inequitable for independent broadcast groups. The basic argument of the broadcasters is that coverage must be on-the-spot, not a subsequent recreation of what occurred, presented after the fact. It seems fairly certain, though, that some feasible method will evolve by which the public will be able to view televised coverage of Congress in action.

8

The Diffident Supreme Court

No Washington institution traditionally has been as reluctant to traffic with the media as the Supreme Court of the United States. The Court is not political—at least not in any official sense—and it does not consider itself part of the federal bureaucracy. It does not hold formal news conferences, has not had a press officer who meets the press for regular briefings (although it maintains an information officer) and does not explain its proceedings or decisions to editors even though in recent years, Chief Justice Warren Burger has shown a greater awareness of the media than his predecessors. Despite the court's publicity aversion, a major court decision can be front page news and is also widely publicized by the broadcast media. The members of the Court rarely give interviews and are seldom quoted. Personal coverage by the news media usually results from a speech, most often by the Chief Justice, less so by an Associate Justice. The Court also receives press coverage in an indirect way, when legal scholars discuss or criticize its decisions. The public is aware through the media, for example, that there were enormous differences in philosophy and in interpretation of the Constitution by the Warren Court as compared to the Burger Court on such issues as free press and fair trial, busing, abortion, the rights of the accused and the privileges of reporters. Through all these and other differences of opinion in the political climate, the Supreme Court goes its serene way, apparently oblivious to any media publicity about it. As for the bureaucracy, the public seldom reads or hears direct criticism from within the government, although criticism is implied when decisions are made with which the President or congressional leaders disagree.

There have been recent recommendations that the broadcasters ought to be permitted—indeed, invited—to televise court proceedings. Richard S. Salant, former president of CBS News, believes that the Supreme Court should permit coverage but that lower court trials should not be televised. He asserted, in an article in *The New York Times* (November 16, 1977) that public knowledge would be at its maximum if radio microphones and subsequently TV cameras were permitted to cover the Supreme Court in action. Since, Mr. Salant claimed, there is neither jury nor witnesses in Supreme Court cases, there would be no question as to the effect on juries, and the problem of free press versus fair trial would simply not be a relevant one.

United States Judge Jack B. Weinstein and Diane L. Zimmerman, a law professor at New York University, presented a similar but not identical viewpoint in *Judicature,* a publication of the American Judicature Society. Their position is that the courts have not been accessible to the public, that people should be given the opportunity "to observe the courts" and that, despite the requirements of the Sixth Amendment for a fair trial, the broadcast press should not be completely excluded from criminal trials. Television cameras are "not subversive of a fair and dignified trial" and controls should not be exercised against the media, but against the officials. In this period of sophistic technology, "barring television from the courts seem increasingly archaic and arbitrary."

Media Coverage and Limitations

If the Supreme Court seems reluctant to engage in publicity about its activities, the media are often equally tentative about the manner in which they disseminate news that may be issued as a result of a court decision. Major decisions, such as the 6–3 determination on publication by the newspapers of the celebrated Pentagon Papers, occasion a flurry of media coverage and discussion. But the in-between periods can be long and relatively silent, punctuated only by an occasional electrifying and highly newsworthy decision. Yet, no action by any government branch or agency, even the White House, can compare in significance with decisions on controversial social or political issues by the highest court. The Supreme Court, by what it decides, can alter the course of government right up to the Presidency, and its influence on the social, economic and political life of the nation is equally enormous.

The significance of the Pentagon Papers from a media standpoint inhered in the attempt to restrain publication in 1971 of the volume entitled *History of the U.S. Decision-Making Process on Vietnam Policy*. The issue was prior restraint, the first in four decades against a newspaper. Whether the basis was political or not, the fact is that *The New York Times* published parts of the Pentagon Papers, and the government obtained an injunction against further publication after the third installment appeared in the paper. What was surprising to the media was the Supreme Court decision to continue the restraining order issued by the lower courts, for this action was felt by many concerned editors to be a violation of both the spirit and the letter of the Bill of Rights. The fact that the highest court ultimately decided (6–3) that publication would not constitute a national security problem did little to reassure the media, because three of the members of the Court, including the Chief Justice, dissented. Unfortunately, the Supreme Court also avoided coming to grips with the basic issue of prior restraint.

The Supreme Court has an information officer, but he does not normally function to explain or interpret decisions to the mass media. That the interpretation is not his responsibility is understandable but, in a sense, it is unfortunate that the press is not given an opportunity to ask questions before printing or airing its story. It is also unfortunate that the Court makes no great effort and has no specific process by which decisions can be explained or discussed. Coverage of the Supreme Court by the correspondents is considered by legal scholars to be grossly inadequate. Over the past decade, only two Washington reporters (James E. Clayton of the *Washington Post* and Anthony Lewis of *The New York Times*) are said to have had some legal background. The assignment, it is claimed by experts, does not demand a law degree but rather sufficient training in general and communications law to enable the reporter to prepare an accurate account and to write an interpretive piece that will be comprehensible to the public. It is not too much to ask, legal scholars complain, that those who report on the Supreme Court have training in political science and particularly in constitutional law and, indeed, some journalism schools have now begun to offer such preparation.

The types of cases argued before the Supreme Court are either *certiorari* (the petition to the Court to hear a case) or an appeal of a case to the Court as the highest authority. If the Court does hear a case, briefs are then filed by respective counsel for the plaintiff and the defendant. The Court then hears the case by oral argument. There are rarely, unlike other institutions, information, backgrounders or "leaks" provided for the media; they must operate strictly on their own. When the Court does hear and decide a case before it, the formidable challenge to the reporter is to convey the decision accurately, completely and intelligently. The Court frequently does not decide the way in which its decision is reported by the media. Nor does the headline, written by a "gatekeeper," always accurately reflect the thrust and meaning of a reporter's account of what transpired. In the processing of Supreme Court news, it is felt that there is far too much reliance on standardized press association copy which, by its very nature, is not always complete or exhaustive. In cases before the highest court, many scholars believe that each newspaper should have firsthand coverage by its own trained reporters. Only a few major newspapers, such as *The New York Times* and the *Washington Post,* make any genuine effort to cover the decisions of the Court, while most of the others accept and print wire copy which is conscientious and accurate, but may be incomplete, owing to deadline limitations.

Information to the Media

The Constitution (Article III, Section 1) provides that "the judicial power of the United States shall be vested in one Supreme Court, and in such inferior Courts as the Congress may from time to time ordain and establish.'' The Supreme Court was created in 1789 and organized in 1790. It is composed of a Chief Justice and eight Associate Justices. Since the power to nominate Justices is vested in the President of the United States, with the ''advice and consent'' of the Senate, appointments to the Court have often resulted in considerable comment by the media, which have on more than one occasion accused presidential choices of being politically motivated. Only rarely, however, has either the Senate or the press raised serious and strenuous objections. Franklin D. Roosevelt's attempt to ''pack'' the Court did arouse nationwide protest. But, more significantly, as a result of excellent investigative reporting by the news media, two successive candidates selected by President Nixon were rejected by the Senate—a rare event and one which came about largely because of the enterprise of the press in investigating the candidates' backgrounds and qualifications.

The *modus operandi* by which the Supreme Court moves information has been clumsy and cumbersome by comparison to other agencies and branches of the federal government. Traditionally, quarters for the press were established on the first level, along with the court public information official. For many decades, pneumatic tubes provided a way for reporters to receive data and these reached the news desks and were distributed out of sight of the bench. In the Burger Court, which appears to have taken greater cognizance of the needs of the media, the reporters' desks were moved to an area where the Justices on the bench are visible. The pneumatic tube arrangement was removed. Unlike other institutions, many of the conventional publicity aids are not available. The press officer issues a report of cases to be heard and a file of briefs, and he also makes available background data on the Justices. The Court's opinion goes to the media only at the time of announcement of a decision from the bench. There are no advance or subsequent briefings. Little, if any, background information is provided. There are no official press releases or other explanatory materials. In short, the Court makes no effort, formal or informal, to deal with the press according to accepted standards for the dissemination of public information.

In the abstract, the Court does not seek publicity for its members or its decisions. It is extremely difficult, in fact virtually impossible, for the correspondents to induce a member of the Court to discuss a case. Press image means little to the Court as an entity. Not only is there virtually no regular contact with the media, there is no apparatus set up for such liaison. Individual Justices, however, may occasionally discuss general philosophical matters. One such instance was the memorable appearance of Justice Hugo L. Black on a CBS program. Likewise, Chief Justice Burger granted an interview with *U.S. News and World Report* in 1970—hardly a "people's magazine" piece. The Chief Justice, however, has made a number of speeches, most about the case load of the courts, which have been adequately reported in the press.

The Director of the Public Information Office of the Supreme Court of the United States, with an assistant, is responsible for the distribution of appropriate materials to the media. According to this source, about 40 correspondents cover the Court "off and on" along with an additional 100 newsmen who do so occasionally. Three correspondents are present on a full-time basis, two from AP and one from UPI. An additional 15 cover half of the time and include *Reuters, Washington Post, The New York Times, Wall Street Journal, Baltimore Sun* and *The Los Angeles Times*. Others cover seven days a month when the Justices are sitting: the commercial television networks, public television, McGraw Hill publications, *Milwaukee Journal, St. Louis Post Dispatch,* Knight papers, *New York Daily News, Chicago Tribune, Journal of Commerce,* Gannett chain, Scripps-Howard, Prentice-Hall publications and *Newsweek.* On special issues, such as education, birth control, religious and international issues, reporters specializing in these areas may cover. In the case of "blockbusters," 200 or 300 correspondents may cover (the Nixon case, the Bakke case, the death penalty).

Court opinions are printed by and available from the Government Printing Office. The Court public information office makes a number of these available to the media. "Within 100 seconds of the time a decision is announced," the full text is made available to some 40 reporters.

In some instances, Opinions are preceded by a "syllabus"—or

headnotes—which is essentially a summary of the case and is released at the same time as the Opinion. (See Nixon decision in Appendix.) The Opinion, including dissents, follows the headnotes. The United States Supreme Court also publishes a brochure of interest to the public, containing significant information on its purpose, structure and function. For internal distribution, as well as for former and retired employees, the information officer produces a ''house organ'' publication known as *The Docket Sheet,* which contains incidental data, personal briefs, historical material, new books in the Court library, news briefs and comments from readers.

The major sources of Supreme Court news then, both for the media and the public, are the ubiquitous press associations which do their usual effective job under limiting conditions. The restrictiveness led former AP executive, Wes Gallagher, to suggest that reporters receive decisions in advance, so that they can be studied and reported without the speed necessitated by the demands of newspaper deadlines. One available source of information to all the media is *United States Reports,* but this volume, running to several hundred pages, is intended more for legal experts than for reporters.

That the Court itself has recognized the need for information was indicated by Justice William J. Brennan's call for a ''national commitment to the principle that debate on public issues should be uninhibited, robust and wide open.'' But the Court's encouragement of public and media debate apparently does not include the need of the institution itself to be more accessible to the media. The AP and UPI usually convey the material to others in the press area where copy is prepared for the bureau office. By the very nature of the procedures, much material which would be valuable to the media is simply not available. The press, for example, may not receive data which are highly relevant to a news story. Had Judge John Sirica, for example, not made certain Watergate data available to the press, the public's right to information might simply have been ignored. Although Judge Sirica did not sit on the Supreme Court, the principle applies.

The diffidence of the Court has been the subject of considerable discussion among legal scholars. Since the infrastructure keeps the press at arm's length, are there any methods by which the media can gain greater understanding of Court decisions, so that reporters can convey information more accurately and intelligently to the public? Legal scholars, opinion leaders and political scientists have offered information and discussion of Court decisions, opinions and dissents, but these have come invariably after the report has appeared in the mass media. While most editors consider wire service reports quite adequate, information problems and gaps still prevail, stemming primarily from lack of effective two-way communication. Among suggestions made are the preparation and distribution of an advance background summary of Court decisions, the appointment of a ''qualified'' individual to answer questions from the press and the possibility—a remote one, if desirable at all—of reporter-lawyers being assigned to cover the Court.

In the Burger Court, there has been a greater realization by the Chief Justice of the needs of the press and some effort has been made to meet those requirements, notably a degree of contact between the Chief Justice and the representatives of the media. But reporting about the Court is still inadequate in terms of the far-reaching significance of its deliberations and opinions. In 1963, the Association of American Law Schools recommended that a committee of professors of law prepare a report or memorandum on cases of unusual news interest to the media. An effort was made to promulgate this recommendation, but the project was abandoned in 1972 because of lack of funds. It has since been renewed, apparently with the implicit and unofficial approval of the Court.

Although Chief Justice Burger has been aware of the requirements of the media, the late Chief Justice Earl Warren also called for ''accurate accounts'' of the work of the Supreme Court. Both the Warren and the Burger Courts, utterly different in philosophy, have received widespread comment by the media. The Warren Court was one of the most discussed in the history of the judiciary and was scored by many for its ''liberalism.'' The Burger Court has come under equally intense criticism for its ''conservatism.'' Thus, while individual decisions may need clarification to the media, there is an overall public perception of the Court, largely as a result of reporting, interpretation and editorializing. The Warren Court was disposed to a broad interpretation of the free speech concept embodied in the First Amendment. The merit and need of a free press was emphasized constantly. The Burger Court has been less consistent—and insistent—on recognizing the rights and privileges of the mass media, particularly in cases where reporters have been subpoenaed before grand juries. Significant attitudes on free press in the Warren Court apparently have not been embraced as enthusiastically by members of the Burger Court. This point was clear in the Court's decision to continue the restraining order in the Pentagon Papers case and in the 6–3 decision on that case. Although Justices Hugo L. Black and William O. Douglas characteristically came out for absolute freedom without any restraint, Chief Justice Burger, along with Justices Harry Blackmun and John Marshall Harlan, dissented and stated that there had not been sufficient time to come to a proper decision.

To Justices Douglas and Black, the Bill of Rights statement that Congress could make no law restricting press freedom meant precisely that. But, as Justice Holmes' "clear and present danger" concept showed, restraint under some circumstances cannot be avoided. The basic questions are concerned with court decisions involving a reporter's right to keep sources confidential and with the right of the press to cover a trial as against the Sixth Amendment affirmation of the need for a fair trial. In recent years, many decisions by the Supreme Court, and by lower courts as well, have not been supportive of the free press argument by the media. Free speech, for example, has never been defined to the satisfaction of all interested parties, nor has the nature of a "clear and present danger," despite the clarity of Justice Holmes' language. Limits have been set on verbal and written expression. The media have exposed cases of clearly illegal surveillance of groups and individuals by government agencies that had no constitutional right to such action. Searches are condoned without a warrant. The "due process" concept is a subject for continuing controversy. All this has an effect on the behavior of the mass media, both in the abstract and particularly on the individual journalist.

Public consciousness and public opinion of the Supreme Court develop in several ways. To begin with, the conception of the Court has always been rather awesome, that of an institution that was the one basic guardian of the ideal of government by consent of the governed.

In its own descriptive brochure, the Court is described as "the highest tribunal in the Nation for all cases and controversies arising under the Constitution or the laws of the United States." As the final arbiter of the law, the Court is charged with ensuring to the American people the promise of equal justice under law and, thereby, also functions as guardian and interpreter of the Constitution. Regardless of the awesomeness of the institution, criticism of the Warren Court was surprisingly aggressive from many quarters, and there is a restiveness about the Burger Court among some legal scholars and in segments of the mass media. The public's image of the Court is influenced by many extraneous factors: the analysis in the media of presidential appointments, the position of the Congress (which can effect legislation even when the Court has taken a contrary position), the opinions of legal scholars in the universities and the information that comes from influential opinion leaders and special interest groups in the two-step flow pattern. All these, in the main, depend fundamentally on reports and analyses of the Supreme Court in the mass media.

More than one student of the Court has come to the conclusion that there is no institution in Washington which is reported on more inadequately and with greater restrictions and less understanding than all the courts in general and the highest court in particular. Several factors are responsible, including the public conception of the Court as a remote body, the attitude of the press officer and the assumption by too many newspaper editors that the public is not particularly interested in the esoteric work of the Supreme Court. Just how the Court can be demystified is a recurrent question, but a problem whose solution will certainly require the close and voluntary cooperation both of the Justices and of the mass media. Justice Felix Frankfurter, a figure much publicized by the press, thought that reporters should not have access to the Supreme Court, that the institution should "not be amenable to the forces of publicity." The reason was that secrecy was necessary if the Court were to function efficiently. This conviction, however, concerns the deliberations of the Justices. It does not apply *after* a case has been decided. At this juncture, the demands of the media should clearly coincide with the desire of the Court that the public receive complete and adequate information.

The continuing and formidable problem is, as always, that of freedom to acquire and disseminate vital information to the people. In the cases decided by the Supreme Court, the people's "right to know" is of particular significance. The First Amendment guarantees no abridgment of speech, but the press cannot report freely if it does not have complete and comprehensible information. In the case of the Supreme Court, the media cannot follow up a story as in other branches and departments, except by going outside to legal experts. The essential and continuing problem is one of overcoming various roadblocks to effective communication between the Court system and the mass media. The Supreme Court could dispense with some of its austerity. The media could make a greater effort to cover the Court more professionally. One helpful method of facilitating informational flow would be to give the media a lead time of an hour or two in which to study a decision and prepare a story. The press also needs a more comprehensive report on the work of the Court, containing summaries and facts and figures. While the press is capable of reporting what happened, it is less able to discuss the significance of the law pertaining to the announced decision. The "why" of Supreme Court deliberations and decisions is seldom proffered to the media, and pieces of this kind must necessarily be speculative and may be wrong as many times as they are right. The Supreme Court (and lower courts as well) is generally free of public and media pressure and properly should be resistant to such pressure. But the decisions of the Court become, in themselves, sources of information which the press can use as a basis for many reports and analyses on a variety of issues.

Prior Restraint

How do the media react to a court decision—and there have been many in the past seven years—where the question of prior restraint conflicts with the press' freedom to function under the First Amendment? This question has formed the basis of several cases before the courts and some have reached the Supreme Court. Most of these cases involve an interpretation of what constitutes freedom of information, of the right of the press to determine and to report the news without restriction by court orders. If that were not the case, there could be a "print by authority" ruling by the government as had prevailed in the

Colonies. The recurrence of such a state of affairs is what the courts are supposed to guard against as indicated in the Bill of Rights. Sir William Blackstone's comment is singularly relevant—that publication ought not to be restrained, but that the publisher must suffer the consequences of his own temerity. The time to punish, therefore, is not before but after the fact of publication. This was the basis of the classic decision in *Near v. Minnesota,* in which the court judged that although the *Saturday Press* was defamatory, prior restraint could conceivably have set a precedent for restrictions on other publications. In the Nixon Administration, however, the Supreme Court upheld a restraining order against *The New York Times* (the Pentagon Papers).

Reporters, traditionally able to maintain confidential sources of information, have also been told that they have no privilege under the First Amendment to keep facts and sources confidential. So acrimonious was this decision that Earl Caldwell, a *New York Times* reporter, was jailed when he refused to respond to a subpoena by a grand jury to release sources for a story on the Black Panthers. Despite the fact that the United States Court of Appeals rescinded a contempt citation against Caldwell, the Supreme Court upheld the original citation.

The Caldwell case alarmed the media, as well it might, for it was followed by several other instances where reporters were jailed for refusing to be responsive to grand jury subpoenas—among them John Lawrence of *The Los Angeles Times* and William Farr of the *Los Angeles Herald-Examiner.* Both refused to disclose information on demand from grand juries. In both cases the Supreme Court refused a hearing. The result has been greater restrictions on the release of information and greater pressure on the reporter to release confidential sources—despite the position of the press that such a demand would have a chilling effect on a free press, would discourage and dry up news sources and is, above all, unconstitutional.

There have, of course, been notable dissents. Justice Brennan saw the Pentagon Papers case as one where the government "sought to enjoin a newspaper from publishing information in its possession." And the late Justice Black noted that the courts were stating that "the First Amendment does not mean what it says, but rather means that the government can halt publication of news of vital importance to the people of this country.'' Justice Black noted further that the government should refrain from prior restraint of the press ''so that the press would remain forever free to censure the government.''

Obscenity and the Court

The assumption that free speech is not an absolute right has been challenged, notably by Justice Black and Justice Douglas, but restraints on speech have been imposed by government ever since the Alien and Sedition Acts, passed in 1798, only seven years after the ratification of the First Amendment. The limits on free speech were established clearly by Justice Holmes in 1919 in *Schenck v. United States,* a case which involved the distribution of materials opposing the draft. Schenck was called in violation of the Espionage Act. Holmes, in the decision, set forth his now classic doctrine of ''clear and present danger,'' which limited freedom of speech under certain circumstances that would ''bring about the substantive evils that Congress has a right to prevent.''

Obscenity as a limitation on freedom of speech is an important issue in government–media relations, because decisions on what is obscene affect the communication of materials in terms of the free speech guarantees of the First Amendment. Few matters have aroused more controversial comment in the mass media, a result essentially of the Supreme Court's ambivalent attitude in defining what is obscene. The Court has waffled persistently over the years on obscenity and the First Amendment, and decisions have shown little consistency of attitude. One Justice stated categorically that while obscenity could not be defined, he knew it when he saw it—a provocative, but subjective, way of viewing a fundamental social problem.

A review of the Court's decisions clearly delineates the lack of consistency in the determination of obscenity. One conclusion, however, appears to emerge: the Court has been unable to arrive at a definition of what is obscene. At the same time, what also emerges is that what is deemed to be obscene, by any standard, is not necessarily protected by the First Amendment. It is this problem that has aroused comment and controversy in the media and among legal scholars.

Differing standards have been applied to a consideration by the

Supreme Court on what constitutes obscenity. The British Hicklin test was considered and abandoned. This test called for a determination to be made on the basis of whether the material was of such a nature as to affect susceptible individuals, such as the very young or the psychopathological. At the heart of the matter, though, is always the effect of a decision on obscenity on freedom of speech and on the First Amendment. Here is where the concerns of the media are paramount. The legal and moral implications have been treated exhaustively in other contexts. Of concern here is the impact of government action on the freedom of the media—*all* media, including books and motion pictures—to function under the guarantees of the Bill of Rights. Most, if not all, of the obscenity cases have involved the federal government and all have revolved around media freedom of expression. In *Roth v. United States* (1957) the Supreme Court upheld a United States Court of Appeals affirmation of Roth's conviction by a lower court for mailing obscene matter. The Court made the firm statement that obscenity simply could not be included in the "area of constitutionally protected speech and press." However, in *Jacobellis v. Ohio* (1964), the highest court, ruling on a case involving the showing of an obscene motion picture, decided the film was not obscene because it had "redeeming social value." The vote, though, was 6–3, an indication that the Court failed to reach unanimity of judgment. In the *Fanny Hill* case (*Memoirs v. Massachussetts,* 1966), the Supreme Court again ruled, reversing a lower court, that the book had "redeeming social importance." In *Ginzburg v. United States* (1966), a case involving the use of the postal service for obscene material, the Supreme Court (5–4) affirmed a lower court conviction, because the thrust of Ginzburg's material had no social value at all. In another case, *Ginsberg v. New York* (1968), involving the sale of obscene matter to a minor, the Supreme Court upheld the conviction because a minor was involved. In *Stanley v. Georgia* (1969), the Court stated that no state could dictate what an individual reads or sees in the privacy of his home. The most recent— and controversial—of Court decisions was that since no national parameters of what constitutes obscenity could be devised, the determination would be based on contemporary community standards. This decision was replete with ambiguity, for each community might have different standards and the First Amendment could not be applied across the board in any future cases. The ambivalence in the Court's position on obscenity was again exemplified early in 1978 when, surprisingly, it agreed to hear an obscenity case, *FCC* v. Pacifica Foundation, involving a recorded monologue by George Carlin on radio station WBAI in New York City. The station contended that the use of "sexual and excretory slang" did not appeal to the prurient interest, but the FCC ruled against the station. The Appeals Court for the District of Columbia did not agree, stating that such a ruling was censorship which, by the same token, would ban parts of Shakespeare and the Bible. The Supreme Court agreed to hear the case, despite the fact that in the past such a case might be found to be bereft of literary or social value.

While it is doubtful that the press would claim that all communications are absolutely protected by the Bill of Rights, it could claim that some standard of what constitutes a "clear and present danger" be established. Otherwise, any effort to apply the First Amendment against arbitrary government restriction becomes an exercise in futility. The basic question regarding obscenity and the restriction of freedom of expression is one which neither the media nor the government has resolved. It is simply whether the government has any right or obligation, legal or otherwise, to suppress what it believes to be without redeeming social value. And, if it has, how is the concept of redeeming social value to be defined so that the government will know when to determine that a communication is obscene? Even though the Supreme Court has noted that "obscenity is not within the area of constitutionally protected speech or press," there is no legal basis either for restraint or regulation. When does freedom of expression cease to be of social value—or educational, or informational? Films that would have resulted in riots in the motion picture theatres ten years ago are shown with impunity today. Do they have more—or less—social value?

One of the criteria, perhaps the best and most democratic, is public opinion. The people themselves, in a pluralistic, democratic society, have not hesitated to express value judgments on various communications and have made their opinion felt to the managers of the mass media. When this consumer pressure occurs, the special interest groups, the federal agencies and the courts usually respond to public demand. A case such as that of *United States v. "Ulysses,"* as far back as 1933, was probably decided, at least in part, by public opinion. *Ulysses,* a book by noted author James Joyce, was banned from the borders of the United States by a government agency, the Customs Bureau. But Judge John M. Woolsey, in a landmark decision, determined that *Ulysses* was not obscene to the average individual.

Widely reported in the media were the recommendations of a commission set up by President Nixon, the Report of the Commission on Obscenity and Pornography (issued by the United States Government Printing Office in 1970). It concluded that social problems stem from a failure to confront sexual matters candidly. Thus, legitimate channels of information are subverted, and illegitimate ones are used. The Commission recommended a widespread program in sex education, including factual, clear-cut sex information, the widest distribution of this information by such government agencies as the National Institute of Health; federal legislation to prevent the mailing of unsolicited promotional materials, allegedly of an offensive nature, to those who have no desire to receive such materials (this was enacted as legislation under the Postal Reorganization Act, 1970); the keeping of lists by the Post Office of those who do not want unsolicited material; and mandating that mailing organizations code their mailings so that they can be returned unopened.

Motion Picture Censorship

Motion pictures are not the press, particularly since the demise of the newsreel as the result of the arrival of television. Indeed, at one juncture, the Supreme Court considered films strictly a "business" and not protected, as were other mass media, by the First Amendment. But the protection of motion pictures is important because restrictions, suppression and prior restraint of film have a direct and chilling effect on other media, such as newspapers, magazines, books, radio and television. All are implicitly (in the case of broadcasting, explicitly) influenced and regulated by government, however indirectly.

The early conclusion of the Court that motion pictures were

purely business was subsequently rescinded. The later opinion was that film was to be included, along with print and broadcasting, as a medium which came under the protection of the First Amendment. In a landmark decision on *The Miracle* (*Joseph Burstyn Inc. v. Wilson,* 1954), the Supreme Court affirmed the new concept, despite some protest against the film as sacrilegious and unworthy of exhibition. The basis for the decision was the First Amendment—that religious conviction could not supersede freedom of speech. At the same time, there was a continuing effort to impose a kind of "Hicklin Rule" on film by judging the acceptability of the parts, rather than the whole— as an aesthetic or informational entity. But, in 1961, the Supreme Court again established a special category for motion pictures by deciding, in a divided opinion, that licensing film—thought to be a form of censorship by free press advocates—was not antagonistic to, or subversive of, the Bill of Rights. Thus, the City or the State could prereview film and issue permits for showing.

Actually, until the so-called sex and violence issue came about as the result of special interest group pressure on the broadcasting industry, motion pictures were the most frequently attacked of media. The Church inveighed against many films and interdicted them from being viewed by its members. A film to be shown late at night on CBS-TV, *The Damned,* was the target of protests from stations and religious groups, although it had been edited carefully and the strictures against it were made *without* the protesters having seen the edited version. When the television critics finally reviewed it, they termed it an innocuous and pallid version of the original theatrical film. The wide swing in what is and is not acceptable in motion pictures can be demonstrated best by a comparison of films today with those shown two decades ago and, above all, by the comparison of the first Motion Picture Code with the rating system for films that is currently in use.

Privacy, Press and Government

Privacy may be invaded by the media as well as by the government. The latter has done so by surveillance, wire- and phone-tapping, the use of secret informers and the illegal exchange of computer information, among other methods. The press invades privacy, at least in theory, when it publishes pictures, exposes heretofore secret information, thrusts microphones in the subject's face and asks embarrassingly personal questions. Privacy is also violated by defamation—the injury to good name or reputation by libel (written defamation) or slander (spoken defamation). Unwarranted and unsolicited publicity in the media is also considered by many to be an invasion of privacy, *even* when public officials are involved.

The major problem confronting the media and the courts is that dissemination of publicity, which in itself may constitute significant news and information for the public, may also be an invasion of privacy. Thus, publication of a picture or a story in the newspaper or on radio or television has drawn more than one irate individual to a lawsuit. But there are parameters as to what clearly is a violation of privacy. For example, should the reporters and photographers force their way into one's home to ask questions and take pictures? Even if the criterion of newsworthiness is met, does not the rule of reason and common courtesy sometimes demand that questions which might be acutely embarrassing or painful be eliminated? There is always the responsibility of the press to be considered, particularly when the demands of a sensational story might give an impression of the subject which turns out to be erroneous. In this case, a retraction has little value once public opinion is established. The media believe, however, that the demands of the news can be so overriding that an invasion of privacy argument has no validity, that they are not in the business of making moral judgments but of reporting the news.

The First Amendment protects freedom of speech and of the press, but the founding fathers had not the remotest idea that privacy could be invaded by a growing battery of technological devices, available primarily to the bureaucracy but also to some extent to the media. Alexander Meiklejohn's theory of the First Amendment in connection with the individual was that the public not only was governed but that it governed itself as well. The people must have freedom of speech and the press must have freedom to report. Both have a need to hear and to be heard. Zechariah Chafee urged that questions of the integrity of the individual and matters of privacy be resolved by a reliance on "public opinion and the conscience of owners and editors." The one fixed idea of the reporter is to obtain accurate and newsworthy information. Since this job is sometimes difficult without intrusiveness, the press has not hesitated to violate privacy with the rationalization that what is sought is in the public interest. At some point, though, what is thought to be information deteriorates into the dissemination of "news" which may be malicious, distorted or untruthful. The heart of the matter is the need for the courts to determine when the publication of information about an individual violates privacy and when it is categorically essential to the "right to know." The media must often make a hard distinction between bona fide news and gossip or scandal. This was a problem that did not appear to bother the Hearst papers in their circulation battle with Pulitzer, and unfortunately there are still a few newspapers which put the sensational above the legitimately newsworthy, particularly where public officials are concerned. The basic issue is the right of the individual to be permitted to have a private life, free from intrusion either by government agencies or the media.

The original intent of the laws concerning defamation was to protect reputation. An individual whose privacy has been violated may claim defamation because of resultant injury to his reputation. Information and news about an individual may be so presented by the mass media as to constitute injury to one's good name, means of livelihood or standing in the community. Since the 1950s, though, it has become exceedingly difficult to establish and win a defamation action, and almost impossible in the case of public figures. In fact, it was President Truman who noted that those who can't stand the heat ought to get out of the kitchen. The Supreme Court has established criteria which make a libel or slander action almost a lost cause from the start. In 1967, in the celebrated *New York Times v. Sullivan* case, the Court decided that the Montgomery, Alabama, Commissioner of Public Affairs did not prove that a civil rights ad which the *Times* ran was either malicious or revealed a reckless disregard for truth. Sullivan, therefore, had no cause for action, particularly as a city government official. The Court declared its conviction that there ought to be no curbs on free, robust, uninhibited debates. This set an unusual precedent for media performance, since it went a long way toward eliminating the concern over possible defamation action. It was certainly a far cry from the

Zenger case and the Alien and Sedition Acts. In another case, General Edmund Walker claimed he had been libeled by the Associated Press, but the Supreme Court held that the general was a public figure and that, in addition, the AP was faced with the need to meet a news deadline. The case concerned AP coverage of General Walker's participation in the events surrounding the admission of James Meredith to the University of Mississippi.

In the opinion of some, even in the media, the Court has gone too far in protecting the press against a libel suit. At present, both public officials and private individuals must show malice before damages can be established. Thus, the newspaper would have to be shown to have published a malicious story or one with a reckless disregard for truth. The Supreme Court has noted, incidentally, that while the media have not always abided by the ethical and professional obligations which are part of freedom of expression, a free press in a democratic society must allow for occasional "abuse," which is not too much of a price for society to pay for freedom of communication. The Court has stated that, out of a multiplicity of ideas (many diverse media), truth can emerge. The broad interpretation of the law of defamation gives the media not only unusual latitude but also an unusual obligation to put the social responsibility of the press to the test. The media constantly are confronted with the recurrent need to make value judgments and can best perform their function in society when limitations are self-imposed, not established by regulatory measures. How much "information" should investigative reporters reveal about an individual's past or private life? Does such reporting, if it is critical, come under the concept of "fair comment"?

Postal Restrictions

The government, through the power invested in the Post Office, has a formidable potential weapon to use against the media. Whether it uses it depends upon several factors, including the social climate, public opinion, the attitude of the administration toward the press and, when cases arise, the courts. Early newspapers in this country were published under the authority of the Postmaster, who could rescind a license to print. The Post Office, by regulating mailing rates, has the power to put fringe publications out of business, as well as to help the publication and distribution of magazines and, on occasion, it has revoked mailing privileges because of allegations of obscenity. The operation of the postal authorities, then, can raise serious questions of First Amendment rights, for the philosophy of the Bill of Rights is plainly that a society can function as a political democracy only if the public has a wide-open opportunity to receive information and the media have latitude in securing information for distribution. But the Post Office has denied facilities to material which it deemed to be deleterious to the common good. Obscenity and sedition have not been constitutionally protected, which has given the Post Office leverage to restrict and to ban mailings.

The purpose of reduced postal rates, on the other hand, is a beneficial one: to encourage the growth of newspapers, magazines and books. But on several occasions, the government has stepped in to restrain and suppress and revoke privileges. Even in the nineteenth century, the Postmaster exercised authority over print and could hold up or deny second class mail permits—the life-blood of most periodicals. In this century, there have also been significant examples of revocation. In *Hannegan v. Esquire* (1946), the Postmaster General revoked the mailing privilege of *Esquire* as immoral and contrary to the good of the public. The Supreme Court, in this instance, unanimously voted down Hannegan, and this decision became a significant one in curtailing unilateral action by the bureaucracy in censoring the mails. A finding for Hannegan conceivably would have given the Postmaster General the right—now by precedent—to make future value judgments of what is a "good" or "bad" publication. In essence, this is censorship and violates the spirit and letter of the First Amendment. In 1967, however, Congress passed a law by which an individual recipient of mail deemed to be offensive could demand that those who distributed the material desist. The recipient can advise the Post Office, which then tells the sender to remove the receiver's name from the mailing list. This position has been reaffirmed by the courts as underscoring the right of an individual to be left alone.

In 1970–71, the Congress passed a postal law regulating obscenity in the mails. The individual can ask the Post Office to place his name on a list of those who do not wish to receive "sexually oriented" material. It may be asked, however, how the establishment of such a list coheres with the principles of freedom of expression? Would such lists simply be used for their expressed purpose—or for other tangential purposes by government? It poses another question which the courts may one day have to confront.

Trial by Media

A source of considerable conflict and controversy between the press and the courts has been the recent exacerbation of a long-standing problem—the question of whether media coverage and publication of a court trial will prove prejudicial to the establishment of a fair trial for the accused. In recent years, the courts, including the highest court, have tended to support the fair trial guarantees inherent in the Sixth Amendment and to brush aside the press' claim of violation of its First Amendment rights. The *major* issue, then, is no longer that of gaining access to government information but how the press can continue to function as a surrogate for the public when it can neither refuse information on confidential sources to grand juries nor cover trials freely when prohibited by the courts. Increasingly over the past seven years, the courts have placed "gag" rules on media activities. In Minnesota, for example, reporters for the *Minneapolis Star and Tribune* have been given instructions by management on possible ways to try to combat restrictive measures by the courts. What motivated this procedure was the fact that judges have continued to close proceedings and have adamantly refused to make legal documents available to accredited reporters. Media in most states have been experiencing identical restrictions on obtaining news of trials.

The position of the media is that the press and broadcasting are entitled to cover and receive information on behalf of the public. More significantly, omission of the press ensures that judges and other participants are responsible to no one. In more than one instance, enterprising reporters have exposed bias, have investigated charges and have proved some to be groundless. To restrict the press, then, is literally a repression of the people's "right to know." In Florida, one of the most conspicuous exercises in restraint of press freedom to cover trials was instituted. United States Senator Edward J. Gurney was indicted while in office, and the press was prohibited by the presiding judge from examining various relevant exhibits. In addition, it was not given any information on conferences between the judge and the litigants. In a case involving a public official in particular, the thwarting of the press from performing its legitimate function is clearly operating against the public interest.

Decisions in restraint of press coverage continue despite the reversal of Justice Blackmun's ruling that a Nebraska judge acted properly in restricting the media from covering a criminal trial. On the issue of free press versus fair trial, the Burger Court has tended generally to rule against the media, although the media are of the conviction that responsible behavior by both the reporters and the trial protagonists (judge, jury, lawyers and police) can overcome any conflict. The courts, however, continue to restrict the media, which suggests that the press itself must continue to demand its privileges under the First Amendment and, in any case, must strive to engender a ground swell of public opinion, which to this point has been lethargic. Support for the free press' position must continue to be developed by appropriate special interest and consumer groups, including the professional organizations of journalists. The Reporters Committee for Freedom of the Press has gone on record and termed the present position of the courts one of "hopeless confusion." Ultimately, the Supreme Court will have to make a firm decision.

In January of 1978, the Supreme Court refused to rescind lower court curbs on the press in criminal trials, leaving "gag orders" standing. The media had challenged two court orders on constitutional grounds in the states of Ohio and South Carolina. The Supreme Court supported the judge's orders, which prohibited either witnesses or jurors from making any statement outside the formal proceedings of the courtroom. The press complained that the ruling was a "gag order" against the media of mass communications. The basis for the highest court's decision was that no First Amendment issues were involved. In effect, this gave lower courts and judges freedom to restrain the media with impunity and without concern of reversal by higher courts. The Supreme Court ruling was termed by Jack C. Landau,

Director of the Reporters' Committee for Freedom of the Press, as leaving "the press, the bar and the bench in a chaotic situation, where nobody really knows with any certainty what the law is."

The issue of fair trial is not without merit, but the position of the media is that the First and Sixth Amendments conflict can be resolved so that neither is subverted or ignored. In effect, the issue came about because of isolated cases of abuse of media privileges, notably in the celebrated Dr. Sam Sheppard trial in 1954, as well as in the cataclysmic series of events following the assassination of President Kennedy. The shooting of Lee Harvey Oswald was brought about, it is claimed, by exploitation by both press and law enforcement agents. The circus atmosphere of the Sheppard trial also brought about demands for greater restrictions on the media. Fundamental questions were raised as a result of these events: whether a fair trial is possible in the face of publicity, whether some method can be devised to compel more responsible behavior by law enforcement agencies and the media, whether some compromise can be constructed between the press and courts as to ground rules. At the same time, some have suggested that the United States follow the custom established in Great Britain which permits no publicity while a trial is in progress. But this suggestion has aroused intense opposition from civil libertarians, who are convinced it would stifle a free press. The American Bar Association has made the recommendation that the Reardon Report be adopted—a recommendation in which publicity on a pre-trial situation would come under court restrictions that would not permit those involved (police and attorneys) to offer any information, unofficially or officially, to the media. In any event, it should now be clear to the media that the courts have raised a formidable barrier to freedom of information and that the media, in insisting on their rights, must also be scrupulously careful to avoid a repetition of a situation like the Sheppard case, where the court concluded that flamboyant and irresponsible coverage did not result in a fair trial.

A distinguished jurist, Harold R. Medina, of the United States Court of Appeals for the Second Circuit, takes a jaundiced view of the recommendations by the American Bar Association to ensure both fair trials and free press. In a seminar of the Practicing Law Institute,

Judge Medina urged the media to stand firmly against the association's position of accommodation. Under the ABA proposal, which encountered opposition from the media, the court must tell reporters the reason for restrictive orders and must show that the public interest is involved. The court must show that press coverage would prevent a fair trial. This was the second set of guidelines issued by the Bar Association. The first was the aforementioned Reardon Report. But Judge Medina, in his demurrer, pointed out that "judge after judge and court after court took these voluntary guidelines and turned them into a piece of concrete." Judge Medina urged that both lawyers and the media reject any guidelines that would vitiate press freedom.

The critical conflict that arises between court and media is but another acute example of the conviction, so often expressed, that a political democracy and a free press system must never be taken for granted and are always open to challenge. Conflict over public policy, free of authoritarianism, is a prime aspect of an open society.

9

Departments and Agencies

EACH DEPARTMENT HEAD and Cabinet member has a press secretary, and all the agencies and quasi-agencies also have an information officer. Some of these are more visible in the media than others because of the nature of their function, particularly the State; Defense; Justice; and Health, Education and Welfare Departments (HEW). But political and economic events also have a way of thrusting a particular department or agency into focus in the press. The Pentagon becomes highly visible at about the time its budget proposals are considered by the White House and the Congress. The abortion and social security issues result in media coverage of HEW. Problems of the economy usually focus media coverage on the Treasury Department. The testimony of former CIA official Richard Helms put the Department of Justice in the press limelight. The proposal to revise the Communications Act draws attention by the media to an agency such as the Federal Communications Commission. And controversy over a new drug will increase visibility of the Food and Drug Administration. In short, the quantity and quality of press coverage depend to a great extent on extraneous and factitious factors. In some cases, however, public and press interest are fairly constant; one such case concerns the Department of State.

147

The State Department

Vastly more conspicuous than the Supreme Court and, in fact, the most ubiquitous of government departments is the Department of State. Next to the White House, the State Department is usually the most fruitful source of news for the media, but it is not as consciously conspicuous as is the White House. The President's press office works assiduously to enhance the "image" of the Chief Executive. The State Department, traditionally and disdainfully termed "Foggy Bottom" by the press, is a source of news, but the news develops in mysterious ways. The Secretary of State is always highly visible, and some secretaries more than others.

John Foster Dulles, with his "agonizing reappraisal," his pontifical attitudes and his fixed opinions was a highly visible and peripatetic Secretary for his time. His foreign policy was under criticism from many segments of the media, and it was widely assumed that Dulles, not President Eisenhower, was the architect of this country's diplomacy. In the Nixon and Ford Administrations, Henry Kissinger became the most publicized and visible Secretary in history. Kissinger was his own public relations counsel—brilliant with the press, often thought testy and autocratic by his subordinates and a superb diplomat in the period of *détente*. Kissinger's successor, Cyrus Vance, a more modest figure, has been thrust stage center by the world situation, particularly the Middle East, but President Carter himself and Zbigniew Brzezinski are active in foreign policy determination.

The Assistant Secretary of State for Public Affairs is one of the few information officers in the government who is widely quoted in the media as a spokesman for the Department of State. This situation is unusual, not prevailing in other government branches and agencies where the press officer is usually not encouraged to permit personal quotation by the media. In a survey dealing with the structure and function of the Office of Press Relations, the office was questioned about the way in which the media covered the Department and were asked whether there were suggestions for improving press coverage. The respondent, a spokesman from the press office, did not address the question of State Department–media relations.

The State Department's Office of Press Relations has responsibilities in two areas: to service to the press information regarding the position of the Department on foreign policy and to be responsive to requests from the press for information. The press office is also supportive of the Secretary of State in matters relating to press relations, such as travel, news conferences, interviews, speeches and congressional testimony. A daily briefing is held for the press by the Assistant Secretary for Public Affairs and other press officers, including a Deputy Spokesman and Director of the Press Office, a Deputy Director and four additional press officers. A monitoring team consisting of two individuals records and transcribes radio and television coverage of State. The Department has five secretaries.

Although this is no precise list of correspondents, about 7(X) are accredited. On a daily basis, some 30 or 40 newsmen attend the briefings. About 35 operate regularly out of the press room. Of these, approximately 6 reporters represent wire services, 14 are from large metropolitan daily newspapers, 4 from the news magazines and 7 from the radio and television networks. Two reporters represent local press, and the foreign press contingent numbers about 9.

Beyond the press officers, the State Department boasts of an enormous staff, with several Under Secretaries, Deputy Under Secretaries, Directors, a Department Counselor, various Assistant Secretaries and Advisers. There appear to be at least 11 Assistant Secretaries, each with a large group of Deputies and Directors. Literally, there is an individual assigned to every country in the world. Subsumed under the State Department are also the Agency for International Development, the Permanent Mission to the Organization of American States and the United States Mission to the United Nations. All of these various officials, through the Secretary of State, function to advise the President on foreign policy and frequently on press relations relating to diplomatic matters. From the point of view of media exposure, it is worthy of note that the Department presents the position of this country at the United Nations and also sends a representative to hundreds of annual international conferences. The enormous potential for visibility with the press by the Secretary is evident, particularly since he is the first-ranking member of the Cabinet.

The State Department issues a considerable quantity of informational materials. These include audio-visual materials (films and discussion guides) on foreign policy. The Department has prepared a four-part film series, available from the Office of Media Services, on the history of United States foreign relations. The Department also holds several national foreign policy seminars and conferences, as well as regional conferences. Public briefings on foreign policy are held at the Department twice weekly, on Tuesday and Friday mornings. Several publications are produced by the State Department, A *Bulletin, Background Notes, Special Reports* and *Current Policy,* among others. Above all, the Freedom of Information Staff, Bureau of Public Affairs, is responsible for the administration of the Freedom of Information Act, and the Privacy Staff of the Foreign Affairs Document and Reference Center administrates the 1974 Privacy Act.

Media coverage of the Department of State carries an obligation as weighty as that of the Supreme Court, but the difference is that more sources of information, official as well as unofficial, are available to the correspondents. The Department holds regular briefings, as well as special conferences when the news warrants this procedure. The Secretary is accompanied by press on his trips abroad. While there are delicate problems in diplomacy to be considered—and press exposure has often proved embarrassing—the Department appears willing, by and large, to assist the news media in their journalistic objectives. One of the major problems in press relations may eventuate out of overlapping of function or lack of communication between the Department and representatives of the White House, the National Security Agency, the Congress or the Department of Defense. One conflicting story in the media can open a veritable Pandora's Box of difficulties, not for the related agencies, but for the State Department. A "leaked" story can arouse the ire of the White House or the Congressional Committee on Foreign Relations as well as foreign diplomats. Correspondents covering State, then, are often faced with value judgments, not so much as whether to run a story but as to what to leave out. Confidential data on delicate negotiations on *détente* and other diplomatic matters often reach the reporter, and it is his judgment which determines whether the public interest will benefit from its release. All institutions, including State, attempt implicitly to influence the news, and that involves subtle pressures to omit as well as to include sensitive data.

It is the opinion of most correspondents that in the State Department, as elsewhere, press briefings are not usually productive of news, which comes more readily from following leads and by interviews, lunches and other more casual methods. The more knowledgeable the correspondent on foreign affairs, the greater the opportunity for productive and newsworthy information. In addition to the daily briefings, reporters receive press releases and background briefings, some for attribution, some not. In a sensitive area such as the State Department, the reporter must exercise a constant and healthy skepticism. There is always the possibility that efforts will be made to use the media as conduits of a carefully prepared position. Such efforts constitute a control of information, and the determination of its news value to the public must be made by the correspondent. If reporters accepted the plea that some material was not in the "national interest," journalists would have little news to report. Here again, the seasoned journalist makes a value judgment. The veteran knows when he is being used to run a "leak" or a "trial balloon." And the only criterion for judgment is news pertinence.

In the State Department, in particular, the elite correspondents tend to have greater access than others. These are the nationally syndicated political columnists and the writers for major metropolitan dailies or national news magazines. This favored treatment, however, can be a two-edged sword. It was certainly difficult for a reporter of the stature of Walter Lippmann to resist the pressure to offer advice in the making of policy. This is a pitfall which most—but unfortunately not all—columnists seek to avoid.

The Department of State, in essence, is an enormous, sprawling, cumbersome, unwieldy apparatus which manages to function despite the ebb and flow of many conflicting currents and areas of responsibility. But the responsibility of the journalist is not to the government; it is to his calling and to the public. The roadblocks in the bureaucracy can be surmounted by a responsible and persistent press.

The Treasury Department

The Department of the Treasury is another large institution, the Secretary of which is a key member of the President's Cabinet. The degree of press coverage accorded to Treasury is not constant and is dependent on a number of variables. News does not flow as easily as from the White House and the State Department. In addition, the media long ago discovered that the public is not interested in the complexities of the budget and the economy and that most readers and viewers, without a background in economics, simply do not understand matters relating to the Federal Reserve System, balance of payments and similar recondite topics. But the Secretary of the Treasury does become a subject for media coverage when an economic crisis which has dramatic impact on the wage-earner occurs: inflation, unemployment, a falling stock market, a weakness of the dollar. Yet, even when the Secretary addresses these problems, he is rarely covered by the electronic media, and the newspapers still tend to emphasize the activities of other, more provocative branches.

The Treasury Department functions primarily to formulate and recommend financial, tax and fiscal policies; it is the official financial agent for the government, operating in the area of law enforcement and responsible for the manufacturing of money. Created by the Congress in 1789, the Department over two centuries has grown into one of the largest institutions in the federal government. Subsumed under the Department of the Treasury are the Office of the Controller of the Currency; the United States Customs Service (which in the past has banned certain books from being shipped into this country); the Bureau of Engraving and Printing; Fiscal Services, the Internal Revenue Service (recently under fire from the press for allegedly violating privacy by politically motivated investigations of individual income tax returns); the Bureau of the Mint; the United States Savings Bond Division; the United States Secret Service; Bureau of Alcohol, Tobacco and Firearms; and the Federal Law Enforcement Training Center.

Information to the media about the Department of the Treasury is distributed by the Assistant Secretary for Public Affairs and the Deputy Assistant. This office issues news releases and texts of speeches by Treasury officials. Examples of releases from the press office are two speeches made by the Secretary before the New York Board of Trade and the Southern Methodist University School of Business Administration. Among the informational brochures prepared by the Treasury are a pamphlet entitled "Facts about United States"; a pamphlet simply called "The Treasury," detailing salient facts about the various sub-departments and activities of the Department; and an educational booklet, "The Engine that Built America—a Treasury Guide for Young Citizens." Each of these publications is essentially promotional, although each is also informational. At the time of the celebration of the Nation's Bicentennial, the Department of the Treasury produced a complete booklet, "The Treasury Story," covering various activities of the Department, intended primarily for students and tourists who visited Washington branches and agencies.

Each of the various sub-departments of the Treasury Department also makes information available relating to its specific function. In such agencies as the Bureau of Engraving and Printing, the public may take self-guided tours through the visitor's galleries. Engraved portraits of the Presidents and engraved and lithographed historical prints may be obtained by mail order. Various publications, intended for the public, but occasionally of some value to the press as syndicated feature material, are available from the sub-departments. The United States Customs Service issues publications on importing and travel and has a speakers' bureau to serve community groups. The Director of the Internal Revenue Service prepares an annual report. The Bureau of the Mint also issues an annual report from the Director and maintains public exhibits.

The Public Affairs officer of the Department of the Treasury responded to a questionnaire on its duties as follows:

Q) What is the particular function of your office?

A) *To keep key Treasury executives informed on a timely basis of pertinent news in all media and to keep the public informed by all means available–news media, response to letters and such of Treasury Department developments.*

Q) Approximately how many press correspondents cover your institution?

    a) How many wire service correspondents?   *5 or 6*

    b) How many representatives of large, national dailies?
        dozens

    c) How many from local papers?   *all*

    d) How many from radio and TV?   *all networks; many individual stations and syndicates*

    e) How many from magazines?   *all business and economic magazines and all others from time to time*

Q) Approximately how many press releases do you distribute weekly?

A) *55 a month average, many of them highly technical*

Q) Is there usually a press officer present when your executives are interviewed by the press?

A) *Sometimes yes, sometimes no. With the Secretary of the Treasury, almost always yes. With others, it depends on different circumstances, including the wishes of the executive and the sensitivity of the subject, or as the case may be, the relationship between the reporter and the executive. No set rule. Very flexible—case by case.*

Q) Do you feel that the media give accurate and knowlegeable information about your institution?

A) *More often yes than no.*

Q) Is there any way in which you feel that the press can improve its coverage of your institution? In what way?

A) *There's always room for improvement both in the press' quest for information and the govenment's obligation and duty to provide it.*

Q) What, in your opinion, is the best way of getting information to the press: press release, interview, press conference?

A) *All three, including public speeches, Sunday TV network talk shows and Q and A sessions after or before public speeches, plus OP-Ed articles and response to requested signed articles from publications.*

An example of the kind of news made by the Treasury Department—although apparently published in a limited number of newspapers and not used on radio or television news programs—is a front-page *New York Times* account from Washington on the acrimonious dispute between the United States and Japan over steel imports at a time when steel company stocks in this country had plummeted. The story, summarized in a key first paragraph, reads: "The Treasury, taking its final action in a case that had focused attention on the increasingly bitter trade dispute between America and Japan, today cut in half the punitive duties it had recommended against five Japanese steel producers." Significantly, this Treasury story came out of the *Times'* Washington bureau and was written by its own correspondent. It is doubtful whether many papers around the country gave it similar exposure, if any, as a result of wire service accounts. Treasury Department news, in short, tends to be basically limited by its very subject matter to those papers that carry business and financial information, although an occasional story has sufficient general interest to run on the front page and, more rarely, on the air.

The Department of Justice

The Justice Department is, in effect, the legal representative of the United States, serving, at least in theory, as general counsel for the public. It is another extremely large government institution, with literally several thousand lawyers, agents and investigators. Its functions are broad and variable and are concerned with criminal justice, law enforcement and protection of the citizen by the drug, naturalization and immigration statutes. Cases in which the federal government is involved and which reach the Supreme Court are argued by the Department of Justice, and, in matters of law, it is an advisory agency to the President of the United States. Established in 1870, it functions under the direction of the Attorney General.

Although other branches list public information officials, the Justice Department has no such designation in the official *Government Manual* and lists a Director of Community Relations Service instead. In the Department's table of organization, however, a Public Information Office reports to the Attorney General. Dealing with media correspondents and issuing press releases on a regular basis, the Public Information Office's stated function is to inform the media and the public about the agency's programs and to be available to answer questions from the media and the public. Comprised of 19 personnel, of which 7 members have liaison with the media and which include a Citizen's Mail Unit, the office arranges news conferences, prepares a newsletter for the Law Enforcement Assistance Administration and co-ordinates Freedom of Information activities of the agency. In 1976, the Public Information Office prepared a total of 900 news releases and news features. It also "monitored" the publication of a bicenten-nial study of the history of crime and criminal justice, *200 Years of American Criminal Justice*.

The Department services include a press room, where four press services maintain reporters on a regular basis: the Associated Press, United Press International, Reuters (the British press association) and the newspaper the *Washington Star*. This representation by the wire services illustrates their importance to newspapers around the country. Although hundreds of correspondents are accredited, only about 40 cover on a fairly regular but not constant basis. The various bureaus also have their own press officials. At this writing, the Justice Depart-ment is preparing a brochure describing its functions and operations.

The Department has numerous divisions, including the Antitrust Division, Civil Division, Civil Rights Division, Criminal Division, Land and Natural Resources Division and Tax Division. The largest bureau is, of course, the Federal Bureau of Investigation, which has its own information apparatus. The Justice Department also includes the Bureau of Prisons, The United States Marshals' Service, the Immigra-tion and Naturalization Service, the Drug Enforcement Administra-tion, the Law Enforcement Assistance Administration and the Board of Immigration Appeals and Parole Commission. Most of these have a public affairs or information officer.

Typical press releases deal variously with such subjects as possi-ble antitrust enforcement against United States oil companies if these companies meet with international tanker owners, because scrapping of old tankers causes pollution; a series of grants from the Depart-ment's Law Enforcement Assistance Administration to establish neigh-borhood Justice Centers (in this release, the Attorney General is quoted as saying that the grants are "one of our efforts to make justice faster, fairer and more accessible to the people"); the results of a study showing that women perform as well as men in police patrol work; a Drug Enforcement Division feature story on the activities of an agent; a news feature on a drug used in veterinary medicine and also used by drug abusers; a release on the negotiations to bring Tong Sun Park from Korea to the United States to be interrogated on the subject of bribery of United States officials; a release charging an industry executive with making false statements before the Securities and Exchange Commission; a release noting the names of persons and firms registered with the Department of Justice under the provisions of the Foreign Agents Registration Act; and a press handout charging a company with conspiracy to fix interstate motor carrier rates.

A survey of several correspondents on which of these press releases was most likely to be used by the news media brought forth on the whole the consensus that the most newsworthy were those dealing with the Korean bribery scandal and with women compared to men in police patrol work. Which news features are or are not printed depend on the traditional journalistic criterion of "what else happened that day."

Information other than news releases is obtainable through the Reading Rooms, which have been established in the various divisions of the Department of Justice. Films on citizenship education are offered by the Immigration and Naturalization Service. The Federal Bureau of Investigation publishes a pamphlet, "The Story of the Federal Bureau of Investigation." Some divisions produce annual reports, but the most official is *The Annual Report of the Attorney General of the United States,* a 240-page paper-bound volume, which is issued by the Attorney General and addressed to the Senate and House of Representatives of the United States. Just how much of this material is read by each congressman remains a moot question. The report is presented as a summary of the highlights and accomplishments of the Department and of the activities of the divisions. Presumably, a patient, dogged and enterprising correspondent can find kernels of news or suggestions for further investigation in the *Annual Report.* For example, the Office of Legal Counsel heads the Department of Justice's

Freedom of Information Committee, which provides advice to other agencies on questions pertaining to the Freedom of Information Act. The information system's staff formulates policies on the use of automatic data processing. The Information and Privacy Section, established in 1975, defends suits brought under the Freedom of Information Act—always a good source of news to the media. The Office of Congressional Liaison functions to promote more effective communication with the Congress.

Following is a questionaire sent to the public information officer, with replies to the questions returned by the Deputy Director.

Q) What is the particular function of your office?

A) *Providing information to the public, mostly through the news media, swiftly and accurately.*

Q) How is your office structured? How many people are assigned to the information function?

A) *Seven professionals are in the office. The office is divided into "beats," with the director having overall supervision.*

Q) Approximately how many press correspondents cover your institution?

    a) How many wire service correspondents?   *3*

    b) How many representatives of large, national dailies?   *12–15*

    c) How many from local papers?   *the local papers really are national*

    d) How many from radio and TV?   *the networks plus PBS*

    e) How many from magazines?   *primarily 3*

Q) Approximately how many press releases do you distribute weekly?

A) *10*

Q) Is there usually a press information officer present when your executives are interviewed by the press?

A) *Usually. However, it depends on the wish of the interviewee. The public information office does not insist on being present.*

Q) Do you feel that the media give accurate and knowledgeable information about your institution?

A) *For the most part, yes. However, because of the nature of the work of the Department, erroneous information is sometimes leaked about sensitive investigations by people with only a piece of the picture. The public information office often is in a position of being able to straighten out the erroneous information because it would be inappropriate to discuss open investigations.*

Q) Is there any way in which you feel that the press can improve its coverage of your institution? In what way?

A) *The reporters covering the Justice Department for the most part are very competent.*

Q) What, in your opinion, is the best way of getting information to the press: press release, interview, press conference?

A) *All three methods are necessary.*

The Department of Defense

From the standpoint of obtaining information, the Defense Department—probably because of its size and ramifications—exemplifies many of the inevitable characteristics of the federal bureaucracy. A letter and questionnaire brought no response, except a copy of the DOD *Annual Report,* a 300-page document dealing with the presentation of defense budget data for the Congress and with interesting, but highly technical, information. A further direct inquiry brought the response that the Department had a policy of not replying to questionnaires. Facts and figures on public information personnel were difficult to come by because of apparent diffusion of officials among various divisions, departments and sub-departments. But a spokesman for the DOD gave the following summary of public information personnel:

The Defense Department assigns a total of 22 personnel to liaison with the print media. Of these, 11 are military professionals and two are on the professional support staff, six are professional civilians and three are in civilian support. Electronic media are serviced by a staff of ten—four military professionals, four civilian professionals and two in the clerical support staff. Heading the Public Affairs Office is an Assistant Secretary for Public Affairs, along with assistants. One of these executives meets with the newsmen twice weekly for briefings. Public Affairs services the media with several thousand releases each year, and often as many as hundreds each week. The DOD makes 40 desks available for the media correspondents. These include United States and foreign wire services, newspapers, electronic media and service and technical journals.

The Army, Navy and Air Corps each has its own information service. The Air Corps, as an example, has a staff of 19 military professionals and seven in clerical support positions.

Subsumed under the Department of Defense are four departments, each of which has a fully staffed information section: Department of the Air Force, Department of the Army, Department of the Navy and Department of Defense Agencies and Joint Service Schools. The Defense Department is responsible for the security of the United States through the Army, Navy, Marine Corps and Air Force. Since the President is also Commander in Chief, the Secretary of Defense exercises his authority under the President. Headquartered in the Pentagon, the Department, in addition to the Secretary at the head, includes the Organization of the Joint Chiefs of Staff who are the military advisers to the Secretary and to the President. Rarely, differences between the Secretary of Defense and the military establishment find their way into the media, owing to well-placed "leaks" or the digging of an enterprising reporter. For example, Robert MacNamara, when Secretary, held strong convictions on civilian control and was alleged to have created considerable resentment in the Pentagon. Budget problems between the Pentagon and the White House also occasionally reach the media. Generally, however, the Department of Defense is not a highly visible one in the media except in times of national crisis or on stories comparing military "hardware" with that of the Soviet Union.

One of the functional areas of the Defense Department is that of Public Affairs. This unit is concerned with public information, with community activities and with what the *United States Government Manual* terms "programs in compliance with the Freedom of Information Act." The Public Affairs division maintains liaison with the mass media. All material, including testimony before congressional committees, undergoes security review as the result of an executive order in 1972. The division also reviews official speeches before release, as well as material for release from other executive agencies, to determine whether there is any conflict with department policy. The Defense Department is responsible for guidance on classified information and matters relating to implementation of the Privacy Act. Sources of information include a Reading Room under the Office of the Deputy Assistant Secretary of Defense. In addition, motion pictures are available for non-profit distribution. The Office of Community Relations arranges for speakers on a variety of subjects.

A widely publicized case in the media was that of a documentary on CBS in 1970 entitled *The Selling of the Pentagon*. The program, prepared by CBS News, was widely praised by the press as a searching study of Pentagon public relations—the use of speakers, films, and exhibits designed to give the public a positive "image" of the work of the Defense Department. The Pentagon, however, as well as congressmen on the Armed Services Committee, felt that *The Selling of the Pentagon* presented a most unflattering depiction of the Defense establishment. An investigation was started and Representative Harley O. Staggers (D. W. Va.) and the committee insisted that CBS make outtakes available. Dr. Frank Stanton, then President of CBS, was adamant in his refusal despite a subpoena. Staggers attempted to have Dr. Stanton cited for contempt, but failed to muster sufficient vote support. The press was consistently supportive of CBS in this vendetta, and the failure to achieve a contempt citation was viewed as a decided victory for freedom of the media under the First Amendment. Of additional significance from a freedom of communication standpoint is that the Pentagon was given time on CBS to offer a rebuttal, and that CBS, despite bitter criticism, rebroadcast the program.

From a reporter's vantage point, the Defense Department presents unique problems and challenges to his ingenuity and, indeed, to his value judgments. Many correspondents have complained about closed-door policies, except at those times when the Pentagon would stand to benefit from stories about the country's defense needs. The CBS documentary *The Selling of the Pentagon* was a searing indictment of the Pentagon's public relations motivation. Other criticisms leveled at the information office have been that news is often withheld, that efforts are made to control news flow, that interviews are avoided whenever possible and that the information officers rely too strongly on such replies as "negative" or "no comment." With these restrictions and with the limitations of wire service copy, it is not difficult to understand the problem in obtaining significant news from this branch of government.

There are, of course, comprehensible problems involving national security, and these must be recognized and appreciated by the media. Furthermore, the Pentagon is often concerned about the effect of news on its relations with the State Department, the Congress and the White House. Thus, efforts to manage news are more likely to occur in the DOD than in other federal institutions. But what correspondents reject are comments such as those from one public affairs official who implied baldly that the Department was not under any categorical obligation always to tell the truth or those of another official who lied about this country's involvement in Southeast Asia. The media also object to the use of "national security" as a device for controlling the news when no genuine problems of security are involved. The Pentagon, reporters claim, should not be a sacrosanct institution, but the press must also recognize its need to keep certain information confidential. There has been, however, too much classification, too much secrecy and too much of an effort to control and direct the free flow of information.

The simple way for the media to process Pentagon news would be to accept press releases and formal briefings uncritically. But this would make the media little more than a conduit for what the Department wanted the public to receive and would be contrary to the traditional function of the media in a free society. Nor should reporters acquiesce to holding back stories until such time as the DOD is ready for general release. It is reprehensible for the Department to ask such favors of the press, and it would be unprofessional for the press to go along.

The media clearly constitute a headache to the Department of Defense on many occasions. The adversarial relationship is that of an enterprising reporter against a tightly knit bureaucracy. Some media observers insist this relationship is healthy and part of the democratic process. One way of circumventing the inevitable diffidence of Pentagon officials is by the "leak" or "backgrounder." But here the reporter is well advised to check other sources discreetly before processing the story. Furthermore, uncritical acceptance of "leaks" involves the correspondent with the source in a kind of conspiracy which is not salutary. Most Pentagon news comes from releases, briefings and occasional conferences. But these constitute no more than the tip of the iceberg to the diligent journalist. Although the information officials can set up roadblocks, they can also be helpful, and effective two-way communication is utterly necessary if the media are to perform their function adequately. The position of the press is clear: the public is entitled to information about all of its government agencies and Defense is no exception. With the exercise of the rule of reason and of sound value judgments, the correspondents must make an intelligent distinction between the security needs of the nation and the legitimate right to function as a surrogate of the people.

The Department of Health, Education and Welfare

One of the largest of government departments, Health, Education and Welfare (HEW), is also one of the more visible in the media. So gigantic is this organization that President Carter proposed, against the alleged objection of the Secretary, the establishment of a separate department of Education, with its own Secretary and full Cabinet status. The media coverage of this department varies, but it manages to achieve publicity in the press and on the air with some degree of constancy and consistency, owing to the nature of its responsibilities. The public has a proprietary interest in the activities of HEW, since many of these activities affect their personal lives and that of their families: social security, education, health care, abortion, smoking and other highly relevant matters of concern to the citizen.

HEW exemplifies bureaucracy in its most massive form, and how well an institution of this kind functions depends to a great degree on the attitude and, indeed, the symbolic significance of the Secretary. Under the Secretary of HEW are Assistant Secretaries in the Office of Human Development and in the Education Division, as well as a Commissioner, who heads the United States Office of Education. There are, in addition, such vital agencies as the Public Health Service, which includes the Alcohol, Drug Abuse and Mental Health Administration; the famous Center for Disease Control, in Atlanta, Georgia; the Food and Drug Administration; the Health Resources Administration; the Health Services Administration; and the National Institute of Health. Among the multiplicity of other agencies is the Social Security Administration, a sprawling bureaucracy in itself.

The *United States Government Manual* aptly describes HEW as a department that "touches the lives of more Americans than any other federal agency." Sources of information on the work of the department are numerous, and most of the related agencies have their own public information personnel. The Department maintains a Reading Room and a Visitors' Information Center, at which numerous publications are available, including "HEW—People Serving People" and "A Common Thread of Service," a brief history of HEW. There are, in addition, pamphlets on "Prenatal Care," "Infant Care" and "No Smoking," among many others available to the public. Various agencies, such as the National Institute of Health, also publish brochures and reports which are available from the Office of Communications, division of Public Information. Speakers, films and exhibits are available to organizations, schools and community groups.

The information service of the Department of Health, Education and Welfare (the "parent" organization, in a sense) is headed by an Assistant Secretary for Public Affairs, along with a Deputy Assistant. The office issues the following table of organization.

The function of the Office of Public Affairs is "to serve as the Secretary's principal public affairs policy adviser; to provide centralized professional leadership and continuous monitoring and evaluation of Department-wide policies, procedures and operating practices regarding public affairs activities; and to administer the Freedom of In-

OFFICE OF THE SECRETARY

OFFICE OF ASSISTANT SECRETARY FOR PUBLIC AFFAIRS

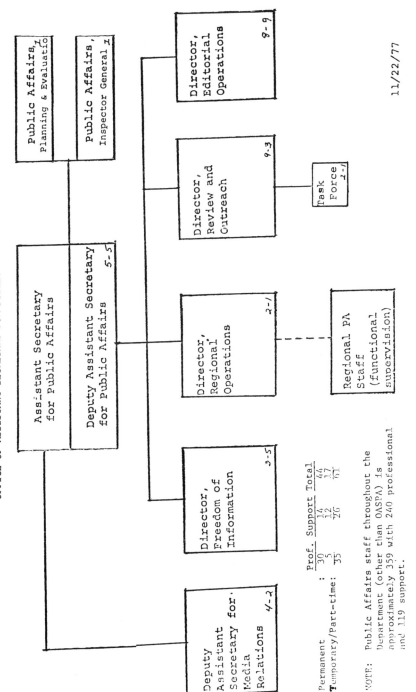

Public Affairs,
Planning & Evaluation

Public Affairs,
Inspector General

Assistant Secretary
for Public Affairs

Deputy Assistant Secretary
for Public Affairs   5-5

Deputy
Assistant
Secretary for
Media
Relations   4-2

Director,
Freedom of
Information   3-5

Director,
Regional
Operations   2-1

Regional PA
Staff
(functional
supervision)

Director,
Review and
Outreach   3-3

Task
Force   2-1

Director,
Editorial
Operations   3-3

	Prof.	Support	Total
Permanent	30	14	44
Temporary/Part-time:	5	12	17
	35	26	61

NOTE: Public Affairs staff throughout the Department (other than OASPA) is approximately 359 with 240 professional and 119 support.

11/22/77

formation Act.'' Under the Assistant Secretary for Public Affairs is the Media Relations Devision and the Editorial Operations Division. Media relations are the responsibility of the Deputy Assistant Secretary for Media Relations. This unit functions to convey public information to the print and electronic media; it prepares news releases and clears releases from HEW components. It ''coordinates and arranges news conferences, briefings, interviews and appearances by the Secretary and other key HEW officials with the press and broadcast media.''

The Office of Public Affairs, in addition to the administration of the Freedom of Information Act, develops policy guidelines for such related legislation as the Privacy Act and the Government in the Sunshine Act. The Editorial Operations Division has among its responsibilities that of preparing, reviewing and editing written materials on HEW policy and editing congressional testimony of departmental officials.

All in all, HEW administers more than 350 programs—an amazing number. Some of the informational activities of the organization have been detailed. Others are included in answers to a questionnaire which was responded to by the Assistant Secretary.

Q) What is the particular function of your office?

A) *Overall public affairs.*

Q) How is your office structured? How many people are assigned to the information function?

A) *This was answered in the table of organization and related information.*

Q) Approximately how many press correspondents cover your institution?

    a) How many wire service correspondents?   *2 AP; 1 UPI*

    b) How many representatives of large, national dailies?   *about 15–18*

    c) How many from local papers?   *5(different areas) from* Washington Post; *2 from* Washington Star

　　d) How many from radio and TV?　　　*all 3 TV networks; many radio*

　　e) How many magazines?　　　Time; Newsweek; U.S. News

Q) Approximately how many press releases do you distribute weekly?

A) *8–10*

Q) Is there usually a press information officer present when your executives are interviewed by the press?

A) *Highly variable.*

Q) Do you feel that the media give accurate and knowledgeable information about your institution?

A) *Some do*—N.Y. Times *excellent;* Washington Star, *Gannett Chain, some others good; wire services, especially AP, distorted and inaccurate.*

Q) Is there any way in which you feel that the press can improve its coverage of your institution? In what way?

A) *Do some work in the substantive issues; stop paying attention chiefly to style; make more serious attempt to be knowledgeable.*

Q) What, in your opinion, is the best way of getting information to the press: press release, interview, press conference?

A) *All are useful.*

Other Branches and Agencies

All of the Cabinet-level departments of the executive branch of the government have information units, but none of these create news as visibly as State, Treasury, Defense, Justice and Health, Education and Welfare. The Department of Agriculture has an Office of Communication, headed by a Director. It, too, has good Reading Rooms and produces publications for farmers, suburbanites and consumers. It has a Speakers' Bureau and makes available films on a variety of agricultural subjects.

The Department of Commerce has a Director of Communications. Subsumed under this Department are agencies like the Maritime Administration, the National Bureau of Standards, the National Oceanic and Atmospheric Administration, the National Technical Information Service, the Patent and Trademark Office, the Bureau of the Census and the Office of Telecommunications. Each has an information service. In addition to Reading Rooms, the Commerce Department issues a large number of publications dealing with business, environmental and technical matters. A *Business Service Checklist,* issued weekly, keep the list updated and may be a source of occasional news.

The Commerce Department issues an *Annual Report,* as well as a descriptive brochure, ''Serving the Nation,'' which details the manifold activities of the Department. Of these many functions, the Secretary of Commerce notes: ''The seeming illogic of Commerce's organizational maze begins to make sense, however, if we view the Department's role in the context of its relation to its overall mission: to facilitate commerce.''

A spokesman for the Commerce Department responded as follows to a questionnaire:

Q) What is the particular function of your office?

A) *These functions are divided into disseminating information to the public, primarily through the media, and providing policy guidance on public affairs matters to the Secretary of Commerce and other executive-level department officials and information staffs of major bureaus. Information is disseminated by press releases, news conferences, radio and television broadcasts, publications, speeches, films and exhibits.*

Q) How is your office structured? How many people are assigned to the information function?

A) *There are two main divisions: the Print Media Division and the Audio-Visual Division. Within the Print Media Division, there is a Departmental News Room, which writes, edits, processes and distributes all the Department's news releases and speeches by top of-*

ficials, arranges news conferences, and prepares bylined Secretarial articles upon request for magazines, newspapers and books. Another unit in the division is the Publications Review Office, which reviews, edits and clears for printing all publications produced by the Department.

The Audio-Visual Division has a Broadcast Media Section, which provides daily news stories and features for radio stations around the country. An audio-visual unit prepares, reviews and clears all departmental films and slide shows, tapes news conferences and other important conferences and prepares or approves other graphic materials.

A Special Projects Office prepares briefings for the Secretary, schedules and coordinates out-of-town public appearances, maintains liaison with the Secretary's representatives in the field, handles the preparation of Sunday news features and Opinion-Editorial Page articles, replies to correspondence of a public affairs nature and provides briefing materials for the White House.

Overall supervision of these units is provided by the Director of Communications and his deputy.

We also supervise the public affairs activities of 15 bureaus. My immediate staff includes 21 professionals engaged in information activities.

Q) Approximately how many press correspondents cover your institution?

    a) How many wire service correspondents?   *5*

    b) How many representatives of large, national dailies?   *75*

    c) How many from local papers?   *14*

    d) How many from radio and TV?   *5*

    e) How many from magazines?   *12*

Q) Approximately how many press releases do you distribute weekly?

A) *45–50*

Q) Is there usually a press information officer present when your executives are interviewed by the press?

A) *We usually have an information officer present for interviews with the Secretary, unless the correspondent objects to this arrangement. Depending on the subject matter—for instance, some sensitive foreign trade matter such as the Arab boycott—we might also have an information officer present. We don't follow any particular rule in this regard, though, but treat each interview according to what we think is required.*

Q) Do you feel that the media give accurate and knowledgeable information about your institution?

A) *On the whole, I would say yes. There have been some isolated incidents in which columnists—unwittingly or knowingly—have distorted the facts. But by and large, the reporting of the Department's activities has been fair and accurate.*

Q) Is there any way in which you feel that the press can improve its coverage of your institution? In what way?

A) *Perhaps the area in which the most improvement of coverage could be made is the reporting of economic stories. Some of the treatment is superficial and banal. Some of it shows a lack of understanding. However, we must share some of the responsibility for this. We are in the process of trying to improve our economic releases and reports by making the prose less arcane and more understandable to the average reader.*

Q) What, in your opinion, is the best way of getting information to the press: press release, interview, press conference?

A) *This depends on the subject matter. If the information is of sufficient importance, or if it is a difficult or controversial topic that raises a number of questions, we prefer holding a news conference or press briefing, although we usually have a press release and background material to pass out at news conferences. There are instances when a complex subject, such as scientific information, is best conveyed in a press release. Interviews permit a more wide-ranging expression of views and also are helpful when a reporter wants to flesh out his story with personal touches.*

The Department of Housing and Urban Development lists an Assistant Secretary for Public Affairs. The Department is responsible for the administration of the Government National Mortgage Association and serves to advise the President on matters relating to federal policy on housing and community development. It maintains a Program Information Center, which provides data concerning available publications and departmental functions and also makes films and speakers available through the office of Public Affairs.

The Department of the Interior has an Assistant to the Secretary and Director, Office of Public Affairs, to handle information matters. Parks, Land and Water Resources, Territorial Affairs, the United States Fish and Wildlife Service, the National Park Service, the Bureau of Mines, the Geological Survey and the Bureau of Indian Affairs are among the agencies which are part of the Interior Department. Of these, Indian Affairs has been in the news over the past few years, and relative periods of quiet are punctuated on occasion by problems arising in the administration of this bureau. The Interior Department maintains a Visitor Information Center, publishes several *Conservation Yearbooks* ("America 200—The Legacy of Our Land," "Our Natural Resources," "Man . . . An Endangered Species," and so on). There is also a museum containing appropriate informational and educational exhibits.

The Department of Labor is a basic source of news to the media on matters relating to statistics on employment, international labor meetings, work programs and so forth. Information services are the responsibility of a Director of the Office of Information, Publications and Reports. The Labor Department advises the President on developing and executing policies relating to laws covering wage earners, working conditions and employment opportunities. Various divisions are concerned with the American work force and with working conditions: among these are the Office of Policy, Evaluation and Research, the National On-the-Job Training Program, programs for older workers, migrant workers, Apprenticeship and training, the Labor-Management Services Administration, the Employment Standards Administration, the Wage and Hour Administration and the Women's Bureau. Sources of information include Reading Rooms, Public Document Rooms, speakers and films and a wide variety of booklets and brochures. The Bureau of Labor Statistics has its own Information Office and offers various publications, some at a moderate cost, some at none. All the Labor Department agencies are used for research and documentation of articles and features by media correspondents, and statistics released by the Department are usually used in the press and occasionally on the air.

The Labor Department publishes a pamphlet called "Information Please"—a guide to acquiring information—in which the public is advised that the Department "publishes a wide variety of press releases, reports, pamphlets and brochures." Records and documents, the announcement states, are available to reporters and other interested parties. But there is also the *caveat* that certain types of information cannot be released, particularly those exempted from disclosure by federal law and those not to be released by executive order, such as matters relating to defense and foreign policy. In addition, the Privacy Act prohibits the release of information concerning internal personnel rules and both medical and investigatory files, as well as confidential trade secrets. The Labor Department also puts out its own *Annual Report,* in which there is a summary of information activities. Following is a table of organization of the Office of Information, Publications and Reports, which has a total of 88 employees.

The Department has described its Public Information Program.

OVERVIEW OF THE PUBLIC INFORMATION PROGRAM

The Office of Information, Publications and Reports (OIPR) is responsible for administering the public information activities of the Department of Labor (DOL) and for establishing and maintaining, on behalf of the Secretary, an internal employee information system utilizing print, audio-visual and electronic media. This office formulates information policies, standards and guidelines for all DOL agencies with prime responsibility for developing and administering public information and publications programs to support their programs. In addition, it also reviews for quality of production audio-visual and graphics materials for internal communications with employees. The office serves as the central point in the Department for media and public inquiry concerning DOL policies, programs and activities.

ATTACHMENT B

OFFICE OF INFORMATION, PUBLICATIONS AND REPORTS

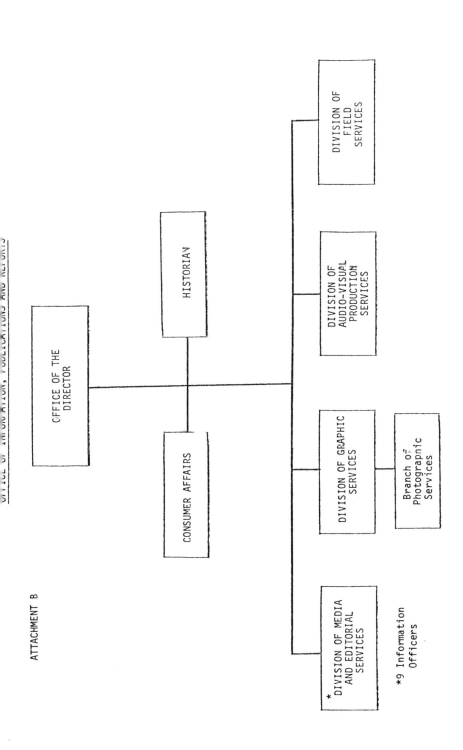

OFFICE OF THE DIRECTOR

HISTORIAN

CONSUMER AFFAIRS

* DIVISION OF MEDIA AND EDITORIAL SERVICES

*9 Information Officers

DIVISION OF GRAPHIC SERVICES

Branch of Photographic Services

DIVISION OF AUDIO-VISUAL PRODUCTION SERVICES

DIVISION OF FIELD SERVICES

A questionnaire that was submitted brought the following response from a Department representative.

Q) What is the particular function of your office?

A) *(See above.)*

Q) How is your office structured? How many people are assigned to the information function?

A) *(See chart above.)*

Q) Approximately how many press correspondents cover your institution?

        a) How many wire service correspondents?   *3*

        b) How many representatives of large, national dailies?   *16*

        c) How many from local papers?   *2*

        d) How many from radio and TV?   *31*

        e) How many from magazines?   *7* (Estimates of those covering on regular basis in Washington, D.C.)

Q) Approximately how many press releases do you distribute weekly?

A) *22*

Q) Is there usually a press information officer present when your executives are interviewed by the press?

A) *Yes, either the Director of OIPR or the Chief of the Division of Media and Editorial Services.*

Q) Do you feel that the media give accurate and knowledgeable information about your institution?

A) *Yes, in general.*

Q) Is there any way in which you feel that the press can improve its coverage of your institution? In what way?

A) *No, in most respects.*

Q) What, in your opinion, is the best way of getting information to the press: press release, interview, press conference?

A) *There are many ways of getting information to the media. Each an-swers specific needs. A release puts into the hands of many reporters or editors a written version of a piece of news in the form the origi-nator wishes. An interview provides a one-on-one opportunity for exchange of information and/or opinions. A news conference allows a number of media representatives to question a news source, and the news source may use the opportunity to present a piece of news to several media representatives at once. We use all three of these devices, as well as others, such as telephone calls and letters, to tell the American public through the media what the Labor Department is doing.*

The Department of Transportation is covered in the press usually when a vital problem concerning railroads or other forms of public carriers arises. Otherwise, it is not usually a productive source of news. But various agencies which are attached to the Department oc-casionally release information of interest to the media and the public. These are, variously, the United States Coast Guard, the Federal Avia-tion Administration (a source of news when a crisis arises concerning aviation safety), the Federal Highway Administration (recently in the news because of the debate over allocation of funds for highways or railroads), the Federal Railroad Administration, the National Highway Traffic Safety Administration, the Urban Mass-Transportation Ad-ministration (in the press of late because of the need for improved in-tercity transportation facilities) and the St. Lawrence Seaway Develop-ment Corporation, among others.

The Department of Transportation has a Director of Public Af-fairs, and of the various agencies noted, each has its own information officers. This branch of the government is the most recently es-tablished. It was activated in 1966 "to assure the coordinated, effec-tive administration of the transportation programs of the federal gov-ernment" and became operative in 1977. The Secretary of Transportation is the principal adviser to the President on matters relat-ing to federal transportation programs. Sources of information are varied. There is a consumer program under the direction of the Assis-tant Secretary for Environment, Safety and Consumer Affairs. This of-fice also has information on activities relating to the environment.

Reading Rooms are available to the public. Speakers will attend to the requests of civic and community groups. A large number of films are also available on subjects relating to transportation. The list of Department publications is fairly large and varied—the publications are available either from the issuing agencies or from the Government Printing Office.

The United States Department of Agriculture achieved press prominence when the country's farmers took the unusual move of going on strike in 1978 to protest the farm policies of the Carter Administration. It is not a highly publicized department, but it performs a function that is far more significant than its publicity value to the media. The stated function of the Agriculture Department is "to improve and maintain farm income and to develop and expand markets abroad for agricultural products." Among its many divisions are those of Rural Development, Rural Electrification Administration, Marketing and Consumer Services, Animal and Plant Health Inspection Service, Food and Consumer Services, Commodity Credit Corporation and Conservation, Research and Education and Forest Service, among others.

Under sources of information, the Department offers various consumer activities, including educational, organizational and financial assistance in rural housing and farm programs and food stamps and school lunch programs. As in other departments, there are Reading Rooms in each departmental division. Speakers and films on agricultural subjects are available and a variety of pamphlets on subjects of interest to farmers and other consumers are issued from the Office of Communication.

According to the Public Information Office, the public relations function has recently undergone reorganization, combining the Office of Communication with other agencies of the Department into a new Office of Governmental and Public Affairs. The following chart indicates the table of organization of the new unit.

The new Office of Governmental and Public Affairs performs a variety of liaison and information functions, some of which are:

1. Liaison with the Congress and the White House on legislative matters of concern to the Department.

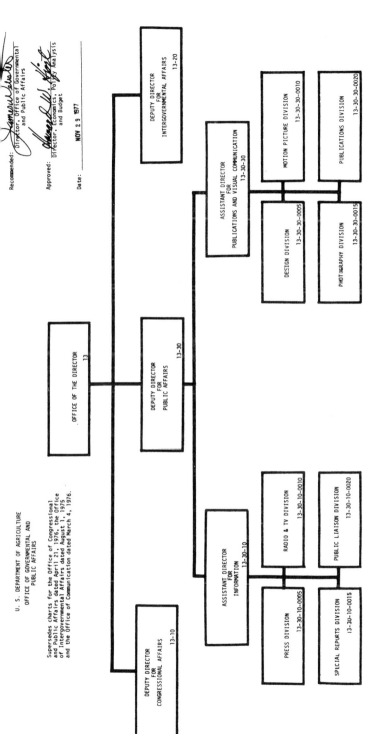

U. S. DEPARTMENT OF AGRICULTURE
OFFICE OF GOVERNMENTAL AND
PUBLIC AFFAIRS

Supersedes charts for the Office of Congressional
and Public Affairs dated April 21, 1976, the Office
of Intergovernmental Affairs dated August 1, 1975
and the Office of Communication dated March 4, 1976.

Recommended:

Director, Office of Governmental
and Public Affairs

Approved:

Director, Economics, Policy Analysis
and Budget

Date: NOV 2 9 1977

OFFICE OF THE DIRECTOR
13

DEPUTY DIRECTOR
FOR
CONGRESSIONAL AFFAIRS
13-10

DEPUTY DIRECTOR
FOR
PUBLIC AFFAIRS
13-30

DEPUTY DIRECTOR
FOR
INTERGOVERNMENTAL AFFAIRS
13-20

ASSISTANT DIRECTOR
FOR
INFORMATION
13-30-10

PRESS DIVISION
13-30-10-0005

RADIO & TV DIVISION
13-30-10-0010

SPECIAL REPORTS DIVISION
13-30-10-0015

PUBLIC LIAISON DIVISION
13-30-10-0020

ASSISTANT DIRECTOR
FOR
PUBLICATIONS AND VISUAL COMMUNICATION
13-30-30

DESIGN DIVISION
13-30-30-0005

MOTION PICTURE DIVISION
13-30-30-0010

PHOTOGRAPHY DIVISION
13-30-30-0015

PUBLICATIONS DIVISION
13-30-30-0020

The mission of the Office of Governmental and Public
Affairs is to coordinate programs involving
governmental and public affairs and emergency
preparedness; maintain liaison with Congress and the
White House on legislative matters and to assist the
Secretary of Agriculture in the development and
execution of Department information policy and programs

2. Counseling of officers on matters relating to public affairs.
3. Directing the activities of the public affairs office, including press relations of the Secretary of Agriculture.
4. Maintaining an emergency center for civil defense or national disaster emergencies and directing the Department's defense program.
5. Serving as the Department contact with the Advisory Commission on Intergovernmental Relations.
6. Representing the Department on information matters relating to the Government Printing Office and with other state agencies.
7. Advising the various officials on the application of information policies to comply with the Freedom of Information Act.
8. Directing and coordinating the formulation and development of policies for the information activities of the Department and its agencies.
9. Maintaining policy clearance and control of all Department publication activities.
10. Assisting the Secretary and other officers in the preparation of speeches to be delivered to the Congress.

The Public Affairs Office, in addition to the Director, has Deputy Directors for Congressional Affairs, Intergovernmental Affairs, Public Affairs, an Assistant Director for Information, a Press Division, a Radio and Television Division, a Special Reports Division, a Public Liaison, an Assistant Director for Public Publications and Visual Communication, a Design Division, a Motion Picture Division, a Photography Division and a Publications Division. Few major corporate industries can boast of an informational structure as large and exhaustive. When multiplied by similar and larger units in most of the other Departments and agencies, it is clear that the government information establishment is, indeed, large, sprawling, bureaucratic and duplicatory. Basic liaison with the press is undertaken by the Press Division, which plans and executes the press information activities of the Department and coordinates relations with newspapers, magazines and trade papers. The Radio and Television Division plans and executes all activities for the broadcast media, including time for appearances by department officials.

A questionnaire on the public information activities of the Department of Agriculture brought the following responses.

Q) What is the particular function of your office?

A) *(See above.)*

Q) How is your office structured? How many people are assigned to the information function?

A) *See above chart. Staff includes about 165 positions—approximately 60 are professional positions.*

Q) Approximately how many press correspondents cover your institution?

    a) How many wire service correspondents?   *4*

    b) How many representatives of large, national dailies?   *78*

    c) How many from local papers?   *6 (more, depending upon conditions)*

    d) How many from radio and TV?   *about 12, including all networks*

    e) How many from magazines?   *about 12 (more, depending upon conditions)*

Q) Approximately how many press releases do you distribute weekly?

A) *75 on the average.*

Q) Is there usually a press information officer present when your executives are interviewed by the press?

A) *No.*

Q) Do you feel that the media give accurate and knowledgeable information about your institution?

A) *Yes.*

Q) Is there any way in which you feel that the press can improve its coverage of your institution? In what way?

A) *Yes, in general; no, when you consider that the "regulars" who cover this Department know pretty well what they are doing. The "yes" applies mostly to individuals who come to the Department only occasionally and don't understand government or agriculture. In other words, agriculture is a science which many journalists simply do not understand.*

Q) What, in your opinion, is the best way of getting information to the press: press release, interview, press conference?

A) *Press releases allow quick access to many correspondents from which they can do their own followups; interviews allow a 1–1 relationship so that a full story can be told more easily and more accurately (if the reporter is willing to learn something); press conferences allow quick announcements to be made on important subjects. So . . . there is no best way . . . we have to use all of them.*

Other Agencies

Beyond the Cabinet-level secretaries and the major branches, departments and their bureaus, there is a multiplicity of federal agencies and quasi-agencies, ranging from regulatory bodies, such as the Federal Communications Commission and the Federal Trade Commission to the National Foundation on the Arts and the Humanities. Altogether, the government lists 59 such agencies from *ACTION* to the Veterans Administration. Quasi-official agencies include the National Academy of Sciences, the Smithsonian Institution and the American National Red Cross. Virtually all of these have a public information official listed under various titles: Public Affairs, Public Communications, Director of Information, Director of Press and Publications and so forth. Most of these deal with the media either directly or through a deputy and most are also responsible for informational and promotional materials.

The National Science Foundation is an example of one of the 59 operating agencies. It functions to "increase the Nation's base of scientific knowledge and strengthen its ability to conduct scientific research" and it supports research in the various scientific disciplines. This was a highly visible agency after the launching of Sputnik by the Soviet Union galvanized this country into a recognition of the need for stimulating additional effort in science education. The Foundation has a Director of Public Programs, a Community Affairs Branch, a Public

Information Branch. The National Science Foundation issues selective grants upon application and has a list of brochures available from the Publications Unit. It publishes a monthly *NSF Bulletin,* which summarizes activities and is of interest to the science reporters, and several other publications descriptive of its programs. Special requests for information under the Freedom of Information Act and the Privacy Act are accepted, respectively, by the Public Information Branch and by the NSF Privacy Act Regulations.

Following is the response to a questionnaire reguarding liaison with the mass media.

Q) What is the particulai function of your office?

A) *To provide information to the public on the programs and activities of the National Science Foundation.*

Q) How is your office structured? How many people are assigned to the information function?

A) *Head, Publication Branch; Deputy Head, PIB; three science writers; one press-aid steno; one Freedom of Information; two clerical.*

Q) Approximately how many press correspondents cover your institution?

A) *30 actively in Washington; about 650 use our news releases.*

    a) How many representatives of large, national dailies?   *15 local; about 400 nationally*

    b) How many from local papers?   *4*

    c) How many from radio and TV?   *4 local*

    d) How many from magazines?   *6 local bureaus; 50–60 nationally*

Q) Approximately how many press releases do you distribute weekly?

A) *2*

Q) Is there usually a press information officer present when your executives are interviewed by the press?

A) *No.*

Q) Do you feel that the media give accurate and knowledgeable information about your institution?

A) *Yes.*

Q) Is there any way in which you feel that the press can improve its coverage of your institution? In what way?

A) *Visit here more often and talk to people about what is going on.*

Q) What, in your opinion, is the best way of getting information to the press: press release, interview, press conference?

A) *Press release reaches the broadest number and has the greatest effect generally. However, special stories get greater coverage from press conferences.*

Still another federal agency, the Securities and Exchange Commission, is covered with reasonable consistency by the media. Although the material from this agency can be rather complex, requiring a background in economics, major decisions of SEC often are printed on the front page, while other activities are noted in the business and financial sections of the newspapers and, particularly, in business and economics periodicals. SEC has an Office of Public Affairs under a Director. The agency functions primarily to provide "disclosure to the investing public" and to protect the public against malpractice in the securities and financial markets. In the course of the past few years, several brokerage firms have received negative exposure in the press owing to the investigatory activities of the Commission, which was created in 1934 as an answer to abuses in the financial markets. It was as a result of the establishment of SEC that regulations on "full and fair disclosure" and other requirements were inaugurated, including regulation of companies controlling electric or gas utilities.

Sources of information for both media and public cover published materials for the potential investor, Reading Rooms and subscriptions to various publications through the Government Printing Office. These include the *SEC Docket,* a weekly compilation of official releases from

SEC, a *News Digest,* a daily report of announcements and decisions, *Statistical Bulletin* and *Monthly Summary* of security transactions.

A questionnaire on the agency and the media was answered as follows.

Q) What is the particular function of your office?

A) *Public information and congressional relations.*

Q) How is your office structured? How many people are assigned to the information function?

A) *Director and Secretary; Deputy Director and 3 professionals; information, 3 clericals; Legislative Counsel.*

Q) Approximately how many press correspondents cover your institution?

      a) How many wire service correspondents?   *4*

      b) How many representatives of large, national dailies?   *6*

      c) How many local papers?   –

      d) How many from radio and TV?   *none on a daily basis*

      e) How many from magazines?   *6*

Q) Approximately how many press releases do you distribute weekly?

A) *Average one press release, plus perhaps a dozen "official" releases which double as press releases.*

Q) Is there usually a press information officer present when your executives are interviewed by the press?

A) *Often, but not always.*

Q) Do you feel that the media give accurate and knowledgeable information about your institution?

A) *Those that cover on a regular basis do, but others are very spotty.*

Q) Is there any way in which you feel that the press can improve its coverage of your institution? In what way?

A) *Assign more personnel to spend more time learning about our work and looking into stories.*

Q) What, in your opinion, is the best way of getting information to the press: press release, interview, press conference?

A) *Interview is the most effective, press conference the most dramatic and press release the quickest and safest.*

One of the major regulatory agencies in Washington is the Federal Communications Commission. This organization, because it functions as the only unit of the government specifically established by the Congress to regulate the broadcast media, is a major source of news, primarily because there is controversy over whether radio and television should be regulated at all, and secondly because its opinions and decisions are almost invariably highly controversial in themselves. At this writing, for example, the House Sub-Committee on Communications, under the Chairmanship of Representative Lionel Van Deerlin (D. Cal.) is determined to revise the Communication Act of 1934, to the consternation of the broadcasters who would like to see matters more or less remain as they have been for the past 30-odd years. The FCC, in addition, has been in the unenviable position of seeing many of its rulings upset by the Supreme Court and its decisions have frequently come under fire from the print media. The broadcasters themselves would like to see certain rules rescinded, with the support of some members of the Congress.

By comparison with other agencies, the FCC is not large, but it does have numerous divisions. There are seven commissioners, all appointed by the President—and usually on political grounds, not in terms of competence or knowledge of broadcast communications. The Commission does more than oversee commercial broadcasting. It regulates interstate and foreign communications by radio, television, wire and cable (although the last is not over-the-air broadcasting). It is responsible for worldwide telephone and telegraph services and also for the promotion of safety through radio and television facilities. All radio and television services are administered by the Broadcast Bureau. Common carrier communications by telephone, telegraph,

FEDERAL COMMISSION USA

ROBERT E. LEE
ABBOTT M. WASHBURN
MARGITA E. WHITE

JAMES H. QUELLO
JOSEPH R. FOGARTY
TYRONE BROWN

Office of Plans & Policy

Office of Opinions & Review

Review Board

Office of Administrative Law Judges

Office of General Counsel

Administrative Rules &
 Procedures Div.
Research &
 Trial Div.
Legislation Div.
Litigation Div.
Public Access Div.

Industry Equal Employment
 Opportunity Unit

Office of Chief Engineer

International &
 Operations Div.
Laboratory Div.
Research &
 Standards Div.
Spectrum Allocations Div.

Planning & Coordination Staff

Office of Executive Director

Administrative Services Div.
Consumer Assistance Office
Data Automation Div.
Emergency Communications Div.
Financial Management Div.
Internal Review & Security Div.
Management Systems Div.
Personnel Div.
Procurement Div.
Public Information Officer
Records Management Div.
The Secretary

Field Operations Bureau

Enforcement Div.
Engineering Div.
Regional Div.
Violations Div.

Field Installations

Broadcast Bureau

Broadcast Facilities Div.
Complaints &
 Compliance Div.
Hearing Div.
License Div.
Office of Network Study
Policy and Rules Div.
Renewal & Transfer Div

Cable Television Bureau

Certificates of
 Compliance Div.
Policy Review &
 Development Div.
Research Div.
Special Relief &
 Microwave D.v.
Records & Systems
 Management Div.

Common Carrier Bureau

Accounting & Audits Div.
Economics Div.
Facilities & Services Div.
Hearing Div.
Mobile Services Div.
Policy & Rules Div
Tariff Div.

Compliance & Litigation
 Task Force

International Programs Staff

Program Evaluation Staff

Field Office

Safety and Special Radio Services Bureau

Aviation & Marine Div.
Industrial & Public
 Safety Facilities Div.
Industrial & Public
 Safety Rules Div.
Land Mobile Spectrum
 Management Div.
Legal Advisory &
 Enforcement Div.
Personal Radio Div.

Regional Branch

radio and satellite are under the Common Carrier Bureau. The FCC provides a pamphlet describing its function and its rules and policies, and its Office of Consumer Assistance explains how the public can participate in the process of decision-making. The Public Information Office offers "Bulletin No.I—Information Services and Publications." Dockets concerning rule-making, information on licenses and grants and other information pertaining to broadcast operations is available from the Public Information Office (including publications, public notices and press releases). On the preceding page is an organizational chart of the FCC.

An FCC source responded to a questionnaire on FCC–media relations.

Q) What is the particular function of your office?

A) *To disseminate information to the news media, general public communications attorneys, public interest groups, the industries the FCC regulates and so on, on all official Commission actions. As a regulatory agency, we do no "puff" publicity. We average 1,000 calls, letters and/or walk-ins per week.*

Q) How is your office structured? How many people are assigned to the information function?

A) *Office Chief, Deputy Chief, Senior Editor, four writers, one editorial assistant, five clericals = 13 total.*

Q) Approximately how many press correspondents cover your institution?

    a) How many wire service correspondents? *3 (AP, UPI, Reuters and* Wall St. Journal *Dow Jones wire)*

    b) How many representatives of large, national dailies? *4*

    c) How many from local papers? *10*

    d) How many from radio and TV? *dozen or more*

    e) How many from magazines? *6 or so*

Q) Approximately how many press releases do you distribute weekly?

A) *more than 100*

Q) Is there usually a press information officer present when your executives are interviewed by the press?

A) *No. This is a wide-open agency and reporters are free to deal directly with staff at all levels, plus the seven commissioners.*

Q) Do you feel that the media give accurate and knowledgeable information about your institution?

A) *Yes.*

Q) Is there any way in which you feel that the press can improve its coverage of your institution?

A) *By actually covering us. AP is here twice a day, UPI was once a day until its reporter left two months ago and no one new has been assigned. Reuters and* Wall Street Journal *check daily;* Washington Star, *two to three times a week;* Washington Post (*TV reporter*), *infrequently; others (business or general assignment), once every week or ten days as need arises. Trade press covers heavily. As for "Sunshine" meetings, advertised a week in advance on both AP and UPI wires the day before and the day of—trades always there, AP too, dailies almost never.*

Q) What, in your opinion, is the best way of getting information to the press: press release, interview, press conference?

A) *We use press release almost exclusively. Many reporters do conduct interviews for their own special needs.*

A federal agency which tends to be somewhat more newsworthy than most is the Environmental Protection Agency. News is generated when EPA announces standards or finds that a company has failed to observe anti-pollution regulations. In some cases, EPA is in the press because the agency comes under attack for allegedly being derelict in enforcing its own standards. The environmentalists have been sufficiently active to insure a number of productive stories in the media. As enacted by Congress, the law calls for the Environmental Protection Agency "to protect and enhance our environment today and for future generations." The basic purpose of EPA is to control pollution and to cooperate with state and local agencies on problems relating to the environment. It is a fairly recent organization, having been established in December, 1970.

The EPA also maintains a Reading Room and makes available films, publications and speakers. Its Press Services Division offers the following description of its functions.

The Division, under the supervision of an Assistant Director for Press Services, performs external services and liaison with news media. Provides newsworthy information to the media to keep the public informed through preparation and dissemination of appropriate press releases and distribution of feature material. Expands the agency's capability to distribute material through the electronic media utilizing agency audio-visual resources. Responds to inquiries from the media and handles other news media services. Internally, the Division initiates and coordinates media attention for the Administrator and Deputy Administrator, including the arrangements for conferences and briefings in Washington. Provides guidance to regional Public Affairs Officers on such media attention. Assists in planning regional conferences, as appropriate. Services and advises the program coordinators in the Office of Public Affairs. Coordinates distribution and participates with the Program Support Divisions and with other components of the office on the content and editorial style of materials going to the media. Serves as the agency focal point (Speakers Bureau) for requests for speech materials and public appearances by key agency staff, develops and disseminates speakers' speech materials and maintains the Agency Calendar.

The EPA responded to questions as follows:

Q) How is your office structured? How many people are assigned to the information function?

A) (*See following organization chart.*)

Q) Approximately how many press correspondents cover your institution?

A) *No full-time correspondents. Varies with story.*

      a) How many wire service correspondents?   *generally 2*

OFFICE OF PUBLIC AWARENESS--ORGANIZATIONAL CHART

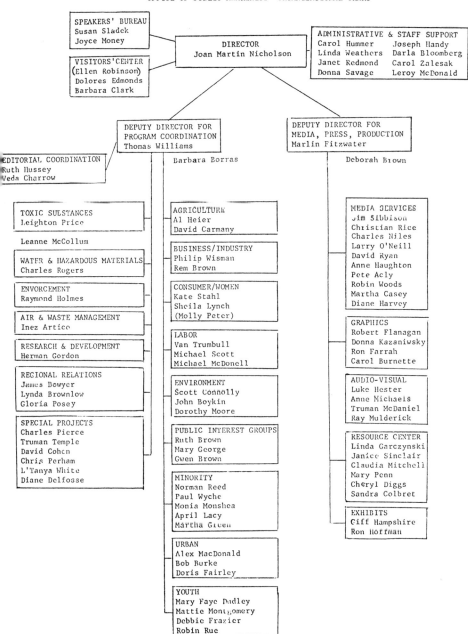

      b) How many representatives of large, national dailies? *generally 2* (Christian Science Monitor; Wall Street Journal)

      c) How many from local papers? *generally 2 big Washington D.C. papers* (Post; Star)

      d) How many from radio and TV? *varies with story*

      e) How many from magazines? *varies with story*

Q) Approximately how many press releases do you distribute weekly?

A) *7*

Q) Is there usually a press information officer present when your executives are interviewed by the press?

A) *No.*

Q) Do you feel that the media give accurate and knowledgeable information about your institution?

A) *Usually.*

Q) Is there any way in which you feel that the press can improve its coverage of your institution? In what way?

A) *Yes. The press should do more background reading on EPA programs, so we don't always have to start from ground zero in explaining important developments to reporters.*

Q) What, in your opinion, is the best way of getting information to the press: press release, interview, press conference?

A) *Depends on the situation.*

Analysis

What emerges from a survey of the branches and agencies that comprise the federal bureaucracy is the enormous number of personnel involved in the public information function. Regardless of whether Senator Scott's count of almost 4,000 publicists is accurate, the estimate of one veteran correspondent may be correct, that there may well be about two P.R. officials for every reporter in Washington. On virtually a ratio of two to one, it is clear that there is bound to be an informational overload from the government. Moreover, only a minimal part of what is released can possibly find its way into print or on the air. Even the material emanating from a single agency can become an information glut.

At the same time, what also emerges is that coverage of the federal government by the media is, in many respects, inadequate. Too few newspapers have Washington bureaus or correspondents and too many rely on the hard-pressed wire services. Even those metropolitan dailies with larger staffs cannot adequately cover the complex political milieu of Washington. No newspaper or network can possibly wade through the plethora of releases that inundate the media. Nor can they cover all the conflicting conferences and special events that are devised in the expectation of achieving media exposure. Additional correspondents will not assure greater use of press releases, but they will enable the media to cover aspects of the bureaucracy that now are not dealt with adequately. It is doubtful that many of the agencies will voluntarily reduce their public information staffs, without a thorough congressional investigation of their budgets and the personnel involved in government public relations. As one journalist put it, if each agency was not busy producing releases and promotional and informational materials, how could it justify its existence? This is precisely the point of Senator Scott's analysis of the size and cost of the information establishment. There may be far too many government publicists at too great a cost to the taxpayer and too little benefit, either to the media or to the public.

10

Access and Control

THE ESSENCE OF THE adversarial relationship between the government and the communications media stems simply from the undeniable fact that the bureaucracy often tries to conceal, manipulate and control news and the media try to pry into informational territory which is considered off limits. At times, the impasse becomes so tight that the government, in frustration and hostility, falls back on "no comment" and the press becomes categorical and strident in its demand for what it feels is being unfairly withheld from it. There would clearly be no adversarial problem if the media accepted the value judgments of the information officials as to what should or should not be disseminated to the public. But the media claim such value judgments as their own inalienable right in a political democracy. Under the social responsibility theory of the press, the media take full consequences for their own temerity in deciding what is significant enough to pass on to readers and viewers.

Newspaper Preservation Act

The government, however healthily adversarial the relationship may be, does not always attempt to control the media and, indeed, has even moved to provide economic relief to the press through the Newspaper Preservation Act. The passage of this Act by the Congress drew a mixed bag of praise and criticism—praise from the publishers, condemnation from critics who were convinced that what Congress did was simply to respond to the powerful publishers' lobby. They labeled the Newspaper Preservation Act as undemocratic in substance and as simply encouraging the growth of monopolies, chains and media conglomerates. The Act provided that (in 22 cities) where a morning and evening paper were published, both papers be permitted to share identical printing facilities, thus cutting costs. This provision was called a shameful capitulation by Congress to a special interest group. This legislation, incidentally, which was passed by a wide margin, rescinded a Supreme Court decision in 1969 that prohibited two newspapers in Arizona from utilizing the same facilities.

The chief complaints of critics of the Act were that it did not "preserve" newspapers but protected publishing interests; that it did not facilitate the flow of news to the reader; that a significant segment of the press opposed it, notably *The New York Times,* the *Washington Post* and even the conservative *Wall Street Journal.* Critics of the Act pointed out that although the newspapers involved were supposed to show economic need, this information was never released to the public by the Judiciary Committee of the Congress. Lobbying on behalf of passage was said to have "set new records." Finally, the Act was called a violation of the anti-trust laws and a supine acquiescence by the Congress to the publishing empires.

Government and Media Controls

The government, however, is also a source of media control, direct in the case of broadcasting and indirect in other areas. A literal interpretation of the First Amendment would appear to indicate that it means precisely what it says—that the Congress cannot, *under any circumstances,* pass a law abridging freedom of speech or press. The Gitlow decision also insured that the amendment was equally applicable to the states. But the fact is that except for those Justices who insisted that the First Amendment was inviolate in all situations, the Supreme Court has decided on more than one occasion that there are extenuating circumstances when freedom of speech must be curtailed.

Only a traditional strict libertarian would insist that the press must enjoy absolute freedom, because the reality is otherwise. The government can, and does, exercise controls, directly and indirectly—although these have been open to challenge. Control is clearly evident in anti-trust actions by the Justice Department against the commercial television networks. And, although television is the one medium regulated by a government agency, the Federal Communications Commission, the other media can still be subjected to controls. Anti-trust actions are one modality. Regulation of second-class mailing privileges by the Post Office Department can prove embarrassing for magazines that are struggling to exist. "Gag rules" by the courts have exerted a powerful controlling lever on the print media. Prior restraint was evident in the Pentagon Papers case. CBS narrowly averted a contempt citation in the Staggers Committee hearings on *The Selling of the Pentagon*. The courts have drastically and seriously restricted coverage of trials by the media. All these procedures, however they may be designated, are methods of media control by the government.

The media have been accused of instituting their own controls at the source, often, critics claim, at the expense of the public. Reporters who "cooperate" with the federal bureaucracy and agree to withhold information exercise source control. The decision not to print the Bay of Pigs story was a clear-cut example of control by the editors of a newspaper. Publishers, who are not hesitant in making their political opinions articulate, influence and control reportorial and editorial judgment, however much they may insist that they do not interfere with the journalistic function of their newspaper. Control of media is evident in monopolies, in cross-ownership of broadcast and print media. Gatekeepers who process the news exercise implicit control over the meaning of the news. Some of these controls are unavoidable and can only be surmounted by ethical diligence and a strong sense of social responsibility.

The very pervasiveness of mass communications and the growing demand for information, for example, have resulted in an unusual and perhaps unhealthy emphasis on investigative journalism. Regardless of government efforts to control news and of control at the source, the press has been more feverish than before in its need to expose. At times, the exposure reveals corruption in high places, as in Watergate, or unethical activities in agencies of the government, as indicated in press reports on many of the activities of the CIA and the FBI. On other occasions, however, this investigatory fever can be quite harmful to the functioning of a responsible press, as the publisher of the *Washington Post* pointed out. Source control also frequently relegates sound information in favor of "bad" news because of a conviction that the reader wants sensation and titillation. Crisis reporting, therefore, takes precedence over many of the less sensational but more significant problems relating to energy, the environment and the nation's health and welfare.

There are times, unfortunately, when the government and the media combine to control news at the source. Because information is not always easy to come by in the federal bureaucracy, the media occasionally tend to cooperate too readily with information sources, even though the "news" may not be accurate or entirely truthful and may be self-serving. In addition, docile and uncritical use of releases or "handouts" makes control of news at the source easier. In this way, the correspondents can drift into a kind of captive audience for the informational bureaucracy. There is no ready solution to the problem of control of news at the source beyond public and consumer group insistence on truthfulness in government and responsibility on the part of the media.

The CIA

There is no instance in recent history which compares in terms of media coverage to the belated exposure by *The New York Times* and other newspapers of the secret maneuvers of the Central Intelligence Agency. Following the revelations of the Watergate scandal and the official lies to the press by so many in the Nixon Administration, the press clearly pursued a far more urgent investigative journalism than ever before. The result was the material that came to light on the activities of the CIA, both at home and abroad. At issue, clearly, was the fact that this government enclave in Virginia was a law unto itself, reporting inadequately and probably falsely to the Congress and totally disregarding any sense of obligation or responsibility either to the media or to the public. Here official secrecy was more than a capricious whim. It was a way of life, a *modus operandi* of the most secretive government agency in American history. Yet, there were many who firmly believed that the CIA could not perform its intelligence function in any other way. Many still share that opinion.

What is notable and significant from the standpoint of government–press relations, however, is that while the CIA refused official information to the media, it did not hesitate to use the press, both to plant propaganda and to obtain information. Technically, the CIA was not permitted under its charter to employ its resources to obtain intelligence within this country. Apparently it did so. Journalistically, it was not considered sound or ethical practice for the CIA to use working reporters to obtain intelligence abroad for the CIA. It did so—and with the cooperation of both reporters and their publishers. Indeed, there are still journalists who argue, albeit lamely, that it was their patriotic duty to be of assistance to an American intelligence agency. Others argue, however, that such cooperation makes them intelligence agents, not journalists, and that the two functions are so divergent in scope and purpose as to be totally antithetical to each other. What is a reporter to do with a story abroad that may reflect unfavorably on the CIA when he is in the process of gathering intelligence for the CIA? Obviously the ethical dilemma is momentous.

On Christmas day, 1977, *The New York Times* revealed a long history of CIA involvement with news management and of a less than salutary relationship between the Central Intelligence Agency and some—but by no means all—of the news media. This was shortly after Richard Helms, former head of the agency, had worked out an apparent agreement with the President and the Attorney General which effectively enabled Helms to plead *nolo contendere* and to avoid testifying on various charges which were leveled against him, including possible perjury. Thus, apart from the clear violation of the principles of political democracy, despite disregard for the responsibilities assumed by a free press system and guaranteed by the First Amendment, the liaison between an intelligence arm of the government and working journalists raises serious problems of news control at the source, of manipulation of information and of the use of the press for purposes totally divergent from its traditional function as a surrogate of the public.

In 1976, following repeated rumors that reporters had worked as intelligence agents for the CIA, the Senate Select Committee on Intelligence revealed that for many years journalists had operated abroad on behalf of the Central Intelligence Agency by gathering information which was then relayed to the agency. This resulted in an uproar in the media and among civil libertarians, as well as in the Congress, although there were cogent and persuasive voices who argued that there was nothing inherently wrong with an exchange of information between reporters and CIA agents if such an arrangement abetted national security and worked to the advantage of the United States. Others, however, found such behavior unethical, reprehensible and at total variance with sound journalistic practice. Both viewpoints were presented before the congressional committee.

The major significance of the CIA involvement of the many media in its intelligence activities was the inevitable effect of the media on public attitudes and opinions. The CIA, it was revealed in a series of articles in *The New York Times,* was secretly the bankroller of a number of periodicals and books, both in English and foreign languages, that purported to be independent journals. In fact, they were owned or subsidized by the Central Intelligence Agency. The *Times'* study revealed that many news and information organizations were actually under the control of the CIA. Since many of the foreign publications were read by American journalists in search of leads, it can readily be seen how a carefully planned propaganda campaign could influence public opinion—and even public policy—in the United States. Not only the newspapers, but other mass media were involved. Several books, produced by reputable American publishers, were written under editorial guidance of the CIA.

The most debated problem, however, was the CIA involvement with the newspapers and with individual journalists. It has now been established that there was extensive financial investment in English language papers abroad and in various news organizations which served as a "front." One news organization, Continental Press Service in Washington, was actually run by a CIA official. This service supplied press credentials "to agency operatives in urgent need of cover." Another service, Forum World Features, published in London and reportedly owned by John Hay Whitney, publisher of the now defunct *New York Herald Tribune,* supplied news to at least 30 American newspapers, including the *Washington Post. The New York Times* noted that it had rejected the service.

Facts revealed that CIA agents passed themselves off as reporters, that legitimate reporters engaged in covert operations for the CIA and that the CIA sought out and used selected journalists who were amenable and who printed the "information" given to them. The number of journalists who had ties to the CIA has not been determined accurately. At least 50 had definite links. Other estimates range upwards of 200 or 300 American correspondents. These included reporters for some of this country's most reputable newspapers and magazines, as well as representatives of radio and television networks. In short, many American journalists, even while continuing to work for newspapers and other news organizations, were paid agents of the CIA and, therefore, in a position to control news at the source. This arrangement, however it may be justified by its defenders on grounds of patriotism and the national interest, inevitably colored the news received by the American people and therefore became propaganda rather than information. It was these disclosures of media–CIA liaison that prompted the House Select Committee on Intelligence to schedule hearings where both apologists and opponents of the CIA–media arrangement could state their views. Some correspondents insisted that the CIA was a legitimate source of news and that the same value judgments should be applied to information supplied by the CIA as to that of any other Washington agency. But this argument, in effect, begs the fundamental question concerning the obligation and responsibility of a journalist working in a free press system.

As a result of these exposés, the CIA lost a great deal of its credibility, and many of its supporters lamented the undeniable fact that it also was both embarrassed and restricted in its intelligence function. On December 2, 1977, Admiral Stanfield Turner, the head of the CIA, announced that new regulations would be effected governing the relationship between the agency and the media correspondents. Henceforth, there would be no use of reporters or news organizations in intelligence operations. A subsequent CIA announcement stated: "The special status afforded the press under the Constitution necessitates a careful policy of self-restraint on the part of the agency in regard to its relations with the United States news media organizations and personnel." As a consequence, the CIA will no longer "enter into any relationship with full or part-time journalists . . . for the purpose of conducting intelligence activities."

Access

In terms of application to the mass media, "access" has at least two connotations. The first, not often used, pertains to the ability or frustration of ability, as the case may be, of the reporter to reach sources of news and to be given relevant information. Access to news flow results from many factors—the ability, reputation and energy of the reporter, the degree of cooperation of public affairs officials and, in some cases, on the availability of confidential sources. Although the federal public information bureaucracy needs the media and seeks their support, reporters often encounter difficulty in securing vital news because high officials are inaccessible and other spokesmen must rely on a "no comment" position or on half-truths. Access, in a journalistic sense, means that the correspondent has open sesame to a free flow of information, that there is always an officer who is available to answer queries and who is capable of answering them, that information in the form of reports and memoranda is not withheld from perusal and use by the media. There has been no law passed by Congress which can guarantee access to information under all circumstances. The Freedom of Information Act, particularly in its amended form, was passed by the Congress for the express purpose of making access to government information more expeditious, both for the public and the press. It has apparently been more successfully invoked by the public than by the media, for the kind of news needed by the press simply cannot be mandated by any branch of the government. It has been helpful to a point to special and business interests, but it has not provided the kind of access which reporters deem necessary for obtaining information for a legitimate news story. Owing to the inevitable adversary relationship between the bureaucracy and the media, it is clear that the press will never be satisfied with government publicity procedures and that the government, because of the institutional nature of the various components, will invariably find itself in the unenviable position of attempting to block access to data which, for various arcane reasons, it feels should not be released to the media.

The second connotation of "access" is more commonly used. It has to do with the controversial problem of opening up the media—newspapers, radio and television—to the public. It is the categorical opinion of Professor Jerome Barron, for example, that the mass media enjoy an information monopoly, while the public and its opinions are almost totally shut out. The problem is easy to delineate, but the solution is difficult. Obviously, it is simply impossible for a multiplicity of voices in a pluralistic society to be given an opportunity to avail themselves of space in the print media or of time on the air. No advocate of access, however vehement, would argue otherwise. Since access to the media cannot conceivably mean access for all, it must imply an opportunity for some to express points of view at variance with those offered in print or on the air. These are the communications influentials whose interest in political and social phenomena make them opinion leaders in the two-step flow process. There are also representatives of consumer organizations, cultural minorities and leaders of special interest groups who want their viewpoint to be read and heard in the media.

As the media now function, critics such as Professor Barron believe, there is virtually no opportunity for differing opinions from citizens to be purveyed to the public. The FCC Fairness Doctrine demands that a station present varying points of view on controversial issues of public significance and that those who may be personally attacked on the air be accorded right of reply. But no such rule governs the newspaper, which is not regulated by a government agency. The media, recognizing that there may be a problem of access, also note that time and space are provided—by a fair and balanced presentation in the broadcast media—by letters to the editor pages in the newspapers and by the technique of having reporters secure quotes and comment from diverse news sources in matters of conflict or controversy.

But these are paltry, access advocates complain, because only a few letters can be printed out of hundreds received, and these at the discretion and judgment of the editor.

In the opinion of some scholars, access can only be achieved if it is mandated by the federal courts so that, in the words of Jerome Barron, "the public, through newspapers and broadcasts, have access to all shades of opinion." Under present restrictive conditions, avenues to the media are all but closed to the people—and not so much by government as by media control. Further, critics claim, the First Amendment is used to protect freedom of the press, but it has not been applied positively to assure citizen access to that press.

Richard Jencks, a former high-level CBS executive, has presented another viewpoint which is germane to the access question. Public access may be a desirable goal in a democratic, pluralistic society, but it is fraught with dangers which may be far more serious than lack of access. In the past few years, for example, the FCC has received a spate of complaint letters from special interest organizations, all asking time under the Fairness Doctrine, but *all* using almost identical language. Many of these groups do not represent the public but simply special and specialized interests that are seeking to influence public opinion toward their own political viewpoints or objectives. Bargains have been struck between station management and these groups, because no television station wants to incur the expense of a hearing before the Federal Communications Commission. This, clearly, is not genuine access, but merely the use of the leverage of an implicit threat to convey a preconceived point of view.

The Red Lion Case, in broadcasting, illustrates how ambivalent the government itself has been on the question of access. A demagogic preacher, the Reverend Billy James Hargis, personally attacked a correspondent, Fred J. Cook, on the air, accusing Cook of being a Communist. The Red Lion Broadcasting Company station WGGB AM-FM, Pennsylvania, refused Cook time for reply, and Cook's petition was rejected by the FCC. But the Supreme Court rescinded the FCC decision, because "the rights of the viewers and listeners," not of the broadcaster, were paramount. This case, however, simply underscores that the citizen who is wrongly accused can turn to the courts for redress. It does not resolve the problem of public access to print or the air. The courts have not been unaware of the need for greater citizen participation in this country's system of mass communications. But no one, in or out of the judiciary, has devised a feasible plan for public access without turning the newspaper into one long series of letters or the airwaves into a cacophony of conflicting voices. Mandating access by turning to the federal judiciary would not resolve the problem and, indeed, poses the distinct danger of government control of communications media. The social responsibility theory of the press in which the media assume full responsibility for what is printed or aired is still, in the opinion of civil libertarians, far better a method than mandated access by government. A public that demands adequate and truthful information, from both government and media, has a good chance of getting that information without intervention from any federal agency. To obtain adequate information, there must be some method for providing feedback from the public, but such a method is difficult to achieve.

Public opinion and reputable consumer organizations, such as Common Cause, have been powerful factors in determining that both government and media contribute to an informed public. Technically, the public has little opportunity for informational input. Neither the reader nor the viewer contributes *directly* to what is in print or on the air. That is why the media serve, in a political democracy, as a surrogate for the public. In indirect ways, however, there is public contribution to public policy. Readers and viewers can reject a newspaper or tune out a station—a powerful weapon if exercised widely. Protests from the public are not disregarded by the media. Our informational system, despite a trend toward contraction of newspapers, is hardly monolithic. There are thousands of radio stations, hundreds of network-affiliated and independent television stations and more daily newspapers than appear in any country in the world. In addition, the development of a nationwide cable system, with many channels and at least one public access channel in each community, will go a long way toward assuring greater public access to the mass communications system. There are those who advocate that the government mandate that broadcast stations devote a specific amount of time to public affairs and discussion, but such a solution raises questions both of constitutionality and government control of the mass media. Others believe that the media should make time and space available to anyone who can pay, but this answer would discriminate against those who cannot pay.

Access is obviously a desirable objective. But none of the proposals advanced thus far have successfully circumvented the very real threat of the imposition of autocratic control, either by government or by special interests. Access applied in an indiscriminate way would also add to the multiplicity of voices and viewpoints and to the informational overflow which already threatens to engulf the reader and viewer. A survey of public opinion on access, while recognizing the problem, would probably conclude—when all aspects are considered—that a responsible press and a free press is still capable of making intelligent value judgments in the interest of the people's "right to know."

Television and the Government

In its relatively short history, television has effected a radical transformation in government–media relations. Presidential press conferences are no longer meetings between reporters and the Chief Executive. They are television events, planned not so much for the correspondents as for the TV cameras. The appearance of the President at a press conference is usually announced the day before, with the added note that the network will carry the conference live. Wherever possible, these meetings with the media are established in prime evening time, carefully chosen to avoid antagonizing audiences for high-rated programs. The correspondents themselves behave with an awareness that they, as well as the President, are "on television." As a result, good reporting tends to suffer.

Many members of the press also feel that television, despite its value as an informational medium, has not contributed substantially to the presidential conference or to other Washington events. The medium has been criticized for obscuring and circumventing normal diplomatic channels for an exercise in instant diplomacy. James Wieghart, of the *New York Daily News'* Washington bureau, returned from a trip abroad with the President with some harsh words for television journalism. "With the all-seeing camera eye," wrote Wieghart, "who needs a second-hand written account from a reporter?" This journalist complains further that reporters are generally pushed around by the presence of television cameras and crews and that print reporters must rely on a small group of "pool" correspondents. The fulcrum of the President's trip was the "overwhelming presence of television," which dominated every one of Mr. Carter's moves. Wieghart, finally, takes the significant position of faulting the White House aides who are obsessed with how the event will look and sound on television.

Despite these criticisms and other critical comments from the print medium, television is a paramount factor in the way in which information flows from federal agencies. Several of the agency information offices have a section devoted exclusively to radio and television. Congressmen use excellent studio facilities to prepare videotaped material to send to their local stations. President Johnson was so intrigued by the medium that he had special studio facilities built in the White House. The reporters were anathema to President Nixon, but he used television with dogged persistence. Broadcasting has radically changed the way in which the government communicates with the public.

Although the government exercises indirect controls over the press through the Congress, the Post Office and the Courts, a specific federal agency, the Federal Communications Commission, was established by Congress in 1934 for the express purpose of regulating broadcast communications. Congress determined that broadcasters did not own the air waves; they were the property of the people. Broadcasting stations, therefore, were licensed by the FCC under the proviso that they operate in "the public interest, convenience and necessity." Licenses are renewed by the commission every three years upon evidence that the station has brought an appropriate amalgam of entertainment, education and information to the community which it serves. Rarely has the FCC rescinded a license, and more often than not, its decisions have been overruled by the Supreme Court. The broadcasting industry is, therefore, in a rather odd position in the area of mass communications. It enjoys partial protection of the First Amendment but not, as the court decision in the *Tornillo v. Miami-Herald* case showed, the same protection as print. Yet, the argument that limited spectrum space demands regulation is no longer valid, because there are sufficient radio and television stations in operation to offer excellent service to the entire country. Cable and satellite communications will add to the growing service. But the federal bureaucracy is ambivalent about television. Washington agencies and officials are delighted when their activities are covered by television cameras. At the same time, they are suspicious of television news and documentaries and show extraordinary sensitivity to any segment that does not—in their opinion—enhance their image. As a result, despite pressure from the broadcasters and from senators like William Proxmire (D. Wis.), the Congress is reluctant to remove some of the now moribund and outdated regulations that apply to the medium.

Lionel Van Deerlin, Chairman of the House Sub-Committee on Communications, is in the process of revising the 1934 Communications Act. Indeed, Representative Van Deerlin was less than pleased when he asked for the cooperation of the broadcasters and was advised that the presently constituted Act did not require revision. Presumably, the broadcast industry would like to leave well enough alone. Mr. Van Deerlin's irritation brought a speedy offer of full cooperation from the National Association of Broadcasters.

The crucial question is whether broadcasting should enjoy identical freedom under the First Amendment as the print media. One viewpoint is that with a multiplicity of stations available, there is no longer a need for regulation. Another is that certain of the FCC rules may be unconstitutional. Still a third is that most FCC commissioners are political appointees with little or no background in broadcast communications. Perhaps the commissioners should be appointments of the Civil Service rather than the choice of the President.

Several aspects of the Communications Act may well be obsolete or at least cumbersome and unnecessary. Recent decisions on obscenity by the Supreme Court would seem to force the FCC to rely solely on community judgment. Under the First Amendment, the government is denied any power to limit or deny free expression, and Section 326 of the Communications Act prohibits the FCC from interfering "with the right of free speech by radio communication." But the

United States Code calls for a fine or imprisonment for uttering obscene language on the air. This contradiction demands clarification—in any revision of the Communications Act—on what constitutes "obscenity" as against interference with "free expression."

In the FCC, the Congress set up a hybrid agency with neither genuine legislative nor judicial authority. The fuzziness of the concept of "public interest, convenience and necessity" has bewildered legal and communications scholars. How do we define the public "convenience"? What is the meaning of public "necessity"? Surely, a revision of the Act requires a more precise definition of what the government expects of broadcasting in the way of public service. The immediate and long overdue elimination of Section 315, the so-called "equal time" rule, ought to be proposed to the Congress without further temporizing. This rule calls for the stations to provide air time during political campaigns to *every* candidate who can get his name on the ballot, if it provides time for one bona fide candidate. When this rule has been invoked, it has been shown to be utterly ludicrous. In no way does it enhance the democratic process, and it serves merely to confuse the public. There is a good argument for scrapping equal time entirely. Its very presence on the books turned the Ford–Carter confrontations into a silly mess by the clumsy device of using an outside organization instead of allowing the news divisions of the networks to perform their journalistic function. Section 315 is an artificial and nonsensical rule, and many believe that the sooner the sub-committee gets rid of it, the better for all concerned.

The Fairness Doctrine is another rule that many feel ought to be rescinded, that Congress would do well to heed Senator Proxmire and get rid of this requirement. The rule may well be unconstitutional. In effect, it gives the FCC an authority which is not mandated by the First Amendment. And here, too, the FCC decisions on fairness have almost invariably been reversed by the courts. The Fairness Doctrine calls for the broadcaster to seek out and present controversial issues of public importance and to assure that all points of view are adequately represented. Even if it were constitutional, there may be considerable validity to the networks' claim that it inhibits genuine controversy or aggressive investigative reporting. Why should television news tackle issues if there is always the possibility of being forced to offer time to pressure groups that might disagree? Furthermore, the Fairness Doctrine does not apply to print journalism. The Supreme Court, in the *Tornillo v. Miami-Herald* case, ruled that a newspaper does not have to give a political candidate space to reply to a critical editorial. Why, indeed, should such a double standard prevail? If editing is what editors are for, as the Supreme Court claimed, the editorial process is no less valid for electronic journalism than it is for print.

If the Congress wants to test the hypothesis that the Fairness Doctrine inhibits the presentation of controversial issues, and if it is chary of rescinding the Doctrine completely, it should, at the very least, declare a three or four year moratorium on the use of the Fairness Doctrine in order to determine whether the networks will put their money where their mouth is and set about increasing the production of documentaries dealing with controversial issues of public policy.

In the opinion of other critics, the House sub-committee should also get rid of the useless prime-time access rule, another roadblock established by the FCC without any clear comprehension of its inevitable consequences. The rule was supposed to stimulate significant cultural programming by local stations through the device of turning a half hour back to the networks' affiliates. In fact, it has simply given the stations the opportunity of picking up valuable commercial time by selling cheap syndicated programs. Since the FCC has no authority over the right of the stations to schedule programs, prime time ought to be revoked. The half hour ought to be returned to the networks with the recommendation—or the admonition—that it be devoted to an expanded network news broadcast. The news divisions claim consistently that they cannot cover all the news in a scant half hour. This change would provide an opportunity to encourage the expansion of news, with the public the clear beneficiary.

The United Church of Christ, a trenchant critic of the broadcasting industry, particularly on questions relating to the employment of women and minorities, has suggested specific ways of revising the Communications Act. This active public interest group has urged the House sub-committee to consider the needs of the consumer, not the broadcasters, and has recommended the following changes in the revised Act: that commercial stations be taxed in order to secure funds in support of public television; that state and local political candidates be afforded air time; that minority groups and women be given greater opportunities to work in broadcasting. Representative Van Deerlin's reaction, in view of his pique at the broadcasters, was predictably favorable. He termed the recommendations both "significant" and "enlightened." Although there has been a proposal to extend licenses from three to five years, the United Church of Christ advocated indefinite renewal, but with the provision that a petition to revoke a license could be instituted at any time, not simply at renewal periods.

One of the major points of conflict in any revision of the Communications Act will center around the double standard which broadcasters claim exists between print and the broadcast media. Both, they insist, should be equally protected by the First Amendment. Additionally, a congressional committee should have no more right to ask networks for outtakes (material which does not appear on the air) than it has the right to ask a newspaper for "overset" copy, which does not run in the paper. The Staggers Committee subpoena of CBS for material not shown on *The Selling of the Pentagon* was considered by many broadcasters to be recriminatory and retaliatory, because the Pentagon found the program distasteful and even harmful to its public relations. Fortunately, the House did not vote a contempt citation, but if the case had ever reached the Supreme Court, it is highly conjectural as to what the decision might have been. The courts in general have not been consistent in determining that the editorial process is always protected by the First Amendment.

Cross-Ownership

One area which has embroiled the industry, the courts and the FCC is that of cross-ownership. This is the control of both broadcasting and newspaper properties by one organization in the same community. This arrangement, critics believe, tends toward the encouragement of monopoly, concentrates control too rigidly and is unduly restrictive of both healthy competition and the development of a diversity of editorial and informational voices. In November of 1977, briefs were filed with the United States Supreme Court by newspaper and broadcasting interests in a legal protest against the imposition by the FCC of restraints on cross-ownership. The claim was that the FCC had gone beyond the limits of its authority and that the United States Court of Appeals in Washington had also done so in refusing to overrule the Commission. This court agreed with the FCC in principle that a company cannot own newspapers and/or radio-television facilities in the same community. However, a public interest organization, The National Citizens Committee for Broadcasting, urged that the Appeals Court uphold the FCC. The Supreme Court has agreed to hear arguments on the case, which includes 16 areas of alleged media monopoly. In all, there are 65 newspaper-television cross-ownerships now extant, and more in radio.

Meanwhile, the media continue to complain that the FCC had exceeded the authority vested in it by Congress. Stations and newspapers involved, however, obviously have some trepidation about the Supreme Court's disposition. To circumvent the problem, *The Washington Post* and *The Detroit News* agreed to exchange television stations. The *Post*'s station, WTOP-TV, will go to the *Detroit News* and the latter's station, WWJ-TV, will go to the Washington paper. Since no taxes are involved, this swapping of stations may be one answer to the cross-ownership dilemma The exchange, however, must receive the approval of the FCC.

The government has been studying cross-ownership arrangements since 1970 At that time, the FCC invited the usual comment from interested parties and, as a result, received responses from some 200 public interest organizations. But the matter did not reach an acute stage until the decision of the Court of Appeals which, as Chief Judge David L. Bazelon phrased it, decided that it was important to insure "a free flow of information from as many divergent sources as possible." Thus, the argument of the court was that cross-ownership was an impediment to diversity of informational flow. The broadcasters have countered with the argument that breaking up cross-ownership would constitute a serious economic dislocation and would not insure diversity. Furthermore, the broadcasters affirm that superior information to the public is provided when the station owners live in the community which the station serves.

The feeling that monopoly arrangements are unhealthy to the public interest is accompanied by a conviction that stations are not properly serving that interest. In 1977, the United States Court of Appeals also directed the FCC to give consideration to a plan that would require the broadcaster to provide the Commission with a list of the ten most controversial subjects which had been broadcast over a stated time period. This list of controversial issues was proposed by Henry Geller, former FCC General Counsel, with the support of the Citizens Communications Center, a public interest organization. The Committee for Open Media also proposed that licensees be forced to reserve one hour weekly for announcements by the public (access) on public issues. The major questions involved in such proposals were whether they would impede, rather than improve, informational flow and, above all, whether they were constitutional, since they constitute an intrusion by government in the editorial process.

Television and the News

Broadcasters have faced some major criticisms in the way they purvey news, and this is particularly true of television news, on both the network and local levels. Admittedly, as Walter Cronkite and others have stated repeatedly, 22 minutes are hardly sufficient to give the public an adequate account of national and international events. Yet, network affiliates are adamant in their refusal to "clear" an extended nightly network news, primarily for economic reasons. With the limited time available, the competition among branches and agencies of the federal bureaucracy for air time is intense, but the networks cannot possibly handle even major stories from the agencies. The result has been predictable coverage by the White House correspondent and, occasionally, reports from the correspondent for the State Department. As a result, network news is scored for failing to convey full and adequate information and for concentrating on the northeastern geographic corridor, the area between Washington and Boston. The fact is, however, as most metropolitan newspapers would agree, that most of the material which journalists consider significant news comes from such centers as New York, Washington, Chicago, Los Angeles and San Francisco.

Both networks and stations have come under criticism for emphasizing sensationalism rather than sobriety. Serious economic and social issues are too seldom discussed on the network news programs and local newscasts have a tendency toward so-called "happy news"—a result of surveys of what kind of news would garner the highest ratings. Because the presentation is necessarily ephemeral and often deliberately sensational, television does not always convey political issues in a way calculated to stimulate public opinion and consensus. Unfortunately, there are few definitive studies on how the viewer reacts to television news—in terms of its effect on attitudes, opinions and behavior—beyond the reported finding that most people turn to television news as the most "believable" of the media. The public also uses media, particularly television, for purposes beyond sheer information. News from Washington, in print and on the air, offers an indirect way of surveillance of the political environment. Some viewers watch the news nightly but cannot recall the broad details of an account relating to the activities of their government. Some tend to accept uncritically statements of the journalistic elite, in print and on the air, as a guide to future action.

In the course of the next decade, owing to the development of cassettes, cable and satellites, there are certainly bound to be changes in the quantity and quality of broadcast news, particularly information emanating from the government. With cable and its many channels, more news of the federal bureaucracy will be forthcoming. Feedback and access by way of public interest channels will be feasible. In the development stage are a number of "super stations"—independent television stations, without network affiliation, to which signals (programs) will be relayed by satellites. Such a phenomenon will set in motion pervasive changes in the development and distribution of information. If such agencies as the wire services become involved in the use of new information systems, using satellites as a mode of distribution, the implications for the dissemination of news and the relationship between government information sources and the media are portentous.

Public Television

Once known as educational television, public television was inaugurated primarily as an alternative and culturally superior service to commercial broadcasting. It has now also become an alternative source of news. Public television offers in-depth reports which analyze significant events in the news that are covered only on the surface by network news broadcasts. It schedules programs on the Washington political scene not ordinarily covered by the commercial networks and stations. It competes directly in carrying special Washington events, such as the President's State of the Union Message to the Congress, and its analysis of such events is more exhaustive than the brief summaries on commercial television.

In April, 1979 the second Carnegie report was published under the title A PUBLIC TRUST The Landmark Report of the Carnegie Commission on the Future of Public Broadcasting. The report reiterates the goals set forth in the first Carnegie report 12 years ago; public broadcasting must be noncommercial, independent and set a standard of excellence for America. The second commission proposes a change from the Corporation for Public Broadcasting to a new entity called the Public Telecommunications Trust. The Trust, a nongovernmental, nonprofit corporation will be the principal agent for the entire system. Under the umbrella of the Trust will be a second organization called the Program Services Endowment whose sole objective will be to support creative excellence.

Funding is again the crux of the whole matter. An increase in general revenues is asked, with the recommendation of the establishment of a fee on licensed uses of the spectrum to help offset the additional increase in general tax revenues. If legislation is passed to set this fee, then the second Carnegie Commission will have succeeded where the first one failed. A public broadcasting system, radio and television, protected from the influence of politics and commercial pressures is the aim of the second commission as it was with the first.

But public television has long been a victim of the federal bureaucracy because it has had to depend upon direct government subsidy for most of its financial support. As a result, the Nixon Administration cut funding drastically and politicized the Corporation for Public Broadcasting. The head of the Office of Telecommunications Policy, Clay Whitehead, baldly stated that public television need not offer news because the networks had a viable and successful service. Although these strictures were rectified to some extent by the Carter Administration, public television still remains a politicized medium. A recent recommendation has been that the government authorize that some of the profits of commercial television be taxed to pay the freight for the operation of the Public Broadcasting System.

President Carter's call for a billion-dollar investment in public television over the next several years will hardly solve the monumental problems facing this alternative broadcasting system. It does not—and cannot—insure that public broadcasting will be insulated from congressional and administration pressures on programming philosophy. Nor does it provide assurance that another Congress and another administration will not rescind Mr. Carter's largesse. In a recent analysis of appointments to the National Endowment for the Humanities, *The New York Times* laments the unfortunate politicization of the administration's commitment to the arts, and there is little reason to believe that a medium like public broadcasting will escape political pressures.

Public television, to flourish in an independent environment, needs a more durable commitment, as the framers of the original Carnegie Commission Report on Public Television saw clearly when they recommended an excise tax as the most feasible way of funding this medium. But these recommendations were never acted upon by the Congress, and it is hardly surprising, therefore, that the underwriting by the Carnegie Corporation of a second commission to evaluate and make recommendations on the future of public television should be greeted with euphoric enthusiasm by public broadcasting executives and by a *pro forma* endorsement from the White House.

The Public Broadcasting System has been locked in a decimating struggle with its "parent" organization, the Corporation for Public Broadcasting. Selection of programs by means of a so-called station cooperative plan has been chaotic and has all but destroyed any genuine national network interconnection. Above all, government funding allocations have been so sparse that PBS has been forced to rely on grants from an ever-increasing number of major national corporations, with the result that public television, in a repudiation of its own mandate, has accepted advertising and industrial sponsorship of its programs. In effect, public television has become corporate television.

The appointment of a second Carnegie Commission, ten years after the publication of the landmark Carnegie Report on Public Television of 1967, implies that the original report was a failure, which is a far cry from the truth. The recommendations in the original document were ignored by the Congress and grossly subverted by Clay Whitehead (then head of the Office of Telecommunications Policy), who, at the urging of Richard Nixon, proceeded to destroy a burgeoning national network and to create a vicious schism between PBS and CPB.

Had the recommendations of the 1967 Carnegie Report been implemented and proved to be unsuccessful or unrealistic, there might be a rationale for a second study. But the "program for action" was never put to the test and the alternatives outlined in the report are still limited by crippling practical considerations. The overriding issue is funding—the lack of money has drawn public television into accepting corporate sponsorship of programs which were, unlike the networks, supposed to be totally free of advertising. With a viable economic base, PBS could have addressed the core of its mandate, which is to produce a creative and innovative program schedule to serve as an alternative to the familiar stereotypes of commercial television.

Political pressures successfully aborted the promulgation of the 1967 Carnegie Report. These came in part from congressmen who feared that public television might prove too independent and "liberal" and from the Nixon Administration, which appointed political hatchet men to the Corporation for Public Broadcasting in an effort to prevent the formulation of a strong network of public television stations and to keep programming bland and innocuous.

The decision to establish a second commission, according to the Carnegie Corporation, was in response to a request by the Corporation for Public Broadcasting. Ironically, the establishment of CPB was a prime recommendation to the Congress in the original Carnegie Report, which urged the establishment of "a federally chartered, nonprofit, nongovernmental corporation" to disburse funds and to "improve public television programming." The request by CPB for a new study, then, can only be viewed as an admission of failure to implement the recommendations of the first Carnegie Report. If, however, no genuine effort has been made to promulgate the 12 recommendations in the 1967 report, can a second commission hope to accomplish anything more than still another cosmetic blueprint for action? An analysis of the objectives of the impending study reveals little more than mild semantic divergences from the first. Unquestionably, the major issue to be considered is funding levels, but the Congress cannot wait for a report that will not be available for almost two years. It is faced with the immediate task of determining a five-year funding plan for the Corporation for Public Broadcasting. As for long range funding for public television, the tenth recommendation in the original Carnegie Report suggested clearly that the Congress "provide the federal funds requested by the Corporation through a manufacturers (graduated) excise tax on television sets." This method of funding, had it been acted upon, would have assured public television not only of economic viability but also of insulation from pressures and controls by either the Congress or the White House. It is difficult to see how a second commission can produce a more palatable method of funding and still assure freedom of action by the Public Broadcasting System. The excise-tax method of funding has worked for the BBC (British Broadcasting Corporation), and although CPB is federally chartered, an excise tax would give public broadcasting a latitude it has not enjoyed by being forced to rely on the dual device of corporate and government handouts. This industrial reliance is hardly the road to political independence.

Without adequate funding, the issue of creative programming is purely academic. But the broad inquiry to be undertaken by the second commission will address itself to "creative programming, public participation, the impact of new technologies." A reading of the immediate action recommendations in the original Carnegie Report reveals a clear call for implementation of each of these objectives. The seventh recommendation urged that the Corporation "encourage and support research and development" toward the end of improving the program service. The eighth recommendation asked support for technical experimentation to "improve present television technology." The second Carnegie study calls for a consideration of similar goals.

Curiously, the notion prevails that the first Carnegie Report sacrificed national interconnection in favor of grass-roots localism. This is a canard. The report plainly recommended that the Corporation provide "as expeditiously as possible facilities for live interconnection" and even went so far as to anticipate the communications satellite as a source of national programming service. The second Carnegie commission may indeed produce a masterful blueprint. But it is difficult to see how—the options being limited—it can improve on the recommendations made in the original report. Advocates of public television believe that it is absurd to wait at least 18 months for a second Carnegie Commission Report. The options are clear. Faced with an immediate decision on funding, Congress is urged in some quarters to approve a graduated excise tax. Indeed, Lionel Van Deerlin, Chairman of the House Sub-Committee on Communications, indicated in a reply to a query that this method of funding would receive serious consideration. With the economic crunch resolved, PBS can then proceed to establish a national network and enlist the talent of this country's creative community.

E.B. White put it clearly in a letter to the first commission, "Noncommercial television should address itself to the ideal of excellence, not the idea of acceptability—once in a while it does, and you get a quick glimpse of its potential."

Had the recommendations in the original Carnegie Report been promulgated, that potential could long have been realized without the need for PBS to demean itself by accepting corporate underwriting, and it might also have prevented CPB from sinking into the mire of Washington politics.

11

Government Obligation:
Media Responsibility

THE FEDERAL GOVERNMENT has an obligation to provide information to the public, as citizens and as taxpayers. This obligation is pursued through direct channels, such as response to mail and phone queries, and through various departmental and agency publications. The government is also obliged to inform the people through the media of mass communication, both voluntarily and at the request of reporters acting as surrogates.

The media have no specific legal obligation to inform. They are not supported by taxpayer funds as are government agencies, except in indirect ways through special postal rates, subsidies and funding of public television. Indeed, a strict libertarian philosophy would claim that the press has no obligation or responsibility to anyone except itself. But the social responsibility concept decrees otherwise. If the media are to function freely and be protected by the First Amendment, they must assume full responsibility for what they print and air. And they must be responsible surrogates of the people, purveying information to meet the people's "right to know."

Both the government and the media also have internal obligations and responsibilities. The government publicist works within a framework of policies set by the establishment—superiors, agency regulations, the Congress. The correspondent works through gatekeepers—editors, other writers, publishers, broadcasting executives. And both the media and the bureaucracy are responsible to each other in a symbiotic relationship, the agency dependent on the media as a conduit and the media looking to the bureaucracy for information. The public affairs officer and the reporter both recognize obligation and responsibility, but each perceives them from a different perspective. It is this difference in perception which creates an adversary relationship between the encoder (government) and decoder (media recipients of government messages).

The Reporter

Information gathering from the apparatus of the bureaucracy is the function of the reporter who, in many instances, now tends to be a product of one of the many schools of journalism, while many are specialists in one or two particular areas. The correspondent's purpose is to evaluate and to process formal news releases, to attend conferences and to ask pertinent questions, to ferret out withheld information and to develop on- and off-the-record reliable sources of intelligence in the complex politics of Washington. Frequently, as in the case of Watergate, reporters work as a team, particularly in investigative journalism. What happens after information is gathered and processed is subject to many variables: "what else happened that day," which might result in the story going into overset; possible unwitting distortion by headline writers or re-write men; changes effected—often irritating to the reporter—by the editors. Although publishers since Hearst have sought more carefully to avoid intrusion on the news flow, it is inevitable that on occasion, political considerations can play an implicit part in coloring the news. Publishers have close relationships with the Congress and often with other high officials and, as in the case of the Newspaper Preservation Act, Washington can be helpful to the economic welfare of the press medium. Thus, there may be an unspoken understanding on the part of editors and reporters of what to include or omit from a political story—an understanding not predicated on the sheer informational value of the news. There is also, in the case of some papers (fortunately in the minority), a reflection of the publisher's political philosophy. This is not to imply that basic news is not covered. No press in the world is as scrupulous—with a few notable exceptions—as American journalism.

The news flow stems from a variety of informational sources in the federal agencies. It is processed by bureaus, correspondents, wire services, columnists, syndicated writers, radio and television correspondents and magazine editors and researchers. Despite cohesive economic interests, there is some assurance of diversity in the gathering and processing of news. But economic considerations also exert an implicit influence on the way in which journalistic responsibility is recognized. The business side of publishing (circulation, advertising and promotion) influences news flow, however indirectly, by determining to some extent how much space is available for editorial content. In broadcast news, the correspondent is held tightly to a strict time limit so that the commercials can be inserted at necessary intervals. Even biographical data, filed in the morgue, can influence a story, depending upon what is left in or excluded. In substance, the number of variables which exert an influence on the amount and quality of information that the public receives is large. And not the least of these variables is the federal publicist. Walter Lippmann noted in 1923, long before there was the present proliferation of information services, that the reporter could not be everywhere. As a consequence, there was a necessary dependence on information specialists as catalysts. There are, finally, other variables and factitious phenomena which influence the news flow—the national and international "climate," public opinion, crisis developments, pressures from economic, educational, religious, social, cultural *and* political groups.

The media are sensitive to, as well as reflective of, the political atmosphere. The conviction of most scholars is that the press reflects developments far more than it influences political action. Yet, political pressures rarely subvert the responsibility of the media as they do in so many countries of the world. In this country, the government treads cautiously in the sensitive area of newspaper content or television programming. Efforts to involve the government in content, at least to this point, have been rejected by the agencies themselves and by the courts. But, particularly in broadcasting, the exercise of potential control is always implicit. Because television is licensed, it is far easier to intimidate stations than newspapers. Broadcasters are sensitive to the prevailing political winds and react to them by rationalizing what they include and what is omitted from content. On the whole, however, the media enjoy and exert a great deal of independence in gathering and distributing the news, and it is their insistence on taking full responsibility for what they print and air that has minimized government interference and further validated the spirit of the First Amendment.

The Bureaucracy

Three questions are posed in the evaluation of any media system: how is it controlled—by government or by the entrepreneur; how and by whom is its content determined; and who exercises supervision? In most countries, the media are owned and operated by the government or they operate under direct bureaucratic control or they are directly subsidized. In the United States, despite direct and indirect modes of control, the media themselves are responsible to the public—to the readers of newspapers and to the listeners and viewers of radio and television programs. Media are privately owned, a situation which has drawn much criticism but few recommendations for changes beyond intrusion by government. The media are totally responsible for content. And the media supervise themselves, subject to minimal regulations and to public opinion as expressed either directly or through "influentials," group leaders and public interest organizations. The resolution of conflict is usually a matter to be settled by the courts. In some instances, voluntary "ombudsman" arrangements or news councils are available, although these have no judicial authority and their impact is essentially that of public pressure and moral suasion.

In its liaison with the media, the government has a clear-cut obligation to contribute to public discussion of political and social issues and toward the formulation of public policy by a truthful and unimpeded flow of intelligence to the mass media. The government, like the media, is an agency of institutional control, but its directive power is limited by the constitutional guarantee of a free press system. Freedom of information, however, has not been interpreted by the courts to mean freedom for every conflicting voice under all circumstances. The Holmes' doctrine underscored a necessary limitation by showing that unrestrained freedom of expression can actually constitute a social hazard and that unrestricted access can actually interfere with the process of both government and media. The government's obligation, apart from facilitating the flow of news, is also to determine when *not* to interfere with the function of the media. One-newspaper cities may not constitute a hazard and, as one study revealed, may actually result in more scrupulous coverage of the news. Cross-ownership is not invariably evil under all circumstances, although healthy competition is obviously a more ideal situation. Small does not necessarily mean better, as the quality of news on many local stations clearly reveals when compared to the network feeds. Experiences with such government-mandated situations as prime-time access (in which the FCC turned back a half hour each evening to affiliated stations) show that such interference may worsen matters, as it has done in the case of prime-time access.

The government aborted, rather than increased, informational flow by its prime-time access rule, for the stations did not use the time for news or cultural programming. They sold syndicated reruns at a handsome profit. Nor does a federal anti-trust action, unless there is clearly demonstrated monopoly and restraint involved, increase the diversity—or quality—of sources of information. And one of the major goals of government is to ascertain that information flows to the public through the media and that there are multiple and pluralistic sources of news. As diversity and pluralism increase, the tendency toward concentration decreases. And over the next decade, with the development of cable and satellites, information sources inevitably will increase. Cable will supply a number of informational channels. Public television, if it is ever funded properly, has a vast and untapped potential for expanded news service to the viewers. These developments will increase the opportunity for greater informational flow from the government simply because there will be more media outlets available to process material from the branches and agencies.

The most crucial problems faced by both the bureaucracy and the media, however, are not those of either technology or control. Since the trauma of Watergate, they are problems of credibility. The public, paradoxically, has not reacted to investigative journalism with greater credence in the media. If the government has faced a credibility gap with both press and public, the media have also had a similar problem with their readers and viewers. The pressures from special interest groups, particularly in the broadcast areas, have eroded public confidence. In print, there is skepticism, perhaps healthy, that it is simply impossible to discover and disseminate "all the news that's fit to print." And there are questions raised as to who determines what is "fit"—the media, the courts or the public. Responsible journalism is a normative process, involving a constant weighing of alternatives and value judgments. That is why a healthy skepticism is necessary to the media's liaison with the government. The bureaucracy cannot resist the need to manipulate information in a way that will reflect favorably on its reputation and credibility. But the press has the responsibility of deciding whether the information offered constitutes legitimate news and whether the public interest is served by printing it.

News Councils

The development of local and national press councils in this country evolved primarily from a feeling of frustration about such questions as access, responsibility and control. In the past decade, the media have come under increasing criticism from both government and public interest organizations. The media now have a credibility gap of their own. The major problems stem from the difficulty in finding a way to ascertain that print, radio and television function responsibly *without* the superimposition of federal controls, which would be unconstitutional and alien to this country's tradition of a free press. Responsible behavior cannot be developed by government authority or by congressional legislation. It must be imposed from within. Yet, the social responsibility theory of the press is under intense challenge.

One method of determining ethical standards is that of the press council. Media "ombudsmen" organizations have worked successfully in several countries abroad, and there have been viable local councils in this country, notably in such states as Minnesota and Hawaii. The best known of the national press councils is that of the British Press Council, established in 1953. Other countries which have organizations to monitor press performance are Norway, Sweden and Denmark, as well as West Germany, Austria and the Netherlands. In Canada, councils operate in the Provinces of Ontario and Quebec.

It was in part the success of these organizations that suggested the establishment of a national council—which eventually became known as the National News Council—in August of 1973. Two years earlier, The Twentieth Century Fund had set up a task force to examine the possibility of establishing press councils in this country. The recommendation was positive and resulted in the National News Council, a national public interest body. The council was not to interfere with the function of the press but would simply rely "on publicity to lend force to its findings." The National News Council noted the pervasive atmosphere of disenchantment with much of the media's performance, as with other institutions. It determined that an independent and national organization, unencumbered by interference from government, could hear complaints about media performance and also examine issues concerning a free press. Its function would be to hear such complaints on fairness and accuracy in reporting the news, and it would be concerned in its investigations with "national suppliers of news—the major wire services, the largest 'supplemental' news services, the national weekly news magazines, national newspaper syndicates, national daily newspapers and the nationwide broadcasting networks." The council would be the only independent organization to which citizens could bring complaints.

Significantly, although the National News Council was established and has been operating for five years, the idea of such an organization did not elicit enthusiastic support from the newspaper publishers, and one paper, *The New York Times,* expressed its opposition to the council. Yet, there was agreement among many media observers that independent grievance machinery was necessary and perhaps long overdue, particularly in the climate of "gag" rules, subpoenas of reporters, demands for outtakes and other restrictive measures. Publishers themselves were concerned by public disaffection with the press. Katherine Graham, president of the Washington Post Company, noted that "the American people do not seem at all happy with their press," and *The Washington Post* had installed its own "ombudsman" to check for fairness and balance in the coverage of news by that newspaper.

The idea for a press council was not new. Such an organization had been suggested by the Commission on Freedom of the Press in 1946, but the publishers generally did not respond favorably to the Commission's proposals in the report, "A Free and Responsible Press." Various professional journalism associations had also suggested a press council, particularly a distinguished journalist, Norman E. Isaacs. After discussion and debate, the National News Council was activated as a nonprofit public interest organization, comprised of 18 members and a relatively modest full-time staff. The council's prerogatives are restricted by certain prohibitions. It has no regulatory or judicial authority. Its lever is publicity. It is funded primarily by foundations. And it receives complaints on inaccuracy and unfairness in the news from both private individuals and organizations. The complaint procedure is simple, requiring a letter to the council, with "supporting information," such as a copy of the news report and publication that is the subject of the complaint or, in the case of broadcasting, the name of the station or network and relevant information on the time and date of the broadcast.

If the National News Council has not had a spectacular success, it has undoubtedly served a most useful purpose. Its decisions have generally been welcomed by critics and it has gained a reputation for independence, fairness and high ethical standards. Of the numerous cases it has investigated, either by request or as part of its own mandate, few are more interesting or illuminating than its attempt to verify charges against the three commercial television networks made by President Nixon at a news conference in October, 1973. Mr. Nixon stated: "I have never heard or seen such outrageous, vicious, distorted reporting in 27 years in public life."

The council decided to review these charges and asked the President to offer specific examples to substantiate his criticism. Although the network news heads agreed to cooperate with the council, the White House was less eager. Wires and other forms of communication were ignored or tabled. Ron Ziegler, the Press Secretary, finally met with representatives of the council but refused to supply a list of the

President's charges, stating that he did not think it would be appropriate for the White House to cooperate. The council finally issued a report, noting that it had been unable over a period of three months to get the White House to substantiate President Nixon's charges and deplored the fact that the President's criticism remained "unsupported by specific details that could then be evaluated objectively by an impartial body." Subsequently, of course, the impeachment hearings took place, and Mr. Nixon resigned from office.

The National News Council's Rules of Procedure, as amended in 1976, include the following:

Rule 1

The National News Council, Inc., is concerned primarily with the freedom, fairness and accuracy of news reporting by the national print and electronic news organizations, namely, the nationwide wire services as well as supplemental wire services, syndicates, the national news magazines, broadcast networks and newspapers significantly national in character. The Council will, however, concern itself with the freedom, fairness, and accuracy of news reporting in all media, whether national or local in initial circulation, if the matter in question is of national significance as news or for journalism and the Council has available to it the necessary resources. The Council concerns itself with editorial comment only insofar as allegations of fact are in dispute.

Credibility

The phrase "credibility gap," which has become part of the language of mass communications, was coined originally to indicate that government officials had attempted to mislead the public by manipulating the mass media. In recent years, the media have had to respond to charges that they, too, face credibility problems. Voices from the political "left" and the "right" score the press for biased news, for omitting data which is crucial and relevant to public understanding, for failing to present a balanced account. Such charges have been made by media critics such as Edith Efron in her study of "news twisters," while others claim that the newspapers and particularly the television medium have failed to give an honest and accurate account of America's defense situation.

Government credibility, however, tends to be far more pervasive than allegations of irresponsibility on the part of the media. Most studies reveal that in general, the majority of viewers and readers place considerable credibility on media performance and, indeed, find television news highly accurate and believable. But the public cynicism about the federal bureaucracy has not diminished; it is, in fact, buttressed by a healthy skepticism on the part of the media. The encounters between government and press inevitably result in a jockeying for position, an occasional trade-off or *quid pro quo* and, more rarely, a strong adversarial controversy. But out of these encounters and occasional antagonisms there develops a two-way communication unique between any government and its media system. The press is aware of the efforts of the bureaucracy to manipulate and control the news, and the media, however uncomfortably, also recognize the effort of the federal bureaucracy to influence and direct the news flow. Thus, some gap in credibility is inevitable. The media expect managed news, and seasoned correspondents must learn to deal with it and go beyond it in order to insure a full and accurate report. The media are also aware of the ability of the government to withhold information or simply to refuse to comment.

For their part, the media, however scrupulous they may be, cannot convey objective and unadulterated information. The very processing of the news includes a degree of subjectivity. The press, for example, influences what the public receives by what it elects to print and by what it omits, by investigative reporting, by personal influence, by editorial policy and by interpretative reporting and news analysis. Information received by the public, as Lippmann wisely noted, may be news, but it may not necessarily be truthful. The Nixon Administration baldly lied to the people, in print and on the air, but it made news. An overt act by government may be newsworthy. It may not be "truth-worthy." Credibility consists in convincing the public that every effort has been made by both government and media to assure that information is not manipulated and that the flow of news is free and unencumbered. But accountability is quite another matter. How can there be assurance that the federal bureaucracy is accountable to the press and that the press is accountable to the public? Congress can legislate a Freedom of Information Act, but it may not always work successfully. And legislation on press accountability by the Congress would not be acceptable in a free society. Critics see a need for more intensive research on the gatekeeping functions of the media and on the intricate and often ambivalent liaison between media and government. Despite investigative reporting, for example, are the media too docile a conduit for the federal information machinery?

Criticism

When he served as Vice-President, the late Hubert H. Humphrey was supposed to have remarked: "I sometimes worry that the information media control the government." This was one of many criticisms leveled at media performance: that government tended to respond to media pressures and that, in this way, there was an inevitable loss of independence. But it might also be said that, conversely, the government controls the media by the very fact that it is an informational source that can withhold as well as release news. In any event, both the bureaucracy and the media have been the subject of critical scrutiny. The government has been accused, among other things, of certain derelictions.

1. The bureaucracy attempts to manipulate and manage the news, instead of giving the media and the public a direct and honest account.
2. Government officials have been known to indulge in misleading information and downright falsehoods to the media.
3. The government has not hesitated to raise the sword of Damocles of controls.
4. Too many federal public information officials proffer a story on a personal friendship basis.
5. Too many officials avoid reporter's questions by falling back on "no comment."
6. Government information officials fabricate pseudo-events in order to try to make news.
7. Top officials in the agencies play favorites among the press, to the embarrassment of many fine reporters.

The media have also received their share of criticism.

1. Too many reporters are apathetic and accept government press handouts uncritically.
2. There has also been an over-zealous emphasis on investigative reporting, even when there is little to investigate.
3. Some reporters tend to "showboat" when asking questions at televised press conferences.
4. Too many correspondents come to conferences inadequately prepared.
5. Reporters, particularly at White House press conferences, ask easy and innocuous questions and avoid crucial issues.
6. Some correspondents agree too readily to *quid pro quo* arrangements with government information officials.
7. Some reporters, conversely, tend to exacerbate the adversarial relationship with the government officials.

A critical factor for both government and media is the number and disposition of personnel. The media, in most instances, simply do not have the correspondents necessary to cover adequately the vast government bureaucracy. Excellent though their services may be, there is too great a reliance by the majority of newspapers on the Associated Press and the United Press International. Neither association has a staff large enough to be everywhere in the complicated maze of Washington politics. Some of this country's largest newspapers have either no bureau in Washington or a woefully understaffed one. The government, on the other hand, has no dearth of publicists. In addition to press personnel, most agencies have publication units, film sections, audio-visual staffs and other varied information personnel. The film operation in the agencies is illuminating, both for cost and for what is produced. Almost every agency has a film program, ranging from material that would be useless under any circumstances to a few good core films that have informational and educational value. Estimates vary, but appraisals by independent observers indicate that the government produces more than two thousand films a year at a cost estimated to be about a half billion dollars. There appears to be no accurate record on the use of these films, which include such exotic subjects as storing apples and climbing poles!

Such make-work projects undoubtedly contribute to credibility problems and to disenchantment with the information establishment. A plethora of motion pictures and publications of dubious value and an overemphasis on "image" over reality also contribute to critical attitudes toward the government by both the media and the public. When the press rejects these obvious public relations ploys by the establishment, the adversary relationship is acute. When reporters accept information handouts placidly, the bureaucracy obviously is relieved of critical pressure. Appraisal of government-issued data should conform to certain specific journalistic parameters. Is it newsworthy? Is it accurate and truthful? Upon analysis, is it legitimate information or self-serving propaganda? The political figure and his press aides constantly probe to determine how amenable and how malleable the press is to managed news. But the well-trained and ethical information source knows that a reputation for integrity with the media must be earned and, once achieved, is of enormous value.

For their part, the media invariably subscribe to the peoples "right to know" concept and, in their relations with the government, insist that a free and responsible press is essential to a democratic, pluralistic society. But each reporter and each medium places various interpretations and values on these concepts. Correspondents view their functions differently. Most reporters see themselves as agents of news and information. Some stress the investigative side of journalism. Others function primarily as news analysts and interpreters, particularly the elite columnists. And a few, unfortunately, cannot avoid seeing themselves as structuralistsdevisers of political policy in conjunction with government. Clearly this attitude warrants criticism. Reporters, if they are to function as surrogates, should not participate in the formulation of legislative or executive policy. Nor should the "new" journalism—the expression of strongly felt opinion—have any place in the media, except in the context of the editorial page.

Correspondents generally are an independent breed. Yet, critics of the Washington press corps deplore the tendency of too many journalists to follow a kind of supine two-step flow process. This entails either a slavish reliance on wire copy or a tendency to follow the lead of a select group of reliable reporters and syndicated columnists and to rewrite their story with minor variations.

With the arrival of the electronic media, the character and style of reporting has changed, but there is still a fetish about "scoops," exclusives, news "leaks" and a race for deadlines. Speed may yet be the undoing of both the press services and radio and television. The urgent push to rush into print or on the air does not encourage careful or reliable reporting in any medium.

Too many of the media correspondents also have an unfortunate predilection on occasion for unwitting "cooperation" with the agency they are assigned to cover. A good news source and a long-standing friendship should not stand in the way of a good story, but frequently they do just that. Thus, while some reporters pursue their adversarial role too strenuously, others are timid about jeopardizing their ongoing contacts with the bureaucracy. The correspondents, particularly in the case of the White House, too rarely ask the tough questions that need to be posed. At a meeting of the Radio and Television News Directors Association, for example, local television station news directors were accused of asking President Nixon "soft" questions at a time when Mr. Nixon's own credibility was a serious public issue. But Senator Patrick Moynihan (D. N.Y.) has also accused reporters of trying to resurrect the old muckraking attitudes that prevailed in the work of Lincoln Steffens and Upton Sinclair. Still other critics, many of them in the media, lament the emphasis in stories and pictures about Amy Carter's tree house, when this admittedly human interest touch could have been eliminated in favor of hard and essential news on problems besetting the economy, the environment or the system of health care. Finally, journalism is criticized for emphasizing entertainment at the expense of news, a process based on the conviction of many editors—particularly local television news directors—that the public thrives on entertainment.

For each criticism leveled at the media, there is always an antithetical viewpoint, often offered in rebuttal by media representatives. It is true that the press is in a curious position, damned by some for what it does and damned by others for what it fails to do. Edith Efron and Patrick Buchanan have scored the media for taking an anti-administration, ultra "liberal" stance in its coverage of the Vietnam conflict. Yet, an equally perceptive journalist, Jules Witcover, claimed that the press, in particular, had failed dismally to give adequate coverage of Vietnam by neglecting to print criticism of this country's involvement and by benign acceptance of government handouts.

Perhaps the most vigorous and trenchant critiques of media performance have been leveled at the conduct of the President's press conference. There are reporters themselves who doubt that the conference contributes to public information or public policy. Since most conferences are televised, the format and timing are necessarily structured. Many reporters arrive ill-prepared and ready to ad lib questions or they rely on the questions posed by others. The press conference is roughly the American analogy of the British Parliament system, except that the President, unlike the Prime Minister, is not often on the defensive and does not often feel a burning need to defend his acts. The President, of course, is dependent on the media, yet he is also in a position of institutional control. Since Watergate, there has been a greater thrust toward hard questions, but critics feel that the press still fails to come to grips with basic issues. Some find the reason for this failure in the persistence of a spirit of "Imperial Presidency," an overruling sense of awe of the Presidential Office. But whatever the reasons, the President's press conferences do not make news because of pertinent questions from the reporters. The President himself makes news by his announcements.

Recommendations: The Media

The media have a responsibility, under a free press system, to provide relevant information to the public. In this respect, because their information often results in consensus and action, the media are molders of public opinion and, to a great extent, of public policy. Because they function under the widely accepted social responsibility theory, newspapers, magazines, radio and television have an awesome responsibility to be certain that the public receives honest, capable, ethical reporting. Only the mass media can report the activities of government intelligently and with a healthy skepticism. In this way, the media are instruments of surveillance of the political environment.

The major problem faced repeatedly by those who appraise media performance is how to determine that the press is functioning responsibly without government control. What instrumentality is there, other than self-analysis, to assure a free and responsible press? The federal courts, often seen as a way of mandating access, do not provide an adequate answer under this country's system of government. Television is the one regulated medium, and the FCC clearly has not influenced program content. Nor should it do so. The media performance in general can now be scrutinized by the National News Council, but the cooperation is voluntary and not binding. Some have urged an annual appraisal and report by a quasi-official and independent agency, but the question arises whether this method would be feasible under this country's communications system. An annual report on media performance would be valuable if an independent agency could be established free of institutional controls. Certainly, some form of surveillance should not be rejected, but it is doubtful whether the necessary cooperation would be forthcoming from either government or media. Ideally, the media should be as accountable to the public as any other institution. But the press is not licensed and bears no official line of responsibility, except to the people. The media insist on indigenous responsibility, on the guarantee that what is conveyed will be exactly as it purports to be. There is, however, no guarantee that this ideal situation is inviolate, and there is no general apparatus for an assessment of media performance.

Apart from media behavior, the question of government news management and control still looms as significant. The federal information establishment is as intrusive on the news process as the media will permit it to be. Here again, an independent agency could appraise the degree and nature of government–media cooperation in the public interest. Unfortunately, no organization—neither the National News Council nor any other—has any judicial authority, except the weapon of publicity. To many critics, that is not a sufficient lever unless the findings are followed up by legal action. A public interest organization is only as important as its findings are respected and its recommendations followed.

What steps can the media take to improve performance? The elite columnists can be less elite and more responsive to public needs. Investigative reporting can be less destructive and less eager for explosive "scoops." There could be less dependence on wire copy and on peer group reporting. There could be established an "ombudsman" on various newspapers to advise management on the integrity of news flow. The media—print and electronic—could be more scrupulous in correcting and retracting mistakes. The media, perhaps paradoxically, could be less truculently adversarial in relation to government and, at the same time, less of a willing conduit for managed news. And the media could remind itself consistently that they serve no interest but that of the public.

The government, in performing its responsibilities, can be somewhat more dedicated to giving the media a straightforward and truthful account of the day's political intelligence. There could be a diminution of competition among agencies. A greater effort could be made to provide information instead of self-serving propaganda. Press officers could be more honestly responsive to the needs of the media. And all government officials might recognize that they have a clear obligation to be available to the media as part of their obligation to serve the public.

It would not be amiss for the Congress to undertake a thorough study of the entire information establishment in all agencies and branches, including its own. If Senator Scott's figures are correct, the number of government publicists and the budget for public information would certainly seem to be excessive. Only a careful and independent appraisal would reveal areas of duplication, unnecessary and wasteful programs and the existence of "make-work" units that do not perform a useful information function, either to the media or to the public.

The public also has both obligations and opportunities. A people can only be assured of a free press system if they respect and demand such a system. Resistance to manipulation and control must come from the public as well as from the media, for the First Amendment was framed to protect both. The "public" is, of course, not a monolith. There are many discrete publics, with varying interests. This diversity is the essence of a political democracy and of a pluralistic society. But it is becoming clear that reliance on the two-step flow, while necessary and important, is not sufficient. Communications influentials and public interest organizations also tend to gravitate toward the proliferation of special and parochial interests. The public—all the people—must be concerned with both government and media performance. This is difficult to achieve, but not impossible. Too few letters and calls from the public are sent to newspapers, magazines and broadcasters. The public places too great a reliance on leaders and influentials without sufficient checks and balances. Too many organizations serve special interests rather than the public interest.

The *New York Times'* Associate Editor, Tom Wicker, quotes William T. Coleman, Jr., former Secretary of Transportation, as noting the enormous contribution of a free press to American society. Coleman properly notes that the press is "the principal source of day-to-day discipline upon office holders and administrators—in many cases the only source," as well as "a source of information and education" for the government.

Despite this recognition of the function of the press, however, there is still powerful criticism from government and special interests and, indeed, the media themselves are concerned over breaches of ethics and integrity. Various safeguards have been offered, among them some suggestions from James C. Thomson, Jr., the Nieman Foundation Curator at Harvard University. Mr. Thomson proposes "self-restraint" based on the following principles:

1. The addition of an ombudsman on newspapers, patterned after *The Washington Post.*
2. A campaign by the media to enhance public support and understanding of the role of a free press.
3. A greater opportunity for journalists to improve their educational and social experiences.
4. The establishment of local press councils to monitor media performance.

These are controversial issues, and many media executives and scholars are not certain that they will exert a salutary influence. It is utterly clear, however, that only a concerted cooperative venture by the government, the media and the public can assure and perpetuate the freedom of communication that was deemed so precious by those who devised the Constitution and the Bill of Rights. The media in the

United States, with their flaws, are one of the few mass communications systems in the world which function free of authoritarian control. Only the triad of government, media and public can assure that they remain that way.

Selected Bibliography

This is a selected bibliography, noting those studies which have particular relevance to the material discussed in this book.

Albig, William. *Modern Public Opinion*. New York: McGraw-Hill Book Co., 1956.

Alsop, Joseph, and Stewart Alsop. *The Reporter's Trade*. New York: Reynall & Co., 1958.

Aronson, James. *Deadline for the Media: Today's Challenges to Press, Radio, and TV*. Indianapolis, Ind.: Bobbs-Merrill, 1973.

Bagdikian, Ben H. *The Information Machines*. New York: Harper and Row, 1971.

Bettinghaus, E.P. *Persuasive Communication*. New York: Holt, Rinehart and Winston, 1968.

Blanchard, Robert O. *Congress and the News Media*. New York: Hastings House, 1974.

Blumer, Jay, and Denis McQuail. *Television in Politics*. Chicago: University of Chicago Press, 1969.

Bower, Robert T. *Television and the Public*. New York: Holt, Rinehart and Winston, 1973.

Carnegie Commission on Educational Television. *Public Television: A Program for Action*. New York: Bantam Books, 1967.

Cater, Douglas. *The Fourth Branch of Government*. Boston: Houghton Mifflin Co., 1959.

Chafee, Zechariah. *Government and Mass Communication,* 2 vols. Chicago: University of Chicago Press, 1947.

Commission on Freedom of the Press. *A Free and Responsible Press.* Chicago: University of Chicago Press, 1947.

Congressional Directory, 95th Congress, 1977–78. Washington D.C.: U.S. Government Printing Office.

Cross, Harold L. *The People's Right to Know.* New York: Columbia University Press, 1953.

De Fleur, Melvin L., and Otto N. Larsen. *The Flow of Information.* New York: Harper and Row, 1958.

Devol, Kenneth, ed. *Mass Media and the Supreme Court: The Legacy of the Warren Years,* rev. ed. New York: Hastings House, 1976.

Doob, Leonard. *Public Opinion and Propaganda.* Hamden, Conn.: Archon Books, 1966.

Emery, Edwin. *The Press and America: An Interpretative History of the Mass Media,* 3rd ed. Englewood Cliffs, N.J.: Prentice-Hall, 1972.

Emery, Walter B. *Broadcasting and Government,* 2nd ed. East Lansing, Mich.: Michigan State University Press, 1971.

Gerald, J. Edward. *The Social Responsibility of the Press.* Minneapolis, Minn.: University of Minnesota Press, 1963.

Gillmor, Donald M., and Jerome A. Barron. *Mass Media and the Law: Cases and Comment,* 2nd ed. St. Paul, Minn.: West Publishing Co., 1974.

Gillmor, Donald M. *Free Press and Fair Trial.* Washington D.C.: Public Affairs Press, 1966.

Government Manual, 1977–78. Washington D.C.: U.S. Government Printing Office.

Hynds, Ernest C. *American Newspapers in the 1970s.* New York: Hastings House, 1975.

Kellcy, Stanley, Jr. *Professional Public Relations and Political Power.* Baltimore, Md.: The Johns Hopkins Press, 1956.

Keogh, James. *President Nixon and the Press.* New York: Funk and Wagnalls, 1972.

Lacy, Dan. *Freedom of Communication.* Urbana, Ill.: University of Illinois Press, 1961.

Lippmann, Walter. *Public Opinion.* New York: Harcourt Brace & Company, 1922.

MacNeil, Robert. *The People Machine: The Influence of Television on American Politics.* New York: Harper and Row, 1968.

McCamy, James L. *Government Publicity.* Chicago: University of Chicago Press, 1939.

Mollenhoff, Clark R. *Washington Cover-Up.* New York: Doubleday and Co., 1962.

Nelson, Harold L. *Freedom of the Press from Hamilton to the Warren Court.* Indianapolis N.Y.: Bobbs-Merrill, 1967.

Nelson, Harold L., and Dwight L. Teeter, Jr. *Law of Mass Communications: Freedom and Control of Press and Broadcast Media,* 2nd ed. Mineola, N.Y.: Foundation Press, 1972.

Nimmo, Dan D. *Newsgathering in Washington.* New York: Atherton Press, 1962.

Pollard, James E. *The Presidents and the Press.* New York: MacMillan, 1947
———. *The Presidents and the Press: Truman to Johnson.* Washington D.C.: Public Affairs Press, 1964.

Rourke, Francis E. *Secrecy and Publicity: Dilemmas of Democracy.* Baltimore, Md.: The Johns Hopkins Press, 1961.

Rucker, Bryce W. *The First Freedom.* Carbondale, Ill.: Southern Illinois Press, 1967.

Schiller, Herbert. *The Mind Managers.* Boston: Beacon Press, 1973.

Schramm, Wilbur. *Responsibility in Mass Communication.* New York: Harper, 1957.

Servan-Screiber, Jean-Louis. *The Power to Inform: Media: The Information Business.* New York: McGraw-Hill, 1974.

Stanley, Robert H., and Charles S. Steinberg. *The Media Environment.* New York: Hastings House, 1976.

Steinberg, Charles S. *The Creation of Consent.* New York: Hastings House, 1975.

Truman, David B. *The Governmental Process.* New York: Alfred A. Knopf, 1958.

Yu, Frederick T.C. *Behavioral Sciences and the Mass Media.* New York: Russell Sage Foundation, 1968.

Appendix I

AMENDMENTS RELEVANT TO FREEDOM OF THE MEDIA

Four of the amendments to the Constitution of the United States (the first ten, known as the Bill of Rights, were ratified on December 15, 1791) are uniquely pertinent to the function of the mass media. These are the first, fifth, sixth, and fourteenth (section 1). The last was ratified on July 9, 1868. The Amendments are included here.

AMENDMENT 1.
Congress shall make no law respecting an establishment of religion, or prohibiting the free exercise thereof; or abridging the freedom of speech, or of the press; or the right of the people peaceably to assemble, and to petition the Government for a redress of grievances.

AMENDMENT 5.
No person shall be held to answer for a capital, or otherwise infamous crime, unless on a presentment or indictment of a Grand Jury, except in cases arising in the land or naval forces, or in the Militia, when in active service in time of War or public danger; nor shall any person be subject for the same offense to be twice put in jeopardy of life or limb; nor shall be compelled in any criminal case to be a witness against himself, nor be deprived of life, liberty or prop-

erty without due process of law; nor shall private property be taken for public use, without just compensation.

AMENDMENT 6.

In all criminal prosecutions, the accused shall enjoy the right to a speedy and public trial, by an impartial jury of the State and district wherein the crime shall have been committed, which district shall have been previously ascertained by law, and to be informed of the nature and cause of the accusation; to be confronted with the witnesses against him; to have compulsory process for obtaining witnesses in his favor, and to have the Assistance of Counsel for his defense.

AMENDMENT 14, SECTION 1.

All persons born or naturalized in the United States, and subject to the jurisdiction thereof, are citizens of the United States and of the State wherein they reside. No State shall make or enforce any law which shall abridge the privileges or immunities of citizens of the United States; nor shall any State deprive any person of life, liberty or property without due process of law; nor deny to any person within its jurisdiction the equal protection of the laws.

Appendix II

FREEDOM OF INFORMATION ACT

The first version of the Freedom of Information Act was enacted by the Congress in 1966. Too many exclusions, however, drew criticism of the Act, particularly from the media. In 1974, an amended version was passed by Congress over the veto of President Gerald Ford. Included here are both versions of the Freedom of Information Act.

PUBLIC INFORMATION—AGENCY RULES, ETC.

For Legislative History of Act, see p. 1196

PUBLIC LAW 90–23; 81 STAT. 54

[H. R. 5357]

An Act to amend section 552 of title 5, United States Code, to codify the provisions of Public Law 89–487.

Be it enacted by the Senate and House of Representatives of the United States of America in Congress assembled, That:

Section 552 of title 5, United States Code,[22] is amended to read:

"**§ 552. Public information; agency rules, opinions, orders, records, and proceedings**

"(a) Each agency shall make available to the public information as follows:

"(1) Each agency shall separately state and currently publish in the Federal Register for the guidance of the public—

"(A) descriptions of its central and field organization and the established places at which, the employees (and in the case of a uniformed service, the members) from whom, and the methods whereby, the public may obtain information, make submittals or requests, or obtain decisions;

"(B) statements of the general course and method by which its functions are channeled and determined, including the nature and requirements of all formal and informal procedures available;

"(C) rules of procedure, descriptions of forms available or the places at which forms may be obtained, and instructions as to the scope and contents of all papers, reports, or examinations;

"(D) substantive rules of general applicability adopted as authorized by law, and statements of general policy or interpretations of general applicability formulated and adopted by the agency; and

"(E) each amendment, revision, or repeal of the foregoing. Except to the extent that a person has actual and timely notice of the terms thereof, a person may not in any manner be required to resort to, or be adversely affected by, a matter required to be published in the Federal Register and not so published. For the purpose of this paragraph, matter reasonably available to the class of persons affected thereby is deemed published in the Federal Register when

22. 5 U.S.C.A. § 552.

incorporated by reference therein with the approval of the Director of the Federal Register.

"(2) Each agency, in accordance with published rules, shall make available for public inspection and copying—

"(A) final opinions, including concurring and dissenting opinions, as well as orders, made in the adjudication of cases;

"(B) those statements of policy and interpretations which have been adopted by the agency and are not published in the Federal Register; and

"(C) administrative staff manuals and instructions to staff that affect a member of the public;

unless the materials are promptly published and copies offered for sale. To the extent required to prevent a clearly unwarranted invasion of personal privacy, an agency may delete identifying details when it makes available or publishes an opinion, statement of policy, interpretation, or staff manual or instruction. However, in each case the justification for the deletion shall be explained fully in writing. Each agency also shall maintain and make available for public inspection and copying a current index providing identifying information for the public as to any matter issued, adopted, or promulgated after July 4, 1967, and required by this paragraph to be made available or published. A final order, opinion, statement of policy, interpretation, or staff manual or instruction that affects a member of the public may be relied on, used, or cited as precedent by an agency against a party other than an agency only if—

"(i) it has been indexed and either made available or published as provided by this paragraph; or

"(ii) the party has actual and timely notice of the terms thereof.

"(3) Except with respect to the records made available under paragraphs (1) and (2) of this subsection, each agency, on request for identifiable records made in accordance with published rules stating the time, place, fees to the extent authorized by statute, and procedure to be followed, shall make the records promptly available to any person. On complaint, the district court of the United States in the district in which the complainant resides, or has his principal place of business, or in which the agency records are situated, has jurisdiction to enjoin the agency from withholding agency records and to order the production of any agency records improperly withheld from the complainant. In such a case the court shall determine the matter de novo and the burden is on the agency to sustain its action. In the event of noncompliance with the order of the court, the district court may punish for contempt the responsible employee, and in the case of a uniformed service, the responsible member. Except as to causes the court considers of greater importance, proceedings before the district court, as authorized by this paragraph, take precedence on the docket over all other causes and shall be assigned for hearing and trial at the earliest practicable date and expedited in every way.

"(4) Each agency having more than one member shall maintain and make available for public inspection a record of the final votes of each member in every agency proceeding.

"(b) This section does not apply to matters that are—

"(1) specifically required by Executive order to be kept secret in the interest of the national defense or foreign policy;

"(2) related solely to the internal personnel rules and practices of an agency;

"(3) specifically exempted from disclosure by statute;

"(4) trade secrets and commercial or financial information obtained from a person and privileged or confidential;

"(5) inter-agency or intra-agency memorandums or letters which would not be available by law to a party other than an agency in litigation with the agency;

"(6) personnel and medical files and similar files the disclosure of which would constitute a clearly unwarranted invasion of personal privacy;

"(7) investigatory files compiled for law enforcement purposes except to the extent available by law to a party other than an agency;

"(8) contained in or related to examination, operating, or condition reports prepared by, on behalf of, or for the use of an agency responsible for the regulation or supervision of financial institutions; or

"(9) geological and geophysical information and data, including maps, concerning wells.

"(c) This section does not authorize withholding of information or limit the availability of records to the public, except as specifically stated in this section. This section is not authority to withhold information from Congress."

Sec. 2. The analysis of chapter 5 of title 5, United States Code, is amended by striking out:

"552. Publication of information, rules, opinions, orders, and public records."

and inserting in place thereof:

"552. Public information; agency rules, opinions, orders, records, and proceedings."

Sec. 3. The Act of July 4, 1966 (Public Law 89–487, 80 Stat. 250),[23] is repealed.

Sec. 4. This Act shall be effective July 4, 1967, or on the date of enactment, whichever is later.

Approved June 5, 1967.

23. 5 U.S.C.A. § 1002.

FREEDOM OF INFORMATION ACT

For Legislative History of Act, see p. 6267

PUBLIC LAW 93–502; 88 STAT. 1561

[H. R. 12471]

An Act to amend section 552 of title 5, United States Code, known as the Freedom of Information Act.

Be it enacted by the Senate and House of Representatives of the United States of America in Congress assembled, That:

(a) The fourth sentence of section 552(a)(2) of title 5, United States Code,[18] is amended to read as follows: "Each agency shall also maintain and make available for public inspection and copying current indexes providing identifying information for the public as to any matter issued, adopted, or promulgated after July 4, 1967, and required by this paragraph to be made available or published. Each agency shall promptly publish, quarterly or more frequently, and distribute (by sale or otherwise) copies of each index or supplements thereto unless it determines by order published in the Federal Register that the publication would be unnecessary and impracticable, in which case the agency shall nonetheless provide copies of such index on request at a cost not to exceed the direct cost of duplication.".

(b)(1) Section 552(a)(3) of title 5, United States Code,[19] is amended to read as follows:

"(3) Except with respect to the records made available under paragraphs (1) and (2) of this subsection, each agency, upon any request for records which (A) reasonably describes such records and (B) is made in accordance with published rules stating the time, place, fees (if any), and procedures to be followed, shall make the records promptly available to any person.".

18. 5 U.S.C.A. § 552(a)(2).
19. 5 U.S.C.A. § 552(a)(3).

(2) Section 552(a) of title 5, United States Code,[20] is amended by redesignating paragraph (4), and all references thereto, as paragraph (5) and by inserting immediately after paragraph (3) the following new paragraph:

"(4)(A) In order to carry out the provisions of this section, each agency shall promulgate regulations, pursuant to notice and receipt of public comment, specifying a uniform schedule of fees applicable to all constituent units of such agency. Such fees shall be limited to reasonable standard charges for document search and duplication and provide for recovery of only the direct costs of such search and duplication. Documents shall be furnished without charge or at a reduced charge where the agency determines that waiver or reduction of the fee is in the public interest because furnishing the information can be considered as primarily benefiting the general public.

"(B) On complaint, the district court of the United States in the district in which the complainant resides, or has his principal place of business, or in which the agency records are situated, or in the District of Columbia, has jurisdiction to enjoin the agency from withholding agency records and to order the production of any agency records improperly withheld from the complainant. In such a case the court shall determine the matter de novo, and may examine the contents of such agency records in camera to determine whether such records or any part thereof shall be withheld under any of the exemptions set forth in subsection (b) of this section, and the burden is on the agency to sustain its action.

"(C) Notwithstanding any other provision of law, the defendant shall serve an answer or otherwise plead to any complaint made under this subsection within thirty days after service upon the defendant of the pleading in which such complaint is made, unless the court otherwise directs for good cause shown.

"(D) Except as to cases the court considers of greater importance, proceedings before the district court, as authorized by this subsection, and appeals therefrom, take precedence on the docket over all cases and shall be assigned for hearing and trial or for argument at the earliest practicable date and expedited in every way.

"(E) The court may assess against the United States reasonable attorney fees and other litigation costs reasonably incurred in any case under this section in which the complainant has substantially prevailed.

"(F) Whenever the court orders the production of any agency

20. 5 U.S.C.A. § 552(a).

records improperly withheld from the complainant and assesses against the United States reasonable attorney fees and other litigation costs, and the court additionally issues a written finding that the circumstances surrounding the withholding raise questions whether agency personnel acting arbitrarily or capriciously with respect to the withholding, the Civil Service Commission shall promptly initiate a proceeding to determine whether disciplinary action is warranted against the officer or employee who was primarily responsible for the withholding. The Commission, after investigation and consideration of the evidence submitted, shall submit its findings and recommendations to the administrative authority of the agency concerned and shall send copies of the findings and recommendations to the officer or employee or his representative. The administrative authority shall take the corrective action that the Commission recommends.

"(G) In the event of noncompliance with the order of the court, the district court may punish for contempt the responsible employee. and in the case of a uniformed service, the responsible member.".

(c) Section 552(a) of title 5, United States Code,[21] is amended by adding at the end thereof the following new paragraph:

"(6)(A) Each agency, upon any request for records made under paragraph (1), (2), or (3) of this subsection, shall—

"(i) determine within ten days (excepting Saturdays, Sundays, and legal public holidays) after the receipt of any such request whether to comply with such request and shall immediately notify the person making such request of such determination and the reasons therefor, and of the right of such person to appeal to the head of the agency any adverse determination; and

"(ii) make a determination with respect to any appeal within twenty days (excepting Saturdays, Sundays, and legal public holidays) after the receipt of such appeal. If on appeal the denial of the request for records is in whole or in part upheld, the agency shall notify the person making such request of the provisions for judicial review of that determination under paragraph (4) of this subsection.

"(B) In unusual circumstances as specified in this subparagraph, the time limits prescribed in either clause (i) or clause (ii) of subparagraph (A) may be extended by written notice to the person making such request setting forth the reasons for such extension and the date on which a determination is expected to be dispatched. No such notice shall specify a date that would result in an extension for

21. 5 U.S.C.A. § 552(a).

more than ten working days. As used in this subparagraph, 'unusual circumstances' means, but only to the extent reasonably necessary to the proper processing of the particular request—

"(i) the need to search for and collect the requested records from field facilities or other establishments that are separate from the office processing the request;

"(ii) the need to search for, collect, and appropriately examine a voluminous amount of separate and distinct records which are demanded in a single request; or

"(iii) the need for consultation, which shall be conducted with all practicable speed, with another agency having a substantial interest in the determination of the request or among two or more components of the agency having substantial subject-matter interest therein.

"(C) Any person making a request to any agency for records under paragraph (1), (2), or (3) of this subsection shall be deemed to have exhausted his administrative remedies with respect to such request if the agency fails to comply with the applicable time limit provisions of this paragraph. If the Government can show exceptional circumstances exist and that the agency is exercising due diligence in responding to the request, the court may retain jurisdiction and allow the agency additional time to complete its review of the records. Upon any determination by an agency to comply with a request for records, the records shall be made promptly available to such person making such request. Any notification of denial of any request for records under this subsection shall set forth the names and titles or positions of each person responsible for the denial of such request.".

Sec. 2. (a) Section 552(b)(1) of title 5, United States Code,[22] is amended to read as follows:

"(1)(A) specifically authorized under criteria established by an Executive order to be kept secret in the interest of national defense or foreign policy and (B) are in fact properly classified pursuant to such Executive order;".

(b) Section 552(b)(7) of title 5, United States Code,[23] is amended to read as follows:

"(7) investigatory records compiled for law enforcement purposes, but only to the extent that the production of such records would (A) interfere with enforcement proceedings, (B) deprive a person of a right to a fair trial or an impartial adjudica-

22. 5 U.S.C.A. § 552(b)(1).
23. 5 U.S.C.A. § 552(b)(7).

tion, (C) constitute an unwarranted invasion of personal privacy, (D) disclose the identity of a confidential source and, in the case of a record compiled by a criminal law enforcement authority in the course of a criminal investigation, or by an agency conducting a lawful national security intelligence investigation, confidential information furnished only by the confidential source, (E) disclose investigative techniques and procedures, or (F) endanger the life or physical safety of law enforcement personnel;".

(c) Section 552(b) of title 5, United States Code,[24] is amended by adding at the end the following: "Any reasonably segregable portion of a record shall be provided to any person requesting such record after deletion of the portions which are exempt under this subsection.".

Sec. 3. Section 552 of title 5, United States Code,[25] is amended by adding at the end thereof the following new subsections:

"(d) On or before March 1 of each calendar year, each agency shall submit a report covering the preceding calendar year to the Speaker of the House of Representatives and President of the Senate for referral to the appropriate committees of the Congress. The report shall include—

"(1) the number of determinations made by such agency not to comply with requests for records made to such agency under subsection (a) and the reasons for each such determination;

"(2) the number of appeals made by persons under subsection (a)(6), the result of such appeals, and the reason for the action upon each appeal that results in a denial of information;

"(3) the names and titles or positions of each person responsible for the denial of records requested under this section, and the number of instances of participation for each;

"(4) the results of each proceeding conducted pursuant to subsection (a)(4)(F), including a report of the disciplinary action taken against the officer or employee who was primarily responsible for improperly withholding records or an explanation of why disciplinary action was not taken;

"(5) a copy of every rule made by such agency regarding this section;

"(6) a copy of the fee schedule and the total amount of fees collected by the agency for making records available under this section; and

---

24. 5 U.S.C.A. § 552(b).
25. 5 U.S.C.A. § 552.

"(7) such other information as indicates efforts to administer fully this section.

The Attorney General shall submit an annual report on or before March 1 of each calendar year which shall include for the prior calendar year a listing of the number of cases arising under this section, the exemption involved in each case, the disposition of such case, and the cost, fees, and penalties assessed under subsections (a)(4)(E), (F), and (G). Such report shall also include a description of the efforts undertaken by the Department of Justice to encourage agency compliance with this section.

"(e) For purposes of this section, the term 'agency' as defined in section 551(1) of this title includes any executive department, military department, Government corporation, Government controlled corporation, or other establishment in the executive branch of the Government (including the Executive Office of the President), or any independent regulatory agency.".

Sec. 4. The amendments made by this Act shall take effect on the ninetieth day beginning after the date of enactment of this Act.

Approved Nov. 21, 1974.

Appendix III

PRIVACY ACT

This Act became a public law, as enacted by Congress, in December, 1974. Its primary purpose was to protect the privacy of the individual from intrusion by the use of new technologies of information storage and retrieval, and to provide individuals with pertinent information concerning personal records and data about them.

Privacy Act of 1974 (88 Stat. 1896; 5 U.S.C. 552a note) Public Law 93–579, December 31, 1974.

An Act

To amend title 5, United States Code, by adding a section 552a to safeguard individual privacy from the misuse of Federal records, to provide that individuals be granted access to records concerning them which are maintained by Federal agencies, to establish a Privacy Protection Study Commission, and for other purposes.

Be it enacted by the Senate and House of Representatives of the United States of America in Congress assembled, That this Act may be cited as the "Privacy Act of 1974".

Sec. 2. (a) The Congress finds that—

(1) the privacy of an individual is directly affected by the collection, maintenance, use, and dissemination of personal information by Federal agencies;

(2) the increasing use of computers and sophisticated information technology, while essential to the efficient operations of the Government, has greatly magnified the harm to individual privacy that can occur from any collection, maintenance, use, or dissemination of personal information;

(3) the opportunities for an individual to secure employment, insurance, and credit, and his right to due process, and other legal protections are endangered by the misuse of certain information systems;

(4) the right to privacy is a personal and fundamental right protected by the Constitution of the United States; and

(5) in order to protect the privacy of individuals identified in information systems maintained by Federal agencies, it is necessary and proper for the Congress to regulate the collection, maintenance, use, and dissemination of information by such agencies.

(b) The purpose of this Act is to provide certain safeguards for an individual against an invasion of personal privacy by requiring Federal agencies, except as otherwise provided by law, to—

(1) permit an individual to determine what records pertaining to him are collected, maintained, used, or disseminated by such agencies;

(2) permit an individual to prevent records pertaining to him obtained by such agencies for a particular purpose from being used or made available for another purpose without his consent;

(3) permit an individual to gain access to information pertaining to him in Federal agency records, to have a copy made of all or any portion thereof, and to correct or amend such records;

(4) collect, maintain, use, or disseminate any record of identifiable personal information in a manner that assures that such action is for a necessary and lawful purpose, that the information is current and accurate for its intended use, and that adequate safeguards are provided to prevent misuse of such information;

(5) permit exemptions from the requirements with respect to records provided in this Act only in those cases where there is an important public

policy need for such exemption as has been determined by specific statutory authority; and

(6) be subject to civil suit for any damages which occur as a result of willful or intentional action which violates any individual's rights under this Act.

Sec. 3. Title 5. United States Code, is amended by adding after section 552 the following new section:

"§ 552a. Records maintained on individuals

"(a) Definitions.—For purposes of this section—

"(1) the term 'agency' means agency as defined in section 552(e) of this title;

"(2) the term 'individual' means a citizen of the United States or an alien lawfully admitted for permanent residence;

"(3) the term 'maintain' includes maintain, collect, use, or disseminate;

"(4) the term 'record' means any item, collection, or grouping of information about an individual that is maintained by an agency, including, but not limited to, his education, financial transactions, medical history, and criminal or employment history and that contains his name, or the identifying number, symbol, or other identifying particular assigned to the individual, such as a finger or voice print or a photograph;

"(5) the term 'system of records' means a group of any records under the control of any agency from which information is retrieved by the name of the individual or by some identifying number, symbol, or other identifying particular assigned to the individual;

"(6) the term 'statistical record' means a record in a system of records maintained for statistical research or reporting purposes only and not used in whole or in part in making any determination about an identifiable individual, except as provided by section 8 of title 13; and

"(7) the term 'routine use' means, with respect to the disclosure of a record, the use of such record for a purpose which is compatible with the purpose for which it was collected.

"(b) Conditions of Disclosure.—No agency shall disclose any record which is contained in a system of records by any means of communication to any person, or to another agency, except pursuant to a written request by, or with the prior written consent of, the individual to whom the record pertains, unless disclosure of the record would be—

"(1) to those officers and employees of the agency which maintains the record who have a need for the record in the performance of their duties;

"(2) required under section 552 of this title;

"(3) for a routine use as defined in subsection (a)(7) of this section and described under subsection (e)(4)(D) of this section;

"(4) to the Bureau of the Census for purposes of planning or carrying out a census or survey or related activity pursuant to the provisions of title 13;

"(5) to a recipient who has provided the agency with advance adequate written assurance that the record will be used solely as a statistical research or reporting record, and the record is to be transferred in a form that is not individually identifiable;

"(6) to the National Archives of the United States as a record which has sufficient historical or other value to warrant its continued preservation by the United States Government, or for evaluation by the Administrator of General Services or his designee to determine whether the record has such value;

"(7) to another agency or to an instrumentality of any governmental jurisdiction within or under the control of the United States for a civil or criminal law enforcement activity if the activity is authorized by law, and if the head of the agency or instrumentality has made a written request to the agency which maintains the record specifying the particular portion desired and the law enforcement activity for which the record is sought;

"(8) to a person pursuant to a showing of compelling circumstances affecting the health or safety of an individual if upon such disclosure notification is transmitted to the last known address of such individual;

"(9) to either House of Congress, or, to the extent of matter within its jurisdiction, any committee or subcommittee thereof, any joint committee of Congress or subcommittee of any such joint committee;

"(10) to the Comptroller General, or any of his authorized representatives, in the course of the performance of the duties of the General Accounting Office; or

"(11) pursuant to the order of a court of competent jurisdiction.

"(c) ACCOUNTING OF CERTAIN DISCLOSURES.—Each agency, with respect to each system of records under its control, shall—

"(1) except for disclosures made under subsections (b)(1) or (b)(2) of this section, keep an accurate accounting of—

"(A) the date, nature, and purpose of each disclosure of a record to any person or to another agency made under subsection (b) of this section; and

"(B) the name and address of the person or agency to whom the disclosure is made;

"(2) retain the accounting made under paragraph (1) of this subsection for at least five years or the life of the record, whichever is longer, after the disclosure for which the accounting is made;

"(3) except for disclosures made under subsection (b)(7) of this section, make the accounting made under paragraph (1) of this subsection available to the individual named in the record at his request; and

"(4) inform any person or other agency about any correction or notation of dispute made by the agency in accordance with subsection (d) of this section of any record that has been disclosed to the person or agency if an accounting of the disclosure was made.

"(d) ACCESS TO RECORDS.—Each agency that maintains a system of records shall—

"(1) upon request by any individual to gain access to his record or to any information pertaining to him which is contained in the system, permit him and upon his request, a person of his own choosing to accompany him, to review the record and have a copy made of all or any portion thereof in a form comprehensible to him, except that the agency may require the individual to furnish a written statement authorizing discussion of that individual's record in the accompanying person's presence;

"(2) permit the individual to request amendment of a record pertaining to him and—

"(A) not later than 10 days (excluding Saturdays, Sundays, and legal public holidays) after the date of receipt of such request, acknowledge in writing such receipt; and

"(B) promptly, either—

"(i) make any correction of any portion thereof which the individual believes is not accurate, relevant, timely, or complete; or

"(ii) inform the individual of its refusal to amend the record in accordance with his request, the reason for the refusal, the procedures established by the agency for the individual to request a review of that refusal by the head of the agency or an officer designated by the head of the agency, and the name and business address of that official;

"(3) permit the individual who disagrees with the refusal of the agency to amend his record to request a review of such refusal, and not later than 30 days (excluding Saturdays, Sundays, and legal public holidays) from the date on which the individual requests such review, complete such review and make a final determination unless, for good cause shown, the head of the agency extends such 30-day period; and if, after his review, the reviewing official also refuses to amend the record in accordance with the request, permit the individual to file with the agency a concise statement setting forth the reasons for his disagreement with the refusal of the agency, and notify the individual of the provisions for judicial review of the reviewing official's determination under subsection (g)(1)(A) of this section;

"(4) in any disclosure, containing information about which the individual has filed a statement of disagreement, occurring after the filing of the statement under paragraph (3) of this subsection, clearly note any portion of the record which is disputed and provide copies of the statement and, if the agency deems it appropriate, copies of a concise statement of the reasons of the agency for not making the amendments requested, to persons or other agencies to whom the disputed record has been disclosed; and

"(5) nothing in this section shall allow an individual access to any information compiled in reasonable anticipation of a civil action or proceeding.

"(e) AGENCY REQUIREMENTS.—Each agency that maintains a system of records shall—

"(1) maintain in its records only such information about an individual as is relevant and necessary to accomplish a purpose of the agency required to be accomplished by statute or by executive order of the President;

"(2) collect information to the greatest extent practicable directly from the subject individual when the information may result in adverse determinations about an individual's rights, benefits, and privileges under Federal programs;

"(3) inform each individual whom it asks to supply information, on the form which it uses to collect the information or on a separate form that can be retained by the individual—

"(A) the authority (whether granted by statute, or by executive order of the President) which authorizes the solicitation of the information and whether disclosure of such information is mandatory or voluntary;

"(B) the principal purpose or purposes for which the information is intended to be used;

"(C) the routine uses which may be made of the information, as published pursuant to paragraph (4)(D) of this subsection; and

"(D) the effects on him, if any, of not providing all or any part of the requested information;

"(4) subject to the provisions of paragraph (11) of this subsection, publish in the Federal Register at least annually a notice of the existence and character of the system of records, which notice shall include—

"(A) the name and location of the system;

"(B) the categories of individuals on whom records are maintained in the system;

"(C) the categories of records maintained in the system;

"(D) each routine use of the records contained in the system, including the categories of users and the purpose of such use;

"(E) the policies and practices of the agency regarding storage, retrievability, access controls, retention, and disposal of the records;

"(F) the title and business address of the agency official who is responsible for the system of records;

"(G) the agency procedures whereby an individual can be notified at his request if the system of records contains a record pertaining to him;

"(H) the agency procedures whereby an individual can be notified at his request how he can gain access to any record pertaining to him contained in the system of records, and how he can contest its content; and

"(I) the categories of sources of records in the system;

"(5) maintain all records which are used by the agency in making any determination about any individual with such accuracy, relevance, timeliness, and completeness as is reasonably necessary to assure fairness to the individual in the determination;

"(6) prior to disseminating any record about an individual to any person other than an agency, unless the dissemination is made pursuant to subsection (b) (2) of this section, make reasonable efforts to assure that such records are accurate, complete, timely, and relevant for agency purposes;

"(7) maintain no record describing how any individual exercises rights guaranteed by the First Amendment unless expressly authorized by statute or by the individual about whom the record is maintained or unless pertinent to and within the scope of an authorized law enforcement activity;

"(8) make reasonable efforts to serve notice on an individual when any record on such individual is made available to any person under compulsory legal process when such process becomes a matter of public record;

"(9) establish rules of conduct for persons involved in the design, development, operation, or maintenance of any system of records, or in maintaining any record, and instruct each such person with respect to such rules and the requirements of this section, including any other rules and procedures adopted pursuant to this section and the penalties for noncompliance;

"(10) establish appropriate administrative, technical, and physical safeguards to insure the security and confidentiality of records and to protect against any anticipated threats or hazards to their security or integrity which could result in substantial harm, embarrassment, inconvenience, or unfairness to any individual on whom information is maintained; and

"(11) at least 30 days prior to publication of information under paragraph (4)(D) of this subsection, publish in the Federal Register notice of any new use or intended use of the information in the system, and provide an opportunity for interested persons to submit written data, views, or arguments to the agency.

"(f) AGENCY RULES.—In order to carry out the provisions of this section, each agency that maintains a system of records shall promulgate rules, in accordance with the requirements (including general notice) of section 553 of this title, which shall—

"(1) establish procedures whereby an individual can be notified in response to his request if any system of records named by the individual contains a record pertaining to him;

"(2) define reasonable times, places, and requirements for identifying an individual who requests his record or information pertaining to him before the agency shall make the record or information available to the individual;

"(3) establish procedures for the disclosure to an individual upon his request of his record or information pertaining to him, including special procedure, if deemed necessary, for the disclosure to an individual of medical records, including psychological records, pertaining to him;

"(4) establish procedures for reviewing a request from an individual concerning the amendment of any record or information pertaining to the individual, for making a determination on the request, for an appeal within the agency of an initial adverse agency determination, and for whatever additional means may be necessary for each individual to be able to exercise fully his rights under this section; and

"(5) establish fees to be charged, if any, to any individual for making copies of his record, excluding the cost of any search for and review of the record.

The Office of the Federal Register shall annually compile and publish the rules promulgated under this subsection and agency notices published under subsection (e)(4) of this section in a form available to the public at low cost.

"(g)(1) CIVIL REMEDIES.—Whenever any agency

"(A) makes a determination under subsection (d)(3) of this section not to amend an individual's record in accordance with his request, or fails to make such review in conformity with that subsection;

"(B) refuses to comply with an individual request under subsection (d)(1) of this section;

"(C) fails to maintain any record concerning any individual with such accuracy, relevance, timeliness, and completeness as is necessary to assure fairness in any determination relating to the qualifications, character, rights, or opportunities of, or benefits to the individual that may be made on the basis of such record, and consequently a determination is made which is adverse to the individual; or

"(D) fails to comply with any other provision of this section, or any rule promulgated thereunder, in such a way as to have an adverse effect on an individual,

the individual may bring a civil action against the agency, and the district courts of the United States shall have jurisdiction in the matters under the provisions of this subsection.

"(2)(A) In any suit brought under the provisions of subsection (g)(1)(A) of this section, the court may order the agency to amend the individual's record in accordance with his request or in such other way as the court may direct. In such a case the court shall determine the matter de novo.

"(B) The court may assess against the United States reasonable attorney fees and other litigation costs reasonably incurred in any case under this paragraph in which the complainant has substantially prevailed.

"(3)(A) In any suit brought under the provisions of subsection (g)(1)(B) of this section, the court may enjoin the agency from withholding the records and order the production to the complainant of any agency records improperly withheld from him. In such a case the court shall determine the matter de novo, and may examine the contents of any agency records in camera to determine whether the records or any portion thereof may be withheld under any of the exemptions set forth in subsection (k) of this section, and the burden is on the agency to sustain its action.

"(B) The court may assess against the United States reasonable attorney fees and other litigation costs reasonably incurred in any case under this paragraph in which the complainant has substantially prevailed.

"(4) In any suit brought under the provisions of subsection (g)(1)(C) or (D) of this section in which the court determines that the agency acted in a manner which was intentional or willful, the United States shall be liable to the individual in an amount equal to the sum of—

"(A) actual damages sustained by the individual as a result of the refusal or failure, but in no case shall a person entitled to recovery receive less than the sum of $1,000; and

"(B) the costs of the action together with reasonable attorney fees as determined by the court.

"(5) An action to enforce any liability created under this section may be brought in the district court of the United States in the district in which the complainant resides, or has his principal place of business, or in which the agency records are situated, or in the District of Columbia, without regard to the amount in controversy, within two years from the date on which the cause of action arises, except that where an agency has materially and willfully misrepresented any information required under this section to be disclosed to an individual and the information so misrepresented is material to establishment of the liability of the agency to the individual under this section, the action may be brought at any time within two years after discovery by the individual of the misrepresentation. Nothing in this section shall be construed to authorize any civil action by reason of any injury sustained as the result of a disclosure of a record prior to the effective date of this section.

"(h) RIGHTS OF LEGAL GUARDIANS.—For the purposes of this section, the parent of any minor, or the legal guardian of any individual who has been declared to be incompetent due to physical or mental incapacity or age by a court of competent jurisdiction, may act on behalf of the individual.

"(i)(1) CRIMINAL PENALTIES.—Any officer or employee of an agency, who by virtue of his employment or official position, has possession of, or access to, agency records which contain individually identifiable information the disclosure of which is prohibited by this section or by rules or regulations established thereunder, and who knowing that disclosure of the specific material is so prohibited, willfully discloses the material in any manner to any person or agency not entitled to receive it, shall be guilty of a misdemeanor and fined not more than $5,000.

"(2) Any officer or employee of any agency who willfully maintains a system of records without meeting the notice requirements of subsection (e)(4) of this section shall be guilty of a misdemeanor and fined not more than $5,000.

"(3) Any person who knowingly and willfully requests or obtains any record concerning an individual from an agency under false pretenses shall be guilty of a misdemeanor and fined not more than $5,000.

"(j) GENERAL EXEMPTIONS.—The head of any agency may promulgate rules, in accordance with the requirements (including general notice) of sections 553 (b)(1), (2), and (3), (c), and (e) of this title, to exempt any system of records within the agency from any part of this section except subsections (b), (c)(1) and (2), (e)(4)(A) through (F), (e)(6), (7), (9), (10), and (11), and (i) if the system of records is—

"(1) maintained by the Central Intelligence Agency; or

"(2) maintained by an agency or component thereof which performs as its principal function any activity pertaining to the enforcement of criminal laws, including police efforts to prevent, control, or reduce crime or to apprehend criminals, and the activities of prosecutors, courts, correctional, probation, pardon, or parole authorities, and which consists of (A) information compiled for the purpose of identifying individual criminal offenders and alleged offenders and consisting only of identifying data and notations of arrests, the nature and disposition of criminal charges, sentencing, confinement, release, and parole and probation status; (B) information compiled for the purpose of a criminal investigation, including reports of informants and investigators, and associated with an identifiable individual; or (C) reports identifiable to an individual compiled at any stage of the process of enforcement of the criminal laws from arrest or indictment through release from supervision.

At the time rules are adopted under this subsection, the agency shall include in the statement required under section 553(c) of this title, the reasons why the system of records is to be exempted from a provision of this section.

"(k) SPECIFIC EXEMPTIONS.—The head of any agency may promulgate rules, in accordance with the requirements (including general notice) of sections 553 (b) (1), (2), and (3), (c), and (e) of this title, to exempt any system of records within the agency from subsections (c)(3), (d), (e)(1), (e)(4) (G), (H), and (I) and (f) of this section if the system of records is—

"(1) subject to the provisions of section 552(b)(1) of this title;

"(2) investigatory material compiled for law enforcement purposes, other than material within the scope of subsection (j)(2) of this section: *Provided however,* That if any individual is denied any right, privilege, or benefit that he would otherwise be entitled by Federal law, or for which he would otherwise be eligible, as a result of the maintenance of such material, such material shall be provided to such individual, except to the extent that the disclosure of such material would reveal the identity of a source who furnished information to the Government under an express promise that the identity of the source would be held in confidence, or, prior to the effective date of this section, under an implied promise that the identity of the source would be held in confidence;

"(3) maintained in connection with providing protective services to the President of the United States or other individuals pursuant to section 3056 of title 18;

"(4) required by statute to be maintained and used solely as statistical records;

"(5) investigatory material compiled solely for the purpose of determining suitability, eligibility, or qualifications for Federal civilian employment, military service, Federal contracts, or access to classified information, but only to the extent that the disclosure of such material would reveal the identity of a source who furnished information to the Government under an express promise that the identity of the source would be held in confidence, or, prior to the effective date of this section, under an implied promise that the identity of the source would be held in confidence;

"(6) testing or examination material used solely to determine individual qualifications for appointment or promotion in the Federal service the disclosure of which would compromise the objectivity or fairness of the testing or examination process; or

"(7) evaluation material used to determine potential for promotion in the armed services, but only to the extent that the disclosure of such material would reveal the identity of a source who furnished information to the Government under an express promise that the identity of the source would be held in confidence, or, prior to the effective date of this section, under an implied promise that the identity of the source would be held in confidence. At the time rules are adodpted under this subsection, the agency shall include in the statement required under section 553(c) of this title, the reasons why the system of records is to be exempted from a provision of this section.

"(l) (1) Archival Records.—Each agency record which is accepted by the Administrator of General Services for storage, processing, and servicing in accordance with section 3103 of title 44 shall, for the purposes of this section, be considered to be maintained by the agency which deposited the record and shall be subject to the provisions of this section. The Administrator of General Services shall not disclose the record except to the agency which maintains the record, or under rules established by that agency which are not inconsistent with the provisions of this section.

"(2) Each agency record pertaining to an identifiable individual which was transferred to the National Archives of the United States as a record which has sufficient historical or other value to warrant its continued preservation by the United States Government, prior to the effective date of this section, shall, for the purposes of this section, be considered to be maintained by the National Archives and shall not be subject to the provisions of this section, except that a statement generally describing such records (modeled after the requirements relating to records subject to subsections (e)(4)(A) through (G) of this section) shall be published in the Federal Register.

"(3) Each agency record pertaining to an identifiable individual which is transferred to the National Archives of the United States as a record which has sufficient historical or other value to warrant its continued preservation by the United States Government, on or after the effective date of this section, shall, for the purposes of this section, be considered to be maintained by the National Archives and shall be exempt from the requirements of this section except subsections (e)(4)(A) through (G) and (e)(9) of this section.

"(m) Government Contractors.—When an agency provides by a contract for the operation by or on behalf of the agency of a system of records to accomplish an agency function, the agency shall, consistent with its authority, cause the requirements of this section to be applied to such system. For purposes of subsection (i) of this section any such contractor and any employee of such contractor, if such contract is agreed to on or after the effective date of this section, shall be considered to be an employee of an agency.

"(n) Mailing Lists.—An individual's name and address may not be sold or rented by an agency unless such action is specifically authorized by law. This provision shall not be construed to require the withholding of names and addresses otherwise permitted to be made public.

"(o) Report on New Systems.—Each agency shall provide adequate advance notice to Congress and the Office of Management and Budget of any proposal to establish or alter any system of records in order to permit an evaluation of the probable or potential effect of such proposal on the privacy and other personal or property rights of individuals or the disclosure of information relating to such individuals, and its effect on the preservation of the constitutional principles of federalism and separation of powers.

"(p) Annual Report.—The President shall submit to the Speaker of the House and the President of the Senate, by June 30 of each calendar year, a consolidated report, separately listing for each Federal agency the number of records contained in any system of records which were exempted from the application of this section under the provisions of subsections (j) and (k) of this section during the preceding calendar year, and the reasons for the exemptions, and such other information as indicates efforts to administer fully this section.

(q) EFFECT OF OTHER LAWS.—No agency shall rely on any exemption contained in section 552 of this title to withhold from an individual any record which is otherwise accessible to such individual under the provisions of this section.".

SEC. 4. The chapter analysis of chapter 5 of title 5, United States Code, is amended by inserting:

"552a. Records about individuals."

immediately below:

"552. Public information; agency rules, opinions, orders, and proceedings.".

SEC. 5. (a) (1) There is established a Privacy Protection Study Commission (hereinafter referred to as the "Commission") which shall be composed of seven members as follows:

(A) three appointed by the President of the United States,

(B) two appointed by the President of the Senate, and

(C) two appointed by the Speaker of the House of Representatives.

Members of the Commission shall be chosen from among persons who, by reason of their knowledge and expertise in any of the following areas—civil rights and liberties, law, social sciences, computer technology, business, records management, and State and local government—are well qualified for service on the Commission.

(2) The members of the Commission shall elect a Chairman from among themselves.

(3) Any vacancy in the membership of the Commission, as long as there are four members in office, shall not impair the power of the Commission but shall be filled in the same manner in which the original appointment was made.

(4) A quorum of the Commission shall consist of a majority of the members, except that the Commission may establish a lower number as a quorum for the purpose of taking testimony. The Commission is authorized to establish such committees and delegate such authority to them as may be necessary to carry out its functions. Each member of the Commission, including the Chairman, shall have equal responsibility and authority in all decisions and actions of the Commission, shall have full access to all information necessary to the performance of their functions, and shall have one vote. Action of the Commission shall be determined by a majority vote of the members present. The Chairman (or a member designated by the Chairman to be acting Chairman) shall be the official spokesman of the Commission in its relations with the Congress, Government agencies, other persons, and the public, and, on behalf of the Commission, shall see to the faithful execution of the administrative policies and decisions of the Commission, and shall report thereon to the Commission from time to time or as the Commission may direct.

(5) (A) Whenever the Commission submits any budget estimate or request to the President or the Office of Management and Budget, it shall concurrently transmit a copy of that request to Congress.

(B) Whenever the Commission submits any legislative recommendations, or testimony, or comments on legislation to the President or Office of Management and Budget, it shall concurrently transmit a copy thereof to the Congress. No officer or agency of the United States shall have any authority to require the Commission to submit its legislative recommendations, or testimony, or comments on legislation, to any officer or agency of the United States for approval, comments, or review, prior to the submission of such recommendations, testimony, or comments to the Congress.

(b) The Commission shall—

(1) make a study of the data banks, automated data processing programs, and information systems of governmental, regional, and private organizations, in order to determine the standards and procedures in force for the protection of personal information; and

(2) recommend to the President and the Congress the extent, if any, to which the requirements and principles of section 552a of title 5, United States Code, should be applied to the information practices of those organizations by legislation, administrative action, or voluntary adoption of such requirements and principles, and report on such other legislative recommendations as it may determine to be necessary to protect the privacy of individuals while meeting the legitimate needs of government and society for information.

(c) (1) In the course of conducting the study required under subsection (b) (1) of this section, and in its reports thereon, the Commission may research, examine, and analyze—

(A) interstate transfer of information about individuals that is undertaken through manual files or by computer or other electronic or telecommunications means;

(B) data banks and information programs and systems the operation of which significantly or substantially affect the enjoyment of the privacy and other personal and property rights of individuals;

(C) the use of social security numbers, license plate numbers, universal identifiers, and other symbols to identify individuals in data banks and to gain access to, integrate, or centralize information systems and files; and

(D) the matching and analysis of statistical data, such as Federal census data, with other sources of personal data, such as automobile registries and telephone directories, in order to reconstruct individual responses to statistical questionnaires for commercial or other purposes, in a way which results in a violation of the implied or explicitly recognized confidentiality of such information.

(2) (A) The Commission may include in its examination personal information activities in the following areas: medical; insurance; education; employment and personnel; credit, banking and financial institutions; credit bureaus; the commercial reporting industry; cable television and other telecommunications media; travel, hotel and entertainment reservations; and electronic check processing.

(B) The Commission shall include in its examination a study of—

(i) whether a person engaged in interstate commerce who maintains a mailing list should be required to remove an individual's name and address from such list upon request of that individual;

(ii) whether the Internal Revenue Service should be prohibited from transfering individually indentifiable data to other agencies and to agencies of State governments;

(iii) whether the Federal Government should be liable for general damages incurred by an individual as the result of a willful or intentional violation of the provisions of sections 552a (g) (1) (C) or (D) of title 5, United States Code; and

(iv) whether and how the standards for security and confidentiality of records required under section 552a (e) (10) of such title should be applied when a record is disclosed to a person other than an agency.

(C) The Commission may study such other personal information activities necessary to carry out the congressional policy embodied in this Act, except that the Commission shall not investigate information systems maintained by religious organizations.

(3) In conducting such study, the Commission shall—

(A) determine what laws, Executive orders, regulations, directives, and judicial decisions govern the activities under study and the extent to which they are consistent with the rights of privacy, due process of law, and other guarantees in the Constitution;

(B) determine to what extent governmental and private information systems affect Federal-State relations or the principle of separation of powers;

(C) examine the standards and criteria governing programs, policies, and practices relating to the collection, soliciting, processing, use, access, integration, dissemination, and transmission of personal information; and

(D) to the maximum extent practicable, collect and utilize findings, reports, studies, hearing transcripts, and recommendations of governmental, legislative and private bodies, institutions, organizations, and individuals which pertain to the problems under study by the Commission.

(d) In addition to its other functions the Commission may—

(1) request assistance of the heads of appropriate departments, agencies, and instrumentalities of the Federal Government, of State and local governments, and other persons in carrying out its functions under this Act;

(2) upon request, assist Federal agencies in complying with the requirements of section 552a of title 5, United States Code;

(3) determine what specific categories of information, the collection of which would violate an individual's right of privacy, should be prohibited by statute from collection by Federal agencies; and

(4) upon request, prepare model legislation for use by State and local governments in establishing procedures for handling, maintaining, and disseminating personal information at the State and local level and provide such technical assistance to State and local governments as they may require in the preparation and implementation of such legislation.

(e) (1) The Commission may, in carrying out its functions under this section, conduct such inspections, sit and act at such times and places, hold such hearings, take such testimony, require by subpena the attendance of such witnesses and the production of such books, records, papers, correspondence, and documents, administer such oaths, have such printing and binding done, and make such expenditures as the Commission deems advisable. A subpena shall be issued only upon an affirmative vote of a majority of all members of the Commission. Subpenas shall be issued under the signature of the Chairman or any member of the Commission designated by the Chairman and shall be served by any person designated by the Chairman or any such member. Any member of the Commission may administer oaths or affirmations to witnesses appearing before the Commission.

(2) (A) Each department, agency, and instrumentality of the executive branch of the Government is authorized to furnish to the Commission, upon request made by the Chairman, such information, data, reports and such other assistance as the Commission deems necessary to carry out its functions under this section. Whenever the head of any such department, agency, or instrumentality submits a report pursuant to section 552a (o) of title 5, United States Code, a copy of such report shall be transmitted to the Commission.

(B) In carrying out its functions and exercising its powers under this section, the Commission may accept from any such department, agency, independent instrumentality, or other person any individually indentifiable data if such data is necessary to carry out such powers and functions. In any case in which the Commission accepts any such information, it shall assure that the information is used only for the purpose for which it is provided, and upon completion of that purpose such information shall be destroyed or returned to such department, agency, independent instrumentality, or person from which it is obtained, as appropriate.

(3) The Commission shall have the power to—

(A) appoint and fix the compensation of an executive director, and such additional staff personnel as may be necessary, without regard to the provisions of title 5, United States Code, governing appointments in the competitive service, and without regard to chapter 51 and subchapter III of chapter 53 of such title relating to classification and General Schedule pay rates, but at rates not in excess of the maximum rate for GS–18 of the General Schedule under section 5332 of such title; and

(B) procure temporary and intermittent services to the same extent as is authorized by section 3109 of title 5, United States Code.

The Commission may delegate any of its functions to such personnel of the Commission as the Commission may designate and may authorize such successive redelegations of such functions as it may deem desirable.

(4) The Commission is authorized—

(A) to adopt, amend, and repeal rules and regulations governing the manner of its operations, organization, and personnel;

(B) to enter into contracts or other arrangements or modifications thereof, with any government, any department, agency, or independent instrumentality of the United States, or with any person, firm, association, or corporation, and such contracts or other arrangements, or modifications thereof, may be entered into without legal consideration, without performance or other bonds, and without regard to section 3709 of the Revised Statutes, as amended (41 U.S.C. 5);

(C) to make advance, progress, and other payments which the Commission deems necessary under this Act without regard to the provisions of section 3648 of the Revised Statutes, as amended (31 U.S.C. 529); and

(D) to take such other action as may be necessary to carry out its functions under this section.

(f)(1) Each [the] member of the Commission who is an officer or employee of the United States shall serve without additional compensation, but shall continue to receive the salary of his regular position when engaged in the performance of the duties vested in the Commission.

(2) A member of the Commission other than one to whom paragraph (1) applies shall receive per diem at the maximum daily rate for GS–18 of the General Schedule when engaged in the actual performance of the duties vested in the Commission.

(3) All members of the Commission shall be reimbursed for travel, subsistence, and other necessary expenses incurred by them in the performance of the duties vested in the Commission.

(g) The Commission shall, from time to time, and in an annual report, report to the President and the Congress on its activities in carrying out the provisions of this section. The Commission shall make a final report to the President and to the Congress on its findings pursuant to the study required to be made under subsection (b)(1) of this section not later than two years from the date on which all of the members of the Commission are appointed. The Commission shall cease to exist thirty days after the date on which its final report is submitted to the President and the Congress.

(h) (1) Any member, officer, or employee of the Commission, who by virtue of his employment or official position, has possession of, or access to, agency records which contain individually identifiable information the disclosure of which is prohibited by this section, and who knowing that disclosure of the specific material is so prohibited, willfully discloses the material in any manner to any person or agency not entitled to receive it, shall be guilty of a misdemeanor and fined not more than $5,000.

(2) Any person who knowingly and willfully requests or obtains any record concerning an individual from the Commission under false pretenses shall be guilty of a misdemeanor and fined not more than $5,000.

SEC. 6. The Office of Management and Budget shall—

(1) develop guidelines and regulations for the use of agencies in implementing the provisions of section 552a of title 5, United States Code, as added by section 3 of this Act; and

(2) provide continuing assistance to and oversight of the implementation of the provisions of such section by agencies.

SEC. 7. (a) (1) It shall be unlawful for any Federal, State or local government agency to deny to any individual any right, benefit, or privilege provided by law because of such individual's refusal to disclose his social security account number.

(2) the provisions of paragraph (1) of this subsection shall not apply with respect to—

(A) any disclosure which is required by Federal statute, or

(B) the disclosure of a social security number to any Federal, State, or local agency maintaining a system of records in existence and operating before January 1, 1975, if such disclosure was required under statute or regulation adopted prior to such date to verify the identity of an individual.

(b) Any Federal, State, or local government agency which requests an individual to disclose his social security account number shall inform that individual whether that disclosure is mandatory or voluntary, by what statutory or other authority such number is solicited, and what uses will be made of it.

SEC. 8. The provisions of this Act shall be effective on and after the date of enactment, except that the amendments made by sections 3 and 4 shall become effective 270 days following the day on which this Act is enacted.

SEC. 9. There is authorized to be appropriated to carry out the provisions of section 5 of this Act for fiscal years 1975, 1976, and 1977 the sum of $1,500,000, except that not more than $750,000 may be expended during any such fiscal year.

Approved December 31, 1974.

Appendix IV

GOVERNMENT IN THE SUNSHINE ACT

First proposed in 1972, the Sunshine Act was not acted upon and promulgated for several years. The Act was designed to open government agency meetings to the public, with certain exceptions such as national security matters, internal management questions, situations that might reflect on one's character or reputation and subjects to be kept confidential under statutory authority. The Sunshine Act was affirmatively passed by the Congress and signed by the President on September 13, 1976.

Public Law 94-409
94th Congress, S. 5
September 13, 1976

An Act

To provide that meetings of Government agencies shall be open to the public, and for other purposes.

Be it enacted by the Senate and House of Representatives of the United States of America in Congress assembled, That this Act may be cited as the "Government in the Sunshine Act".

Government in the Sunshine Act. 5 USC 552b note.

DECLARATION OF POLICY

SEC. 2. It is hereby declared to be the policy of the United States that the public is entitled to the fullest practicable information regarding the decisionmaking processes of the Federal Government. It is the purpose of this Act to provide the public with such information while protecting the rights of individuals and the ability of the Government to carry out its responsibilities.

5 USC 552b note.

OPEN MEETINGS

SEC. 3. (a) Title 5, United States Code, is amended by adding after section 552a the following new section:

"§ 552b. Open meetings

"(a) For purposes of this section—

5 USC 552b. Definitions.

"(1) the term 'agency' means any agency, as defined in section 552(e) of this title, headed by a collegial body composed of two or more individual members, a majority of whom are appointed to such position by the President with the advice and consent of the Senate, and any subdivision thereof authorized to act on behalf of the agency;

5 USC 552.

"(2) the term 'meeting' means the deliberations of at least the number of individual agency members required to take action on behalf of the agency where such deliberations determine or result in the joint conduct or disposition of official agency business, but does not include deliberations required or permitted by subsection (d) or (e); and

"(3) the term 'member' means an individual who belongs to a collegial body heading an agency.

(b) Members shall not jointly conduct or dispose of agency business other than in accordance with this section. Except as provided in subsection (c), every portion of every meeting of an agency shall be open to public observation.

"(c) Except in a case where the agency finds that the public interest requires otherwise, the second sentence of subsection (b) shall not apply to any portion of an agency meeting, and the requirements of subsections (d) and (e) shall not apply to any information pertaining to such meeting otherwise required by this section to be disclosed to the public, where the agency properly determines that such portion or portions of its meeting or the disclosure of such information is likely to—

"(1) disclose matters that are (A) specifically authorized under criteria established by an Executive order to be kept secret in the interests of national defense or foreign policy and (B) in fact properly classified pursuant to such Executive order;

"(2) relate solely to the internal personnel rules and practices of an agency:

5 USC 552.
"(3) disclose matters specifically exempted from disclosure by statute (other than section 552 of this title), provided that such statute (A) requires that the matters be withheld from the public in such a manner as to leave no discretion on the issue, or (B) establishes particular criteria for withholding or refers to particular types of matters to be withheld;

"(4) disclose trade secrets and commercial or financial information obtained from a person and privileged or confidential;

"(5) involve accusing any person of a crime, or formally censuring any person:

"(6) disclose information of a personal nature where disclosure would constitute a clearly unwarranted invasion of personal privacy;

"(7) disclose investigatory records compiled for law enforcement purposes, or information which if written would be contained in such records, but only to the extent that the production of such records or information would (A) interfere with enforcement proceedings, (B) deprive a person of a right to a fair trial or an impartial adjudication, (C) constitute an unwarranted invasion of personal privacy, (D) disclose the identity of a confidential source and, in the case of a record compiled by a criminal law enforcement authority in the course of a criminal investigation, or by an agency conducting a lawful national security intelligence investigation, confidential information furnished only by the confidential source, (E) disclose investigative techniques and procedures, or (F) endanger the life or physical safety of law enforcement personnel;

"(8) disclose information contained in or related to examination, operating, or condition reports prepared by, on behalf of, or for the use of an agency responsible for the regulation or supervision of financial institutions;

"(9) disclose information the premature disclosure of which would—

"(A) in the case of an agency which regulates currencies, securities, commodities, or financial institutions, be likely to (i) lead to significant financial speculation in currencies, securities, or commodities, or (ii) significantly endanger the stability of any financial institution; or

"(B) in the case of any agency, be likely to significantly frustrate implementation of a proposed agency action.

except that subparagraph (B) shall not apply in any instance where the agency has already disclosed to the public the content or nature of its proposed action, or where the agency is required by law to make such disclosure on its own initiative prior to taking final agency action on such proposal; or

"(10) specifically concern the agency's issuance of a subpena, or the agency's participation in a civil action or proceeding, an action in a foreign court or international tribunal, or an arbitration, or the initiation, conduct, or disposition by the agency of a particular case of formal agency adjudication pursuant to the
5 USC 554.
procedures in section 554 of this title or otherwise involving a determination on the record after opportunity for a hearing.

"(d)(1) Action under subsection (c) shall be taken only when a majority of the entire membership of the agency (as defined in subsection (a)(1)) votes to take such action. A separate vote of the agency members shall be taken with respect to each agency meeting a portion or portions of which are proposed to be closed to the public pursuant to subsection (c), or with respect to any information which is proposed to be withheld under subsection (c). A single vote may be taken with respect to a series of meetings, a portion or portions of which are proposed to be closed to the public, or with respect to any information concerning such series of meetings, so long as each meeting in such series involves the same particular matters and is scheduled to be held no more than thirty days after the initial meeting in such series. The vote of each agency member participating in such vote shall be recorded and no proxies shall be allowed.

Recorded voting.

"(2) Whenever any person whose interests may be directly affected by a portion of a meeting requests that the agency close such portion to the public for any of the reasons referred to in paragraph (5), (6), or (7) of subsection (c), the agency, upon request of any one of its members, shall vote by recorded vote whether to close such meeting.

"(3) Within one day of any vote taken pursuant to paragraph (1) or (2), the agency shall make publicly available a written copy of such vote reflecting the vote of each member on the question. If a portion of a meeting is to be closed to the public, the agency shall, within one day of the vote taken pursuant to paragraph (1) or (2) of this subsection, make publicly available a full written explanation of its action closing the portion together with a list of all persons expected to attend the meeting and their affiliation.

Copies, availability.

"(4) Any agency, a majority of whose meetings may properly be closed to the public pursuant to paragraph (4), (8), (9)(A), or (10) of subsection (c), or any combination thereof, may provide by regulation for the closing of such meetings or portions thereof in the event that a majority of the members of the agency votes by recorded vote at the beginning of such meeting, or portion thereof, to close the exempt portion or portions of the meeting, and a copy of such vote, reflecting the vote of each member on the question, is made available to the public. The provisions of paragraphs (1), (2), and (3) of this subsection and subsection (e) shall not apply to any portion of a meeting to which such regulations apply: *Provided*, That the agency shall, except to the extent that such information is exempt from disclosure under the provisions of subsection (c), provide the public with public announcement of the time, place, and subject matter of the meeting and of each portion thereof at the earliest practicable time.

Meeting closure, regulation.

Public announcement.

"(e)(1) In the case of each meeting, the agency shall make public announcement, at least one week before the meeting, of the time, place, and subject matter of the meeting, whether it is to be open or closed to the public, and the name and phone number of the official designated by the agency to respond to requests for information about the meeting. Such announcement shall be made unless a majority of the members of the agency determines by a recorded vote that agency business requires that such meeting be called at an earlier date, in which case the agency shall make public announcement of the time, place, and subject matter of such meeting, and whether open or closed to the public, at the earliest practicable time.

Scheduling, public announcement.

"(2) The time or place of a meeting may be changed following the public announcement required by paragraph (1) only if the agency publicly announces such change at the earliest practicable time. The

Scheduling changes, public announcement.

subject matter of a meeting, or the determination of the agency to open or close a meeting, or portion of a meeting, to the public, may be changed following the public announcement required by this subsection only if (A) a majority of the entire membership of the agency determines by a recorded vote that agency business so requires and that no earlier announcement of the change was possible, and (B) the agency publicly announces such change and the vote of each member upon such change at the earliest practicable time.

"(3) Immediately following each public announcement required by this subsection, notice of the time, place, and subject matter of a meeting, whether the meeting is open or closed, any change in one of the preceding, and the name and phone number of the official designated by the agency to respond to requests for information about the meeting, shall also be submitted for publication in the Federal Register.

"(f)(1) For every ·meeting closed pursuant to paragraphs (1) through (10) of subsection (c), the General Counsel or chief legal officer of the agency shall publicly certify that, in his or her opinion, the meeting may be closed to the public and shall state each relevant exemptive provision. A copy of such certification, together with a statement from the presiding officer of the meeting setting forth the time and place of the meeting, and the persons present, shall be retained by the agency. The agency shall maintain a complete transcript or electronic recording adequate to record fully the proceedings of each meeting, or portion of a meeting, closed to the public, except that in the case of a meeting, or portion of a meeting, closed to the public pursuant to paragraph (8), (9)(A), or (10) of subsection (c), the agency shall maintain either such a transcript or recording, or a set of minutes. Such minutes shall fully and clearly describe all matters discussed and shall provide a full and accurate summary of any actions taken, and the reasons therefor, including a description of each of the views expressed on any item and the record of any rollcall vote (reflecting the vote of each member on the question). All documents considered in connection with any action shall be identified in such minutes.

"(2) The agency shall make promptly available to the public, in a place easily accessible to the public, the transcript, electronic recording, or minutes (as required by paragraph (1)) of the discussion of any item on the agenda, or of any item of the testimony of any witness received at the meeting, except for such item or items of such discussion or testimony as the agency determines to contain information which may be withheld under subsection (c). Copies of such transcript, or minutes, or a transcription of such recording disclosing the identity of each speaker, shall be furnished to any person at the actual cost of duplication or transcription. The agency shall maintain a complete verbatim copy of the transcript, a complete copy of the minutes, or a complete electronic recording of each meeting, or portion of a meeting, closed to the public, for a period of at least two years after such meeting, or until one year after the conclusion of any agency proceeding with respect to which the meeting or portion was held, whichever occurs later.

"(g) Each agency subject to the requirements of this section shall, within 180 days after the date of enactment of this section, following consultation with the Office of the Chairman of the Administrative Conference of the United States and published notice in the Federal Register of at least thirty days and opportunity for written comment by any person, promulgate regulations to implement the requirements of subsections (b) through (f) of this section. Any person may bring a [Judicial proceeding.] proceeding in the United States District Court for the District of Columbia to require an agency to promulgate such regulations if such agency has not promulgated such regulations within the time period specified herein. Subject to any limitations of time provided by law, any person may bring a proceeding in the United States Court of Appeals for the District of Columbia to set aside agency regulations issued pursuant to this subsection that are not in accord with the requirements of subsections (b) through (f) of this section and to require the promulgation of regulations that are in accord with such subsections.

"(h)(1) The district courts of the United States shall have jurisdic- [Jurisdiction.] tion to enforce the requirements of subsections (b) through (f) of this section by declaratory judgment, injunctive relief, or other relief as may be appropriate. Such actions may be brought by any person against [Civil actions.] an agency prior to, or within sixty days after, the meeting out of which the violation of this section arises, except that if public announcement of such meeting is not initially provided by the agency in accordance with the requirements of this section, such action may be instituted pursuant to this section at any time prior to sixty days after any public announcement of such meeting. Such actions may be brought in the district court of the United States for the district in which the agency meeting is held or in which the agency in question has its headquarters, or in the District Court for the District of Columbia. In such actions a defendant shall serve his answer within thirty days after the service of the complaint. The burden is on the defendant to sustain his action. In deciding such cases the court may examine in camera any portion of the transcript, electronic recording, or minutes of a meeting closed to the public, and may take such additional evidence as it deems necessary. The court, having due regard for orderly administration and the pub- [Relief.] lic interest, as well as the interests of the parties, may grant such equitable relief as it deems appropriate, including granting an injunction against future violations of this section or ordering the agency to make available to the public such portion of the transcript, recording, or minutes of a meeting as is not authorized to be withheld under subsection (c) of this section.

"(2) Any Federal court otherwise authorized by law to review [Inquiry.] agency action may, at the application of any person properly participating in the proceeding pursuant to other applicable law, inquire into violations by the agency of the requirements of this section and afford such relief as it deems appropriate. Nothing in this section authorizes any Federal court having jurisdiction solely on the basis of paragraph (1) to set aside, enjoin, or invalidate any agency action (other than an action to close a meeting or to withhold information under this section) taken or discussed at any agency meeting out of which the violation of this section arose.

"(i) The court may assess against any party reasonable attorney [Litigation costs, assessment.] fees and other litigation costs reasonably incurred by any other party who substantially prevails in any action brought in accordance with the provisions of subsection (g) or (h) of this section, except that costs may be assessed against the plantiff only where the court finds that the suit was initiated by the plantiff primarily for frivolous or dilatory purposes. In the case of assessment of costs against an agency, the costs may be assessed by the court against the United States.

"(j) Each agency subject to the requirements of this section shall [Report to Congress.] annually report to Congress regarding its compliance with such requirements, including a tabulation of the total number of agency meetings open to the public, the total number of meetings closed to the public, the reasons for closing such meetings, and a description of any litigation brought against the agency under this section, including any costs assessed against the agency in such litigation (whether or not paid by the agency).

"(k) Nothing herein expands or limits the present rights of any person under section 552 of this title, except that the exemptions set forth in subsection (c) of this section shall govern in the case of any request made pursuant to section 552 to copy or inspect the transcripts, recordings, or minutes described in subsection (f) of this section. The requirements of chapter 33 of title 44, United States Code, shall not apply to the transcripts, recordings, and minutes described in subsection (f) of this section.

"(l) This section does not constitute authority to withhold any information from Congress, and does not authorize the closing of any agency meeting or portion thereof required by any other provision of law to be open.

"(m) Nothing in this section authorizes any agency to withhold from any individual any record, including transcripts, recordings, or minutes required by this section, which is otherwise accessible to such individual under section 552a of this title.".

(b) The chapter analysis of chapter 5 of title 5, United States Code, is amended by inserting:

"552b. Open meetings."

immediately below:

"552a. Records about individuals.".

EX PARTE COMMUNICATIONS

SEC. 4. (a) Section 557 of title 5, United States Code, is amended by adding at the end thereof the following new subsection:

"(d)(1) In any agency proceeding which is subject to subsection (a) of this section, except to the extent required for the disposition of ex parte matters as authorized by law—

"(A) no interested person outside the agency shall make or knowingly cause to be made to any member of the body comprising the agency, administrative law judge, or other employee who is or may reasonably be expected to be involved in the decisional process of the proceeding, an ex parte communication relevant to the merits of the proceeding;

"(B) no member of the body comprising the agency, administrative law judge, or other employee who is or may reasonably be expected to be involved in the decisional process of the proceeding, shall make or knowingly cause to be made to any interested person outside the agency an ex parte communication relevant to the merits of the proceeding;

"(C) a member of the body comprising the agency, administrative law judge, or other employee who is or may reasonably be expected to be involved in the decisional process of such proceeding who receives, or who makes or knowingly causes to be made, a communication prohibited by this subsection shall place on the public record of the proceeding:

"(i) all such written communications;

"(ii) memoranda stating the substance of all such oral communications; and

Margin notes:

5 USC 552.

44 USC 3301.

5 USC 552a.
5 USC prec.
500.

"(iii) all written responses, and memoranda stating the substance of all oral responses, to the materials described in clauses (i) and (ii) of this subparagraph;

"(D) upon receipt of a communication knowingly made or knowingly caused to be made by a party in violation of this subsection, the agency, administrative law judge, or other employee presiding at the hearing may, to the extent consistent with the interests of justice and the policy of the underlying statutes, require the party to show cause why his claim or interest in the proceeding should not be dismissed, denied, disregarded, or otherwise adversely affected on account of such violation; and

"(E) the prohibitions of this subsection shall apply beginning at such time as the agency may designate, but in no case shall they begin to apply later than the time at which a proceeding is noticed for hearing unless the person responsible for the communication has knowledge that it will be noticed, in which case the prohibitions shall apply beginning at the time of his acquisition of such knowledge. — Applicability.

"(2) This subsection does not constitute authority to withhold information from Congress.".

(b) Section 551 of title 5, United States Code, is amended—

(1) by striking out "and" at the end of paragraph (12);

(2) by striking out the "act." at the end of paragraph (13) and inserting in lieu thereof "act; and"; and

(3) by adding at the end thereof the following new paragraph:

"(14) 'ex parte communication' means an oral or written communication not on the public record with respect to which reasonable prior notice to all parties is not given, but it shall not include requests for status reports on any matter or proceeding covered by this subchapter.". — "Ex parte communication."

(c) Section 556(d) of title 5, United States Code, is amended by inserting between the third and fourth sentences thereof the following new sentence: "The agency may, to the extent consistent with the interests of justice and the policy of the underlying statutes administered by the agency, consider a violation of section 557(d) of this title sufficient grounds for a decision adverse to a party who has knowingly committed such violation or knowingly caused such violation to occur.". — 5 USC 557.

CONFORMING AMENDMENTS

SEC. 5. (a) Section 410(b)(1) of title 39, United States Code, is amended by inserting after "Section 552 (public information)," the words "section 552a (records about individuals), section 552b (open meetings),".

(b) Section 552(b)(3) of title 5, United States Code, is amended to read as follows:

"(3) specifically exempted from disclosure by statute (other than section 552b of this title), provided that such statute (A) requires that the matters be withheld from the public in such a manner as to leave no discretion on the issue, or (B) establishes particular criteria for withholding or refers to particular types of matters to be withheld;".

(c) Subsection (d) of section 10 of the Federal Advisory Committee Act is amended by striking out the first sentence and inserting in lieu thereof the following: "Subsections (a)(1) and (a)(3) of this section shall not apply to any portion of an advisory committee meeting where — 5 USC app. I.

the President, or the head of the agency to which the advisory committee reports, determines that such portion of such meeting may be closed to the public in accordance with subsection (c) of section 552b of title 5, United States Code.".

EFFECTIVE DATE

5 USC 552b note.

SEC. 6. (a) Except as provided in subsection (b) of this section, the provisions of this Act shall take effect 180 days after the date of its enactment.

(b) Subsection (g) of section 552b of title 5, United States Code, as added by section 3(a) of this Act, shall take effect upon enactment.

Approved September 13, 1976.

LEGISLATIVE HISTORY:

HOUSE REPORTS: No. 94- 880, Pt. I and No. 94-880, Pt. 2, accompanying
H.R. 11656 (Comm. on Government Operations) and
No. 94-1441 (Comm. of Conference).
SENATE REPORTS: No. 94-354 (Comm. on Government Operations), No. 94
381 (Comm. on Rules and Administration) and No. 94-1
(Comm. of Conference).
CONGRESSIONAL RECORD:
Vol. 121 (1975): Nov. 5, 6, considered and passed Senate.
Vol. 122 (1976): July 28, considered and passed House, amended, in
lieu of H.R. 11656.
Aug. 31, House and Senate agreed to conference rep
WEEKLY COMPILATION OF PRESIDENTIAL DOCUMENTS:
Vol. 12, No. 38 (1976): Sept. 13, Presidential statement.

Appendix V

NEWSPAPER PRESERVATION ACT

The Newspaper Preservation Act was passed by the Congress in order to permit two newspapers (morning and evening) in the same city to use joint printing and publishing facilities as an economy measure in order for each to continue to publish and remain economically viable.

NEWSPAPER PRESERVATION ACT

For Legislative History of Act, see p. 3547

PUBLIC LAW 91–353; 84 STAT. 466

[S. 1520]

An Act to exempt from the antitrust laws certain combinations and arrangements necessary for the survival of failing newspapers.

Be it enacted by the Senate and House of Representatives of the United States of America in Congress assembled, That:

Section 1. This Act may be cited as the "Newspaper Preservation Act".

DECLARATION OF POLICY

Sec. 2. In the public interest of maintaining a newspaper press editorially and reportorially independent and competitive in all parts of the United States, it is hereby declared to be the public policy of the United States to preserve the publication of newspapers in any city, community, or metropolitan area where a joint operating arrangement has been heretofore entered into because of economic distress or is hereafter effected in accordance with the provisions of this Act.

DEFINITIONS

Sec. 3. As used in this Act—

(1) The term "antitrust law" means the Federal Trade Commission Act and each statute defined by section 4 thereof (15 U.S.C. 44) as "Antitrust Acts" and all amendments to such Act and such statutes and any other Acts in pari materia.

(2) The term "joint newspaper operating arrangement" means any contract, agreement, joint venture (whether or not incorporated), or other arrangement entered into by two or more newspaper owners for the publication of two or more newspaper publications, pursuant to which joint or common production facilities are established or operated and joint or unified action is taken or agreed to be taken with respect to any one or more of the following: printing; time, method, and field of publication; allocation of production facilities; distribution; advertising solicitation; circulation solicitation; business department; establishment of advertising rates; establishment of circulation rates and revenue distribution: *Provided,* That there is no merger, combination, or amalgamation of editorial or reportorial staffs, and that editorial policies be independently determined.

(3) The term "newspaper owner" means any person who owns or controls directly, or indirectly through separate or subsidary corporations, one or more newspaper publications.

(4) The term "newspaper publication" means a publication produced on newsprint paper which is published in one or more issues weekly (including as one publication any daily newspaper and any Sunday newspaper published by the same owner in the same city, community, or metropolitan area), and in which a substantial portion of the content is devoted to the dissemination of news and editorial opinion.

(5) The term "failing newspaper" means a newspaper publication which, regardless of its ownership or affiliations, is in probable danger of financial failure.

(6) The term "person" means any individual, and any partnership, corporation, association, or other legal entity existing under or authorized by the law of the United States, any State or possession of the United States, the District of Columbia, the Commonwealth of Puerto Rico, or any foreign country.

ANTITRUST EXEMPTION

Sec. 4. (a) It shall not be unlawful under any antitrust law for any person to perform, enforce, renew, or amend any joint newspaper operating arrangement entered into prior to the effective date of this Act, if at the time at which such arrangement was first entered into, regardless of ownership or affiliations, not more than one of the newspaper publications involved in the performance of such arrangement was likely to remain or become a financially sound publication: *Provided*, That the terms of a renewal or amendment to a joint operating arrangement must be filed with the Department of Justice and that the amendment does not add a newspaper publication or newspaper publications to such arrangement.

(b) It shall be unlawful for any person to enter into, perform, or enforce a joint operating arrangement, not already in effect, except with the prior written consent of the Attorney General of the United States. Prior to granting such approval, the Attorney General shall determine that not more than one of the newspaper publications involved in the arrangement is a publication other than a failing newspaper, and that approval of such arrangement would effectuate the policy and purpose of this Act.

(c) Nothing contained in the Act shall be construed to exempt from any antitrust law any predatory pricing, any predatory practice, or any other conduct in the otherwise lawful operations of a joint newspaper operating arrangement which would be unlawful under any antitrust law if engaged in by a single entity. Except as provided in this Act, no joint newspaper operating arrangement or any party thereto shall be exempt from any antitrust law.

PREVIOUS TRANSACTIONS

Sec. 5. (a) Notwithstanding any final judgment rendered in any action brought by the United States under which a joint operating arrangement has been held to be unlawful under any antitrust law, any party to such final judgment may reinstitute said joint newspaper operating arrangement to the extent permissible under section 4(a) hereof.

(b) The provisions of section 4 shall apply to the determination of any civil or criminal action pending in any district court of the United States on the date of enactment of this Act in which it is alleged that any such joint operating agreement is unlawful under any antitrust law.

SEPARABILITY PROVISION

Sec. 6. If any provision of this Act is declared unconstitutional or the applicability thereof to any person or circumstance is held invalid, the validity of the remainder of this Act, and the applicability of such provision to any other person or circumstance, shall not be affected thereby.

Approved July 24, 1970.

Appendix VI

GOVERNMENT INFORMATION PERSONNEL AND BUDGET

Senator William L. Scott (r. Va.) has disputed the figures of the government General Accounting Office on the costs of various government public information activities. Senator Scott's remarks on government publicity are excerpted here, as printed in the *Congressional Record* dated July 26, 1977:

SENATE

SENATOR SCOTT SUGGESTS INVESTIGATION OF GOVERNMENT PUBLIC RELATIONS

Mr. SCOTT. Mr. President, I believe every Member of Congress at one time or another has expressed concern about the cost of Government and the duplication of Government programs. We recognize the need for Government to provide a variety of services but would want to eliminate nonessential ones. In this connection, I contacted the General Accounting Office and requested information regarding the cost of and number of Federal employees handling public affairs; congressional relations; military recruitment; Government audio-visual programs: Government publications distributed without direct cost to the recipient; advertising the availability of Government funds and programs, such as agriculture's outreach relating to food stamps. None of these activities if considered alone would constitute a sizeable portion of the overall Federal budget but when consolidated and when complimentary mementos and token gifts provided by Government officials, both military and civilian, are considered the total could well run into billions of dollars annually. Therefore, our office requested the comptroller general to examine into expenditures of this nature and to advise of any suggestions he might have to eliminate nonessential Government expenditures. I ask unanimous consent that a copy of the response of the Comptroller General be printed at this point in the RECORD.

There being no objection, the material was ordered to be printed in the RECORD, as follows:

COMPTROLLER GENERAL
OF THE UNITED STATES,
Washington D.C., June 10, 1977.
HON. WILLIAM L. SCOTT,
U.S. Senate.

DEAR SENATOR SCOTT: By letter dated November 29, 1976, you requested that we obtain information on costs associated with various Federal programs such as public relations and audiovisual activities. After meeting with your office, we agreed to obtain:

The number of Federal employees in public affairs and congressional relations and the salaries for these employees in the 20 largest Government agencies.

The amount spent for recruitment by the military.

Government audiovisual costs, if available from the General Services Administration.

The development and printing costs of the Agriculture Yearbook bicentennial issue, and the farmers' bulletins cost, and the number of copies of both distributed free by the Government.

The cost of the Department of Agriculture's Food Stamp Outreach program for fiscal year 1976.

Advertising costs in the Federal Government.

Agency-supplied data is presented below. As agreed with your office, we did not verify the accuracy of information furnished by the various agencies.

DATA ON FEDERAL EMPLOYEES
WORKING IN PUBLIC AFFAIRS
AND CONGRESSIONAL RELATIONS

Since there is no Government-wide definition of public affairs, each agency defined public affairs and congressional relations itself to determine which employees to include in each category. We requested that the agencies include support staff as well as professional employees.

Information submitted by the 20 agencies is as shown on the chart below.

Enclosure I is an index of the agencies, their personnel and salaries. The number of public affairs and congressional relations employees reported by the agencies and shown in the index varied widely. For example, the Department of Transportation, which had a $4.3 billion fiscal year 1976 budget, reported 281 public affairs employees for fiscal year 1976 while the Department of Agriculture, with a $11.8 billion budget in fiscal year 1976, reported only 8 employees in public affairs.

Department of Agriculture

A previous GAO report on public affairs costs (B–161939, Sept. 30, 1975) ex-

	Fiscal year 1976 (actual)		Fiscal year 1977 (budgeted)	
	Personnel	Salary	Personnel	Salary
Public affairs	3,496	$62,414,557	3,366	$65,464,085
Congressional relations	950	19,693,888	934	20,126,275

plained the Department of Agriculture's philosophies that distinguishes public affairs from public information activities. At that time, Agriculture had 21 offices (which varied from 1 to 123 employees) which disseminated information to the public. Agriculture refers to these offices as public information, not public affairs activities, because these offices explain agriculture programs to the public. Therefore, public information activities employees are not included in Agriculture's public affairs costs.

Department of Defense

For both fiscal years 1976 and 1977 the Department of Defense reported over $20 million for public affairs costs. This figure included employee benefits as well as straight salary costs. Public Law 94–419 imposes a $24 million ceiling on the Defense Department's public affairs expenditures. In view of the small difference between the 1976 expenditure and the legal limitation we asked the Defense Department for total public affairs costs for fiscal year 1976. The Defense Department reported that total public affairs expenditures—programs and people —exceeded $23 million.

Our previous report to the Senate Foreign Relations Committee, "Expenditures for Public Affairs Activities" (B–161939, July 30, 1973), reported that Defense did not include operating costs for all promotion activities in public affairs expenditures, nor did it record all personnel costs for such activities. We reviewed selected activities which were at least partly promotional and found that costs for special aerial teams, military ceremonial bands, service museums, service-related exhibits, the Defense Information School, and Industrial College of the Armed Forces seminars were not reported by Defense as public affairs costs.

We recommended that the Defense Department reexamine its position on what it considered public affairs costs since many activities mentioned in our report met the Defense definition of public information and community relations. We also suggested that the Foreign Relations Committee clarify the types of Defense activities it expected to be reported under the limitation.

In commenting on our report, Defense stated that they believe their decision to not report costs for these other activities to the Foreign Relations Committee as public affairs costs is proper. Defense further explained that the Congressional Appropriations Committees are aware of the Defense definition of public affairs but have not suggested broadening its scope.

Others

The Civil Service Commission and General Services Administration also reported few employees in these categories. We asked officials in these agencies if they had included all employees in their figures. According to these officials, all public affairs and congressional relations employees had been reported.

As a matter of interest to you, there is no requirement that agencies specifically identify public affairs costs— programs and people—so no central location exists in the Government where this information can be obtained. Total Government public affairs costs have previously been obtained by special studies or one-time reporting with the criteria for methods and definitions established by each report. To our knowledge, the last special study for public affairs was requested by the Office of Management and Budget in 1970, which showed public affairs obligations to be $153 million in fiscal year 1969. These costs included supplies, materials, and equipment, as well as personnel services and travel costs.

MILITARY RECRUITMENT COSTS

According to the Department of Defense, about $516 million was spent for military recruiting during fiscal year 1976. This amount includes recruiting costs for both active duty and reserve forces.

A Defense official stated that the recruitment expenditures were:

[Expenditure in millions]

Active forces recruitment:
Military salaries for recruiters and headquarters-level employees who monitor the recruitment program $182.6
Salaries for civilian support 25.9
Recruiting support, such as travel, printing, auto leasing, utilities . 71.4
Leasing facilities for recruiting stations 25.1
Costs for recruitment advertising 68.8
Enlistment bonuses presently offered by the Army and the Marine Corps 68.5
Travel and per diem costs for recruiter aides, who are sent to their home neighborhoods for a few weeks to assist recruiting 6.2

Subtotal 448.5

Reserve forces recruitment:
Military salaries 36.4
Civilian salaries 8.7
Recruiting support, including leasing facilities 22.6

67.7

Total 516.21

AUDIOVISUAL COSTS

Audiovisual activities are defined in this report as those functions which produce and distribute audiovisual products such as motion picture films, still photos, television services, and audio services.

The General Services Administration and the Office of Management and Budget have limited information on Government audiovisual costs. Neither agency has information on annual operating costs requested by your office. An Office of Management and Budget official stated that the agencies' annual operating costs cannot be obtained because the agency accounting systems are not designed to report the information.

However, the Office of Management and Budget provided some information on audiovisual costs which they obtained from studies completed in 1974 and 1977. The first study was prepared by the Office of Telecommunications Policy and reported cost data for fiscal year 1972 from the 15 largest users of audiovisual media in the Federal Government. The second study, prepared by the Office of Management and Budget, shows costs for fiscal year 1976 and includes information on 19 Federal agencies.

Both reports contain information on the cost of obtaining audiovisual services from outside sources and the volume of in-house and contract production for different audiovisual media. We extracted data on 15 agencies from both reports so you may compare audiovisual production for fiscal years 1972 and 1976. In-house audiovisual production, contract production, and contract costs for the 15 audiovisual users are:

	Inhouse running time (minimum)		Contract running time (minimum)		Contract cost	
	1972	1976	1972	1976	1972	1976
Television productions	22,338	126,212	651	47,105	$ 309,000	$11,377,356
Motion picture productions	7,453	9,249	14,192	22,100	17,555,000	16,999,361
Mixed media productions	(¹)	273,404	(¹)	101,219	1,444,000	2,899,413
Total					19,308,000	31,276,130

¹Mixed media running time not reported in fiscal year 1972 data report.

In addition to these contract costs, the Office of Telecommunications Policy reported in January 1974 that the acquisition value of equipment owned by the 15 agencies included in their study was $431 million as of June 30, 1972.

In a December 1975 report, the General Services Administration estimated the total Government investment in audiovisual facilities equipment and inventories to be $1 billion and annual operating costs to be $500 million. We could not obtain this report's backup information and therefore cannot comment on the accuracy of these estimated costs.

Our current audit plans include reviewing the utilization and effectiveness of audiovisual activities managed by agencies and the feasibility of consolidating audiovisual activities in certain geographic areas.

AGRICULTURE YEARBOOK AND FARMERS'
BULLETINS COSTS

The Department of Agriculture produces both the Agriculture Yearbook and farmers' bulletins. The Agriculture Yearbook is published yearly and is part two of the annual report of the Secretary of Agriculture. The 1976 Agriculture Yearbook, "The Face of Rural America," is a hard cover publication 284 pages long. In contrast to prior yearbooks which contained reports and papers on various agricultural subjects, the 1976 yearbook mainly contained photographs of American agriculture.

Farmers' bulletins are reprints of articles on different agricultural subjects written mainly by Agriculture employees. Farmers' bulletins cover many subjects, such as home and garden bulletins, or leaflets such as "How to Raise Strawberries," "Foundations For Farm Buildings," and "Home Canning of Fruits and Vegetables." The bulletins vary from one to several pages long and are produced in single page or pamphlet form.

Both the Agriculture Yearbook and farmers' bulletins are published primarily for delivery to, or distribution for, Members of Congress.

Agriculture Yearbook

The cost of the 1976 yearbook consists of both the materials development cost and the printing cost. Total cost is approximately $577,000.

Agriculture officials stated that the development cost of the 1976 yearbook was $56,000, which is the salary cost for the 3 employees who put together the yearbook material. According to these officials, the reason why only employee salaries were considered development costs was that the yearbook is a collection of materials that have previously been produced by the Department or donated by land grant colleges. The Agriculture Department stated it would have reproduced this data even if no yearbook were published.

Printing cost was the major production cost of the 1976 yearbook. Actual year-

Billed to	Number of copies	Billed cost[1]
Department of Agriculture:		
Copies for the Congress	233,450	$442,434
Copies for Agriculture	30,000	41,682
Superintendent of Documents:		
Copies for sales	15,000	24,434
Copies for depository libraries	1,175	1,937
Copies for international exchange..........	135	205
Other agencies	7,003	10,115
Total	286,763	520,807

[1] This includes freight costs.

book printing was procured from a commercial printer by the Government Printing Office. According to Government Printing Office records, 286,763 yearbooks were printed costing $520,807. This includes freight costs. The yearbooks were printed for the Department of Agriculture, the Superintendent of Documents, and other Government agencies. The number of copies and billed costs on chart pg. 283.

The Superintendent of Documents and the other agencies paid less per copy of the yearbook than the Department of Agriculture. This is because of differences in freight costs and a cheaper printing add-on rate, which the contractor charges for printing additional copies.

The majority of yearbooks were distributed to recipients free of charge. As shown, 271,763 yearbooks were distributed to:

Congress:

Senate (100 members and 3 Senate officers—550 copies each)	56,650
House of Representatives (435 members, 4 delegates, and 3 House officers—400 copies each)	176,800
Subtotal	233,450
Department of Agriculture . .	30,000
Superintendent of Documents	1,310
Other agencies	7,003
Total free copies	271,763

Yearbook distribution to the Congress and copies retained by the Department of Agriculture is permitted by 44 U.S.C. 1301, which allows printing up to about 470,000 yearbooks for the Congress and 30,000 yearbooks for the Department of Agriculture. The minimum number of copies for the Congress for fiscal year 1977 must be no less than 232,250.

The copies made available to Members of Congress are for distribution to constituents. The copies retained by the Department of Agriculture are distributed to the press, visiting dignitaries, and various department bureaus, who in turn distribute the yearbook to land grant colleges, Department of Agriculture and Future Farmers of America libraries, and other recipients.

The Superintendent of Documents distributed 1,310 yearbooks free of charge, as required by law. Depository libraries and the Library of Congress received 1,175 and 135 respectively. The Superintendent of Documents is required by 44 U.S.C. 1905 to distribute copies of Government publications to designated depository libraries throughout the country, and 44 U.S.C. 1718 directs that copies of Government publications be furnished the Library of Congress for official use in the District of Columbia and for publications exchange with other nations.

Yearbooks printed for other agencies were for distribution overseas or internal use. The United States Information Agency had 5,000 copies printed for distribution overseas to give key contacts in other countries a pictorial view of American agriculture. The Department of Interior required 1,113 yearbooks, which were distributed to various department offices and bureaus. Many other agencies had small quantities of the yearbook printed for their internal use.

Only 15,000 yearbooks were not given away or used internally by agencies. These were printed for sale by the Superintendent of Documents. These yearbooks are sold at the Government Printing Office bookstores or by mail by the Superintendent of Documents for $7.30 per copy.

FARMERS' BULLETINS

Funds are appropriated annually to the Department of Agriculture for production of farmers' bulletins. As authorized by 7 U.S.C. 417, four-fifths of the bulletins are to be made available to, or sent out for,

Members of Congress. According to Department of Agriculture officials, in fiscal year 1976 the Department spent about $578,000 on bulletin production, however, this cost does not include distribution and mailing costs, which we were unable to obtain.

The farmers' bulletins are distributed free by the Agriculture Department for the Congress, in response to letters requesting information and through the Department Extension Service and Visitors Center. During fiscal year 1976, 9.3 million farmers' bulletins were distributed. Although four fifths of these were available to the Congress, only 3.3 million were delivered to or sent out for Members of Congress. According to Agriculture officials, 3.3 million represented the total publications requested by the Congress. The remaining 6 million publications were made available for distribution to the public through:

The Department's Extension Service, where County agents and State universities give the publications to individuals requesting information.

The Department's Visitors Center, where the general public can obtain publications in person.

Responding to letters from individuals.

DEPARTMENT OF AGRICULTURE COST
FOR THE OUTREACH PROGRAM

The Food Stamp Outreach Program was authorized as part of the Food Stamp Act of 1964 as amended. The act states "* * * the State agency shall undertake effective action, including the use of services provided by other federally funded agencies and organizations, to inform low-income households concerning the availability and benefits of the food stamp program and insure the participation of eligible households * * *."

To achieve the Outreach Program's purposes, the State agencies initiate and monitor efforts to reach all potentially eligible households and provide eligible households with reasonable and convenient access to the program. In fiscal year 1976 all States, plus the District of Columbia, Guam, Puerto Rico, and, the Virgin Islands participated in the Outreach Program.

The Outreach Program's cost is divided between the Federal Government and participating States. The act states "* * * the Secretary is authorized to pay to each State agency an amount equal to 50 per centum of all administrative costs including * * * the outreach * * * requirements of Section 10 of this Act * * *."

According to Department of Agriculture officials, the Department reimbursed State agencies $968,604 for costs the State agencies incurred during fiscal year 1976. These payments partially reimbursed State agencies for the salaries of program coordinators and employees working on Outreach.

We asked Agriculture officials how they control the funds given to the States in the Outreach Program. We were told that the States must submit to Agriculture a semiannual plan of Outreach activities and a semiannual performance report. Agriculture also performs an annual financial management review of each State's use of funds.

FEDERAL ADVERTISING COSTS

The information you requested is not readily available and would require gathering data from each Government agency and bureau. To answer a similar congressional inquiry in 1975, we obtained, from 31 agencies their total advertising cost. We trust this data will meet your needs.

These 31 agencies spent $141.6 million for advertising by private agencies in fiscal year 1974 and estimated that $145.5 million would be spent in fiscal year 1975. In addition, the agencies spent $47.5 million for in-house advertising during fiscal year 1974 and estimated $53.3 million in costs for in-house advertising for fiscal year 1975. Therefore, these 31 agencies spent about $189 million and $199 million for fiscal years 1974 and 1975.

Sincerely yours,

ELMER B. STAATS,
*Comptroller General
of the United States.*

Mr. SCOTT. Mr. President, it will be noted that more than $85 million is budgeted for the current fiscal year for public affairs and congressional relations personnel for 20 departments and agencies. Doubt was expressed, however, by the Comptroller General as to the completeness of the information submitted by the various agencies. He felt that there was not a common agreement as to what was considered to be expenditures for public affairs or for congressional relations. Mr. President, a reading of the report indicates that no one in Federal Government knows how much is being spent each year for public relations and other promotional activities.

Military recruitment costs for fiscal year 1976 were estimated to amount to $516 million. The General Services Administration estimated that the total Government investment in audiovisual facilities, equipment and, inventories was $1 billion, with annual operating costs of $500 million; but the General Accounting Office was unable to obtain backup information and declined to comment on the accuracy of these estimated audiovisual costs.

For many years the Department of Agriculture has issued agricultural bulletins and yearbooks, many of them distributed through the congressional offices. The Comptroller General indicates the total cost for the 1976 yearbooks was $577,000 for 286,000 copies, of which all but 15,000 were distributed free of charge. He also indicated that 9,300,000 farmer's bulletins were distributed, four-fifths of these through Members of Congress and the remainder distributed to the public through the extension services of the Department of Agriculture, the Visitors' Center, and in response to letters from constituents at a total cost of $578,000. Of course, the cost of franking the agriculture yearbooks and bulletins is not included in these figures.

With regard to the cost of advertising the availability of food stamps, or the Outreach program, the Comptroller General indicated that the Federal cost amounted to $968,604 last year but that the annual Federal advertising costs were not readily available.

The General Accounting Office has informally advised our office that since Congress does not specifically require an accounting of mementos or souvenirs of the various departments and agencies distributed free of charge, there is no way that Office can provide an estimate of these costs. The Comptroller General's letter does not include items such as cufflinks, pocketknives, symbols of a given organization or headquarters, personal souvenirs, photographs, plaques of various types, and other promotional items distributed free of charge to visitors by various officials and agencies of Government.

It would, therefore, seem reasonable for the Committee on Governmental Affairs, or the Appropriations Committee, to conduct hearings or otherwise investigate the costs of the items mentioned by the General Accounting Office, and other promotional activities, to determine whether it is in the public interest to revise some of the laws with regard to continuing such practices at taxpayers' expense. Therefore, I am contacting the chairmen and ranking members of both committees with the suggestion that they make such investigation as appears warranted to determine if some unnecessary expenditures can be eliminated.

ENCLOSURE I

| Department or Agency | Fiscal year 1976 | | | | Fiscal year 1977 | | | |
| | Public affairs | | Congressional relations | | Public affairs | | Congressional relations | |
	Number of employees	Salary	Number of employees	Salary	Number of employees	Salary	Number of employees	Salary
Department of Agriculture	8	$ 207,962	22	$ 523,255	10	$ 218,594	28	$ 655,317
Department of Commerce	143	3,334,054	43	901,763	145	3,409,124	40	961,820
Department of Defense[1]	1,404	20,016,000	332	7,500,000	1,322	20,721,000	333	7,400,000
Department of Health, Education, and Welfare[2]	352	7,511,306	97	1,702,792	293	7,892,689	76	1,587,441
Department of Housing and Urban Development	39	923,399	26	503,854	38	983,420	27	550,370
Department of Interior	128	2,934,208	37	873,113	29	3,120,881	40	905,284
Department of Justice	113	2,436,164	55	1,144,674	21	2,648,435	61	1,375,600
Department of Labor	157	2,614,512	16	329,828	160	2,797,352	16	327,000
Department of State	130	2,850,500	35	853,700	126	3,012,600	35	941,700
Department of Transportation	281	4,300,141	24	478,672	256	4,632,254	24	488,684
Department of the Treasury	258	4,372,977	47	725,087	222	4,329,789	48	720,642
Civil Service Commission	4	60,197	5	81,983	4	81,674	5	83,116
Energy Research and Development Administration	74	1,824,000	25	602,000	73	2,000,000	33	740,000
Environmental Protection Agency	67	1,703,000	37	679,000	67	1,750,000	38	243,000
Federal Energy Administration[3]	47	807,897	48	841,825	39	775,841	24	543,000
General Services Administration	8	163,000	11	210,400	8	174,900	11	246,700
National Aeronautics and Space Administration	166	3,535,116	13	385,000	166	3,983,000	13	452,000
U.S. Information Agency	15	375,270	4	76,266	15	452,732	3	71,900
U.S. Postal Service	59	1,461,040	51	815,100	55	1,409,800	57	858,000
Veterans' Administration	46	993,814	22	465,576	47	1,070,000	22	474,701
Total	3,496	62,414,557	950	19,693,888	3,366	65,464,085	934	20,126,275

[1] Department of Defense salary costs include employee benefits.

[2] The Department of Health, Education, and Welfare budgeted salary costs for fiscal year 1977 may include some travel, employee benefits, and/or training costs.

[3] Although a few agencies had larger budgets than the Federal Energy Administration, this agency has been included at your request.

Appendix VII

THE NATIONAL NEWS COUNCIL

The function of the National News Council is to receive and to investigate and evaluate complaints against the media and to render a nonjudicial opinion. The major value of the Council's opinions is that of publicizing the findings and exerting moral strictures. Included here is a complaint received by the Council which was examined by the Grievance Committee.

The National News Council

ONE LINCOLN PLAZA
NEW YORK, N.Y. 10023

(212) 595-9411

COMPLAINT NO. 26

ASHBROOK, ex rel. MARTIN
    against
THE NEW YORK TIMES

Nature of Complaint: Representative John M. Ashbrook of Ohio asked
    the Council to investigate the allegations contained in a
    cablegram received by the State Department from U.S. Ambassador
    to South Vietnam Graham Martin critical of an article which
    appeared in The New York Times on February 25, 1974. The
    article, by David Shipler, summarized the current status of
    the U.S. aid program in South Vietnam. Ambassador Martin charged
    in his cablegram, which had been made public prior to the
    Council's investigation, that the article "contained numerous
    inaccuracies and half-truths." Specifically, he alleged that
    the article:

    1) gave a "slanted impression that the United States
    and South Vietnam are grossly violating the cease-fire
    agreement."

    2) omitted or treated skeptically the flagrant Communist
    violations of the Paris accords.

    3) did not place sufficient emphasis on the training role
    of American technicians in South Vietnam.

    4) wrongly asserted that U.S. liaison officers were giving
    military advice to the South Vietnamese in contravention
    of the Paris Agreement.

    5) wrongly asserted that U.S. advisers were continuing
    to aid the South Vietnamese police force.

6)   did not take into consideration in its contention
that South Vietnamese forces were using excessive amounts
of ammunition in their combat with the Vietcong the fact
that the South Vietnamese have fixed bases to defend and
therefore need more ammunition to defend them against
Communist attacks.

7)   was incorrect on the point that "military aid comes
in through economic programs that dump millions into the
Saigon government's defense budget."

Mr. Shipler noted in the article that he had attempted to
interview the Ambassador and members of his staff in the preparation of the article but had been refused such interviews. Ambassador Martin admits that and contends that to have allowed
his staff or himself to be interviewed would have permitted
"their reputations for integrity to be used as a platform to
grossly deceive the American people."

Response of News Organization: The New York Times declined to
cooperate with the Council or to provide any information.
David Shipler, however, voluntarily expressed a desire to
cooperate with the Council and submitted background information in support of his article as well as a detailed response
to Ambassador Martin's cable.

Conclusion of the Council: The Council concludes that the article
was factually accurate in all material respects. It may be
that some of the statements in that article, although factual,
were subject to interpretations different from the inferences
drawn by Mr. Shipler. But Mr. Shipler found it necessary to
draw his own conclusions from the facts available to him,

made inevitable by the refusal of Ambassador Martin to make himself personally available.

The Grievance Committee of the National News Council closely examined Mr. Shipler's original article in The New York Times of February 25, 1974, as well as Ambassador Martin's reaction to that article expressed in a lengthy cable to the Secretary of State dated March 7. Members of the Council's staff conducted a personal interview with Ambassador Martin in Washington, D.C. on August 5. Mr. Shipler provided the Council with his own rebuttal of the Ambassador's charges in a letter dated August 13. A pertinent staff report of the Senate Foreign Relations Committee also was examined.

Obviously, factual inaccuracy cannot be excused. But the journalist is entitled to draw reasonable inferences from facts available to him. If the significance of the reported facts could have been better understood with a further explanation from Ambassador Martin, even though received after publication of the original story, those views should also be made available to the public.

The committee suggests that, because the article contained much interpretive reporting (including some that must have been known to be controversial), a labelling of the article as "News Analysis" would have been appropriate, and in keeping with a practice followed regularly by The New York Times and many other newspapers. Moreover, in the interest of completeness, the news story that reported Ambassador Martin's cable of complaint should have also reported the Ambassador's specific complaints of inaccuracy in the original Times article.

Because the Council concludes that the original news report was not inaccurate in any material element, the criticism was unwarranted.

<u>Dissenting Opinion</u>: I cannot agree with the majority opinion's assessment of the original article as basically accurate. An article is not really accurate if it is (so to speak) "accurate as far as it goes," but creates a given impression and omits facts that would give a quite different impression. The <u>Times</u> article does this repeatedly, and while that is its perfect right, the result can hardly be called "accurate".

For example, the article reports the highly relevant assertion of U.S. intelligence officials that North Vietnam has massively augmented its forces in the south, squarely in violation of the settlement, but follows this immediately with a paragraph that seems to contradict the assertion effectively:

> Yet in battle the Communists appear more frugal with ammunition than the Government troops, who have been seen recently by Western correspondents spraying artillery across wide areas under Vietcong control as if there was no end to the supply of shells. This difference has bolstered the view of some diplomats that China and the Soviet Union, unwilling to support an all-out offensive now, have placed limits on the rate of resupply to Hanoi.

Ambassador Martin convincingly refutes the implication of the quoted paragraph as follows:

> ...ARVN positions are fixed to defend bases and populated areas. Their location is known to the enemy. Therefore, few rounds are needed for effective fire. The enemy still hits and runs. His permanent bases are outside ARVN artillery range and ARVN gunners must search for targets, register and then fire for effect, all of which requires more ammunition.

All the writer of the article can find to say, in response, is that the Ambassador's point is "well taken, and would have

been mentioned in the story if he had allowed me to interview
him or his subordinates."

But this excuse, is, to put it gently, disingenious. The
high ammunition requirements of fixed positions are hardly
unfamiliar to able correspondents and, even if they were,
Mr. Shipler was scarcely cut off from all access to official
information on the subject. In the Ambassador's letter of
February 5 to Senator Fulbright, he states that his aim is
to provide "a senior, experienced and highly capable officer
who will either obtain and make available the information if
it is readily accessible or arrange for an interview with a
senior official responsible for the area with which the
question deals." The individual described by Mr. Martin is
John F. Hogan, Jr., Counselor of Embassy for Press Affairs,
and Mr. Shipler in his August 13 letter to Mr. Arthur states
that "virtually every statistic in the piece" came either from
Mr. Hogan or Mrs. Ann Battorff, public information officer in
the Office of the Defense Attache; so at least these two routes
were available to him, and were freely availed of. Yet the
false implication was created that the higher ammunition usage
of the South Vietnamese forces was somehow proof of profligacy.
And, interestingly, it was not even corrected in the Times'
subsequent story on Ambassador Martin's complaint, when the
Times was chargeable with knowledge that the implication was
false.

Moreover, the whole tone of the article is at variance with
the minimal requirements of objective reportage. To say that
certain economic programs "dump millions in cash into the
Saigon Government's defense budget" is, like the statement
on ammunition, misleading. The reference is not really to

"cash" contributions at all, but to contributions of food and other goods under the Commercial Import Program and Food for Peace, some of which are sold by the South Vietnamese government to its population, with our full knowledge and approval, for piasters then spent on defense. But the statement is not only misleading; its whole tone is pejorative: "dump", "millions", "cash". This is the rhetoric of propaganda, nothing more.

We must remember that this controversy is merely an episode -- and a late episode at that -- in the running battle between the Saigon press corps and our diplomatic establishment there, which in turn is only one skirmish in the great national controversy of the last decade over our military presence in Southeast Asia. To assume that the _Times_ correspondent was simply balked, in his attempt to write a balanced story, by the unmotivated malice of a crusty diplomatic bureaucrat would be a distortion of the true situation far greater than any achieved by Mr. Shipler.

RUSHER.

Appendix VIII

THE SUPREME COURT

The nation's highest court issues no formal press releases as a general rule. Included here is the Opinion of the Court in *United States v. Nixon, President of the United States, et al.* This is prefaced by a syllabus (headnote) which provides a summary of the case.

(Slip Opinion)

NOTE: Where it is feasible, a syllabus (headnote) will be released, as is being done in connection with this case, at the time the opinion is issued. The syllabus constitutes no part of the opinion of the Court but has been prepared by the Reporter of Decisions for the convenience of the reader. See *United States* v. *Detroit Lumber Co.*, 200 U.S. 321, 337.

SUPREME COURT OF THE UNITED STATES

Syllabus

UNITED STATES *v.* NIXON, PRESIDENT OF THE UNITED STATES, ET AL.

CERTIORARI TO THE UNITED STATES COURT OF APPEALS FOR THE DISTRICT OF COLUMBIA CIRCUIT BEFORE JUDGMENT

No. 73–1766. Argued July 8, 1974—Decided July 24, 1974*

Following indictment alleging violation of federal statutes by certain staff members of the White House and political supporters of the President, the Special Prosecutor filed a motion under Fed. Rule Crim. Proc. 17 (c) for a subpoena *duces tecum* for the production before trial of certain tapes and documents relating to precisely identified conversations and meetings between the President and others. The President, claiming executive privilege, filed a motion to quash the subpoena. The District Court, after treating the subpoenaed material as presumptively privileged, concluded that the Special Prosecutor had made a sufficient showing to rebut the presumption and that the requirements of Rule 17 (c) had been satisfied. The court thereafter issued an order for an *in camera* examination of the subpoenaed material, having rejected the President's contentions (a) that the dispute between him and the Special Prosecutor was nonjusticiable as an "intra-executive" conflict and (b) that the judiciary lacked authority to review the President's assertion of executive privilege. The court stayed its order pending appellate review, which the President then sought in the Court of Appeals. The Special Prosecutor then filed in this Court a petition for a writ of certiorari before judgment (No. 73–1766) and the President filed a cross-petition for such a writ challenging the grand-jury action (No. 73–1834). The Court granted both writs. *Held:*

1. The District Court's order was appealable as a "final" order under 28 U. S. C. § 1291, was therefore properly "in," 28 U. S. C. § 1254, the Court of Appeals when the petition for certiorari before

---

*Together with No. 73–1834, *Nixon, President of the United States* v. *United States,* also on certiorari before judgment to the same court.

Syllabus

judgment was filed in this Court, and is now properly before this Court for review. Although such an order is normally not final and subject to appeal, an exception is made in a "limited class of cases where denial of immediate review would render impossible any review whatsoever of an individual's claims," *United States* v. *Ryan*, 402 U. S. 530, 533. Such an exception is proper in the unique circumstances of this case where it would be inappropriate to subject the President to the procedure of securing review by resisting the order and inappropriate to require that the District Court proceed by a traditional contempt citation in order to provide appellate review. Pp. 5–7.

2. The dispute between the Special Prosecutor and the President presents a justiciable controversy. Pp. 7–12.

(a) The mere assertion of an "intra-branch dispute," without more, does not defeat federal jurisdiction. *United States* v. *ICC*, 337 U. S. 426. P. 8.

(b) The Attorney General by regulation has conferred upon the Special Prosecutor unique tenure and authority to represent the United States and has given the Special Prosecutor explicit power to contest the invocation of executive privilege in seeking evidence deemed relevant to the performance of his specially delegated duties. While the regulation remains in effect, the Executive Branch is bound by it. *Accardi* v. *Shaughnessy*, 347 U. S. 260. Pp. 9–11.

(c) The action of the Special Prosecutor within the scope of his express authority seeking specified evidence preliminarily determined to be relevant and admissible in the pending criminal case, and the President's assertion of privilege in opposition thereto, present issues "of the type which are traditionally justiciable," *United States* v. *ICC, supra,* at 430, and the fact that both litigants are officers of the Executive Branch is not a bar to justiciability. P. 12.

3. From this Court's scrutiny of the materials submitted by the Special Prosecutor in support of his motion for the subpoena, much of which is under seal, it is clear that the District Court's denial of the motion to quash comported with Rule 17 (c) and that the Special Prosecutor has made a sufficient showing to justify a subpoena for production *before* trial. Pp. 13–17.

4. Neither the doctrine of separation of powers nor the generalized need for confidentiality of high-level communications, without more, can sustain an absolute, unqualified presidential privilege of

Syllabus

immunity from judicial process under all circumstances. See, e. g., Marbury v. Madison, 1 Cranch 137, 177; Baker v. Carr, 369 U. S. 186, 211. Absent a claim of need to protect military, diplomatic, or sensitive national security secrets, the confidentiality of presidential communications is not significantly diminished by producing material for a criminal trial under the protected conditions of in camera inspection, and any absolute executive privilege under Art. II of the Constitution would plainly conflict with the function of the courts under the Constitution. Pp. 18–22.

5. Although the courts will afford the utmost deference to presidential acts in the performance of an Art. II function, United States v. Burr, 25 Fed. Cas. 187, 190, 191–192 (No. 14,694), when a claim of presidential privilege as to materials subpoenaed for use in a criminal trial is based, as it is here, not on the ground that military or diplomatic secrets are implicated, but merely on the ground of a generalized interest in confidentiality, the President's generalized assertion of privilege must yield to the demonstrated, specific need for evidence in a pending criminal trial and the fundamental demands of due process of law in the fair administration of justice. Pp. 22–28.

6. On the basis of this Court's examination of the record, it cannot be concluded that the District Court erred in ordering in camera examination of the subpoenaed material, which shall now forthwith be transmitted to the District Court. Pp. 28–29.

7. Since a President's communications encompass a vastly wider range of sensitive material than would be true of an ordinary individual, the public interest requires that presidential confidentiality be afforded the greatest protection consistent with the fair administration of justice, and the District Court has a heavy responsibility to ensure that material involving presidential conversations irrelevant to or inadmissible in the criminal prosecution be accorded the high degree of respect due a President and that such material be returned under seal to its lawful custodian. Until released to the Special Prosecutor no in camera material is to be released to anyone. Pp. 29–31.

No. 73–1766, —— F. Supp. ——, affirmed; No. 73–1834, certiorari dismissed as improvidently granted.

BURGER, C. J., delivered the opinion of the Court, in which all Members joined except REHNQUIST, J., who took no part in the consideration or decision of the cases.

NOTICE : This opinion is subject to formal revision before publication in the preliminary print of the United States Reports. Readers are requested to notify the Reporter of Decisions, Supreme Court of the United States, Washington, D.C. 20543, of any typographical or other formal errors, in order that corrections may be made before the preliminary print goes to press.

SUPREME COURT OF THE UNITED STATES

Nos. 73–1766 AND 73–1834

United States, Petitioner,
73–1766   *v.*
Richard M. Nixon, President
    of the United States,
        et al.

Richard M. Nixon, President
    of the United States,
        Petitioner,
73–1834   *v.*
    United States.

On Writs of Certiorari to the United States Court of Appeals for the District of Columbia Circuit before judgment.

[July 24, 1974]

MR. CHIEF JUSTICE BURGER delivered the opinion of the Court.

This case (No. 73–1766) presents for review the denial of a motion, filed on behalf of the President of the United States, in the case of *United States* v. *Mitchell* (D. C. Crim. No. 74–110), to quash a third-party subpoena *duces tecum* issued by the United States District Court for the District of Columbia, pursuant to Fed. Rule Crim. Proc. 17 (c). The subpoena directed the President to produce certain tape recordings and documents relating to his conversations with aides and advisers. The court rejected the President's claims of absolute executive privilege, of lack of jurisdiction, and of failure to satisfy the requirements of Rule 17 (c). The President appealed to the Court of Appeals. We granted the United States' petition for certiorari before judgment,[1] and also the President's respon-

---

[1] See 28 U. S. C. §§ 1254 (1) and 2101 (e) and our Rule 20. See, *e. g., Youngstown Sheet & Tube Co.* v. *Sawyer*, 343 U. S. 937, 579,

sive cross-petition for certiorari before judgment,[2] because of the public importance of the issues presented and the need for their prompt resolution. —— U. S. ——, —— (1974).

On March 1, 1974, a grand jury of the United States District Court for the District of Columbia returned an indictment charging seven named individuals[3] with various offenses, including conspiracy to defraud the United States and to obstruct justice. Although he was not designated as such in the indictment, the grand jury named the President, among others, as an unindicted co-

---

584 (1952); *United States* v. *United Mine Workers*, 329 U. S. 708, 709, 710 (1946); 330 U. S. 258, 269 (1947); *Carter* v. *Carter Coal Co.*, 298 U. S. 238 (1936); *Rickert Rice Mills* v. *Fontenot*, 297 U. S. 110 (1936); *Railroad Retirement Board* v. *Alton R. Co.*, 295 U. S. 330, 344 (1935); *United States* v. *Bankers Trust Co.*, 294 U. S. 240, 243 (1935).

[2] The cross-petition in No. 73–1834 raised the issue whether the grand jury acted within its authority in naming the President as an unindicted coconspirator. Since we find resolution of this issue unnecessary to resolution of the question whether the claim of privilege is to prevail, the cross-petition for certiorari is dismissed as improvidently granted and the remainder of this opinion is concerned with the issues raised in No. 73–1766. On June 19, 1974, the President's counsel moved for disclosure and transmittal to this Court of all evidence presented to the grand jury relating to its action in naming the President as an unindicted coconspirator. Action on this motion was deferred pending oral argument of the case and is now denied.

[3] The seven defendants were John N. Mitchell, H. R. Haldeman, John D. Ehrlichman, Charles W. Colson, Robert C. Mardian, Kenneth W. Parkinson, and Gordon Strachan. Each had occupied either a position of responsibility on the White House staff or a position with the Committee for the Re-Election of the President. Colson entered a guilty plea on another charge and is no longer a defendant.

[4] The President entered a special appearance in the District Court on June 6 and requested that court to lift its protective order regarding the naming of certain individuals as coconspirators and to any additional extent deemed appropriate by the Court. This motion of the President was based on the ground that the disclosures to

conspirator.[4] On April 18, 1974, upon motion of the Special Prosecutor, see n. 8, *infra,* a subpoena *duces tecum* was issued pursuant to Rule 17 (c) to the President by the United States District Court and made returnable on May 2, 1974. This subpoena required the production, in advance of the September 9 trial date, of certain tapes, memoranda, papers, transcripts, or other writings relating to certain precisely identified meetings between the President and others.[5] The Special Prosecutor was able to fix the time, place and persons present at these discussions because the White House daily logs and appointment rec ords had been delivered to him. On April 30, the President publicly released edited transcripts of 43 conversations; portions of 20 conversations subject to subpoena in the present case were included. On May 1, 1974, the President's counsel filed a "special appearance" and a motion to quash the subpoena, under Rule 17 (c). This motion was accompanied by a formal claim of privilege. At a subsequent hearing,[6] further motions to expunge the grand jury's action naming the President as an unindicted coconspirator and for protective orders against the disclosure of that information were filed or raised orally by counsel for the President.

the news media made the reasons for continuance of the protective order no longer meaningful. On June 7, the District Court removed its protective order and, on June 10, counsel for both parties jointly moved this Court to unseal those parts of the record which related to the action of the grand jury regarding the President. After receiving a statement in opposition from the defendants, this Court denied that motion on June 15, 1974, except for the grand jury's immediate finding relating to the status of the President as an unindicted coconspirator. — U. S. — (1974).

[5] The specific meetings and conversations are enumerated in a schedule attached to the subpoena. 42a–46a of the App.

[6] At the joint suggestion of the Special Prosecutor and counsel for the President, and with the approval of counsel for the defendants, further proceedings in the District Court were held *in camera.*

On May 20, 1974, the District Court denied the motion to quash and the motions to expunge and for protective orders. —— F. Supp. —— (1974). It further ordered "the President or any subordinate officer, official or employee with custody or control of the documents or objects subpoenaed," *id.*, at ——, to deliver to the District Court, on or before May 31, 1974, the originals of all subpoenaed items, as well as an index and analysis of those items, together with tape copies of those portions of the subpoenaed recordings for which transcripts had been released to the public by the President on April 30. The District Court rejected jurisdictional challenges based on a contention that the dispute was nonjusticiable because it was between the Special Prosecutor and the Chief Executive and hence "intra-executive" in character; it also rejected the contention that the judiciary was without authority to review an assertion of executive privilege by the President. The court's rejection of the first challenge was based on the authority and powers vested in the Special Prosecutor by the regulation promulgated by the Attorney General; the court concluded that a justiciable controversy was presented. The second challenge was held to be foreclosed by the decision in *Nixon* v. *Sirica,* —— U. S. App. D. C. ——, 487 F. 2d 700 (1973).

The District Court held that the judiciary, not the President, was the final arbiter of a claim of executive privilege. The court concluded that, under the circumstances of this case, the presumptive privilege was overcome by the Special Prosecutor's prima facie "demonstration of need sufficiently compelling to warrant judicial examination in chambers . . . ." —— F. Supp., at ——. The court held, finally, that the Special Prosecutor had satisfied the requirements of Rule 17 (c). The District Court stayed its order pending appellate review on condition that review was sought before 4 p. m., May 24. The court further provided that matters filed under seal remain under seal when transmitted as part of the record.

On May 24, 1974, the President filed a timely notice of appeal from the District Court order, and the certified record from the District Court was docketed in the United States Court of Appeals for the District of Columbia Circuit. On the same day, the President also filed a petition for writ of mandamus in the Court of Appeals seeking review of the District Court order.

Later on May 24, the Special Prosecutor also filed, in this Court, a petition for a writ of certiorari before judgment. On May 31, the petition was granted with an expedited briefing schedule. — U. S. — (1974). On June 6, the President filed, under seal, a cross-petition for writ of certiorari before judgment. This cross-petition was granted June 15, 1974, — U. S. — (1974), and the case was set for argument on July 8, 1974.

I

JURISDICTION

The threshold question presented is whether the May 20, 1974, order of the District Court was an appealable order and whether this case was properly "in," 28 U. S. C § 1254, the United States Court of Appeals when the petition for certiorari was filed in this Court. Court of Appeals jurisdiction under 28 U. S. C. § 1291 encompasses only "final decisions of the district courts." Since the appeal was timely filed and all other procedural requirements were met, the petition is properly before this Court for consideration if the District Court order was final. 28 U. S. C. § 1254 (1); 28 U. S. C. § 2101 (e).

The finality requirement of 28 U. S. C. § 1291 embodies a strong congressional policy against piecemeal reviews, and against obstructing or impeding an ongoing judicial proceeding by interlocutory appeals. See, *e. g., Cobbie-*

dick v. *United States,* 309 U. S. 323, 324–326 (1940). This requirement ordinarily promotes judicial efficiency and hastens the ultimate termination of litigation. In applying this principle to an order denying a motion to quash and requiring the production of evidence pursuant to a subpoena *duces tecum,* it has been repeatedly held that the order is not final and hence not appealable. *United States* v. *Ryan,* 402 U. S. 530, 532 (1971); *Cobbledick* v. *United States,* 309 U. S. 322 (1940); *Alexander* v. *United States,* 201 U. S. 117 (1906). This Court has

> "consistently held that the necessity for expedition in the administration of the criminal law justifies putting one who seeks to resist the production of desired information to a choice between compliance with a trial court's order to produce prior to any review of that order, and resistance to that order with the concomitant possibility of an adjudication of contempt if his claims are rejected on appeal." *United States* v. *Ryan,* 402 U. S. 530, 533 (1971).

The requirement of submitting to contempt, however, is not without exception and in some instances the purposes underlying the finality rule require a different result. For example, in *Perlman* v. *United States,* 247 U. S. 7 (1918), a subpoena had been directed to a third party requesting certain exhibits; the appellant, who owned the exhibits, sought to raise a claim of privilege. The Court held an order compelling production was appealable because it was unlikely that the third party would risk a contempt citation in order to allow immediate review of the appellant's claim of privilege. *Id.,* at 12–13. That case fell within the "limited class of cases where denial of immediate review would render impossible any review whatsoever of an individual's claims." *United States* v. *Ryan, supra,* at 533.

Here too the traditional contempt avenue to immediate appeal is peculiarly inappropriate due to the unique setting in which the question arises. To require a President of the United States to place himself in the posture of disobeying an order of a court merely to trigger the procedural mechanism for review of the ruling would be unseemly, and present an unnecessary occasion for constitutional confrontation between two branches of the Government. Similarly, a federal judge should not be placed in the posture of issuing a citation to a President simply in order to invoke review. The issue whether a President can be cited for contempt could itself engender protracted litigation, and would further delay both review on the merits of his claim of privilege and the ultimate termination of the underlying criminal action for which his evidence is sought. These considerations lead us to conclude that the order of the District Court was an appealable order. The appeal from that order was therefore properly "in" the Court of Appeals, and the case is now properly before this Court on the writ of certiorari before judgment. 28 U. S. C. § 1254; 28 U. S. C. § 2101 (e). *Gay* v. *Ruff,* 292 U. S. 25, 30 (1934).[7]

II

JUSTICIABILITY

In the District Court, the President's counsel argued that the court lacked jurisdiction to issue the subpoena because the matter was an intra-branch dispute between a subordinate and superior officer of the Executive Branch and hence not subject to judicial resolution.

---

[7] The parties have suggested this Court has jurisdiction on other grounds. In view of our conclusion that there is jurisdiction under 28 U. S. C. § 1254 (1) because the District Court's order was appealable, we need not decide whether other jurisdictional vehicles are available.

That argument has been renewed in this Court with emphasis on the contention that the dispute does not present a "case" or "controversy" which can be adjudicated in the federal courts. The President's counsel argues that the federal courts should not intrude into areas committed to the other branches of Government. He views the present dispute as essentially a "jurisdictional" dispute within the Executive Branch which he analogizes to a dispute between two congressional committees. Since the Executive Branch has, exclusive authority and absolute discretion to decide whether to prosecute a case, *Confiscation Cases,* 7 Wall. 454 (1869), *United States* v. *Cox,* 342 F. 2d 167, 171 (CA5), cert. denied, 381 U. S. 935 (1965), it is contended that a President's decision is final in determining what evidence is to be used in a given criminal case. Although his counsel concedes the President has delegated certain specific powers to the Special Prosecutor, he has not "waived nor delegated to the Special Prosecutor the President's duty to claim privilege as to all materials . . . which fall within the President's inherent authority to refuse to disclose to any executive officer." Brief for the President 47. The Special Prosecutor's demand for the items therefore presents, in the view of the President's counsel, a political question under *Baker* v. *Carr,* 369 U. S. 186 (1962), since it involves a "textually demonstrable" grant of power under Art. II.

The mere assertion of a claim of an "intra-branch dispute," without more, has never operated to defeat federal jurisdiction; justiciability does not depend on such a surface inquiry. In *United States* v. *ICC,* 337 U. S. 426 (1949), the Court observed, "courts must look behind names that symbolize the parties to determine whether a justiciable case or controversy is presented." *Id.,* at 430. See also: *Powell* v. *McCormack,* 395 U. S. 486 (1969); *ICC* v. *Jersey City,* 322 U. S. 503 (1944); *United States ex rel. Chapman* v. *FPC*, 345 U. S. 153 (1953); *Secretary of Agriculture* v. *United States*, 347 U. S. 645 (1954); *FMB* v. *Isbrandsten Co.*, 356 U. S. 481, 482 n. 2 (1958); *United States* v. *Marine Bancorporation*, —— U. S. —— (1974), and *United States* v. *Connecticut National Bank*, —— U. S. —— (1974).

Our starting point is the nature of the proceeding for which the evidence is sought—here a pending criminal prosecution. It is a judicial proceeding in a federal court alleging violation of federal laws and is brought in the name of the United States as sovereign. *Berger* v. *United States*, 295 U. S. 78, 88 (1935). Under the authority of Art. II, § 2, Congress has vested in the Attorney General the power to conduct the criminal litigation of the United States Government. 28 U. S. C. § 516. It has also vested in him the power to appoint subordinate officers to assist him in the discharge of his duties. 28 U. S. C. §§ 509, 510, 515, 533. Acting pursuant to those statutes, the Attorney General has delegated the authority to represent the United States in these particular matters to a Special Prosecutor with unique authority and tenure.[8] The regulation gives the

-----

[8] The regulation issued by the Attorney General pursuant to his statutory authority, vests in the Special Prosecutor plenary authority to control the course of investigations and litigation related to "all offenses arising out of the 1972 Presidential Election for which the Special Prosecutor deems it necessary and appropriate to assume responsibility, allegations involving the President, members of the White House staff, or Presidential appointees, and any other matters which he consents to have assigned to him by the Attorney General." 38 Fed. Reg. 30739, as amended by 38 Fed. Reg. 32805. In particular, the Special Prosecutor was given full authority, *inter alia*, "to contest the assertion of 'Executive Privilege' . . . and handl[e] all aspects of any cases within his jurisdiction." *Ibid.* The regulation then goes on to provide:

"In exercising this authority, the Special Prosecutor will have the greatest degree of independence that is consistent with the Attorney-General's statutory accountability for all matters falling within the

Special Prosecutor explicit power to contest the invocation of executive privilege in the process of seeking evidence deemed relevant to the performance of these specially delegated duties.[9] 38 Fed. Reg. 30739.

---

jurisdiction of the Department of Justice. The Attorney General will not. countermand or interfere with the Special Prosecutor's decisions or actions. The Special Prosecutor will determine whether and to what extent he will inform or consult with the Attorney General about the conduct of his duties and responsibilities. In accordance with assurances given by the President to the Attorney General that the President will not exercise his Constitutional powers to effect the discharge of the Special Prosecutor or to limit the independence he is hereby given, the Special Prosecutor will not be removed from his duties except for extraordinary improprieties on his part and without the President's first consulting the Majority and Minority Leaders and Chairman and ranking Minority Members of the Judiciary Committees of the Senate and House of Representatives and ascertaining that their consensus is in accord with his proposed action."

[9] That this was the understanding of Acting Attorney General Robert Bork, the author of the regulation establishing the independence of the Special Prosecutor, is shown by his testimony before the Senate Judiciary Committee:

"Although it is anticipated that Mr. Jaworski will receive cooperation from the White House in getting any evidence he feels he needs to conduct investigations and prosecutions, it is clear and understood on all sides that he has the power to use judicial processes to pursue evidence if disagreement should develop."

Hearings before the Senate Judiciary Committee on the Special Prosecutor, 93d Cong., 1st Sess., pt. 2, at 470 (1973). Acting Attorney General Bork gave similar assurances to the House Subcommittee on Criminal Justice. Hearings before the House Judiciary Subcommittee on Criminal Justice on H. J. Res. 784 and H. R. 10937, 93d Cong., 1st Sess. 266 (1973). At his confirmation hearings, Attorney General William Saxbe testified that he shared Acting Attorney General Bork's views concerning the Special Prosecutor's authority to test any claim of executive privilege in the courts. Hearings before the Senate Judiciary Committee on the nomination of William B. Saxbe to be Attorney General, 93d Cong., 1st Sess. 9 (1973).

So long as this regulation is extant it has the force of law. In *Accardi* v. *Shaughnessy*, 347 U. S. 260 (1953), regulations of the Attorney General delegated certain of his discretionary powers to the Board of Immigration Appeals and required that Board to exercise its own discretion on appeals in deportation cases. The Court held that so long as the Attorney General's regulations remained operative, he denied himself the authority to exercise the discretion delegated to the Board even though the original authority was his and he could reassert it by amending the regulations. *Service* v. *Dulles*, 354 U. S. 363, 388 (1957), and *Vitarelli* v. *Seaton*, 359 U. S. 535 (1959), reaffirmed the basic holding of *Accardi*.

Here, as in *Accardi*, it is theoretically possible for the Attorney General to amend or revoke the regulation defining the Special Prosecutor's authority. But he has not done so.[10] So long as this regulation remains in force the Executive Branch is bound by it, and indeed the United States as the sovereign composed of the three branches is bound to respect and to enforce it. Moreover, the delegation of authority to the Special Prosecutor in this case is not an ordinary delegation by the Attorney General to a subordinate officer: with the authorization of the President, the Acting Attorney General provided in the regulation that the Special Prosecutor was not to be removed without the "consensus" of eight designated leaders of Congress. Note 8, *supra*.

---

[10] At his confirmation hearings Attorney General William Saxbe testified that he agreed with the regulation adopted by Acting Attorney General Bork and would not remove the Special Prosecutor except for "gross impropriety." Hearings, Senate Judiciary Committee on the nomination of William B. Saxbe to be Attorney General, 93d Cong., 1st Sess., 5–6, 8–10 (1973). There is no contention here that the Special Prosecutor is guilty of any such impropriety.

The demands of and the resistance to the subpoena present an obvious controversy in the ordinary sense, but that alone is not sufficient to meet constitutional standards. In the constitutional sense, controversy means more than disagreement and conflict; rather it means the kind of controversy courts traditionally resolve. Here at issue is the production or nonproduction of specified evidence deemed by the Special Prosecutor to be relevant and admissible in a pending criminal case. It is sought by one official of the Government within the scope of his express authority; it is resisted by the Chief Executive on the ground of his duty to preserve the confidentiality of the communications of the President. Whatever the correct answer on the merits, these issues are "of a type which are traditionally justiciable." *United States* v. *ICC*, 337 U. S., at 430. The independent Special Prosecutor with his asserted need for the subpoenaed material in the underlying criminal prosecution is opposed by the President with his steadfast assertion of privilege against disclosure of the material. This setting assures there is "that concrete adverseness which sharpens the presentation of issues upon which the court so largely depends for illumination of difficult constitutional questions." *Baker* v. *Carr*, 369 U. S., at 204. Moreover, since the matter is one arising in the regular course of a federal criminal prosecution, it is within the traditional scope of Art. III power. *Id.*, at 198.

In light of the uniqueness of the setting in which the conflict arises, the fact that both parties are officers of the Executive Branch cannot be viewed as a barrier to justiciability. It would be inconsistent with the applicable law and regulation, and the unique facts of this case to conclude other than that the Special Prosecutor has standing to bring this action and that a justiciable controversy is presented for decision.

III

RULE 17 (c)

The subpoena *duces tecum* is challenged on the ground that the Special Prosecutor failed to satisfy the requirements of Fed. Rule Crim. Proc. 17 (c), which governs the issuance of subpoenas *duces tecum* in federal criminal proceedings. If we sustained this challenge, there would be no occasion to reach the claim of privilege asserted with respect to the subpoenaed material. Thus we turn to the question whether the requirements of Rule 17 (c) have been satisfied. See *Arkansas-Louisiana Gas Co. v. Dept. of Public Utilities,* 304 U. S. 61, 64 (1938); *Ashwander* v. *Tennessee Valley Authority,* 297 U. S. 288, 346–347 (1936). (Brandeis, J., concurring.)

Rule 17 (c) provides:

> "A subpoena may also command the person to whom it is directed to produce the books, papers, documents or other objects designated therein. The court on motion made promptly may quash or modify the subpoena if compliance would be unreasonable or oppressive. The court may direct that books, papers, documents or objects designated in the subpoena be produced before the court at a time prior to the trial or prior to the time when they are to be offered in evidence and may upon their production permit the books, papers, documents or objects or portions thereof to be inspected by the parties and their attorneys."

A subpoena for documents may be quashed if their production would be "unreasonable or oppressive," but not otherwise. The leading case in this Court interpreting this standard is *Bowman Dairy Co.* v. *United States,* 341 U. S. 214 (1950). This case recognized certain fundamental characteristics of the subpoena *duces tecum* in criminal cases: (1) it was not intended to provide a means of discovery for criminal cases. *Id.,* at 220; (2) its chief innovation was to expedite the trial by providing a time and place *before* trial for the inspection of subpoenaed materials.[11] *Ibid.* As both parties agree, cases decided in the wake of *Bowman* have generally followed Judge Weinfeld's formulation in *United States* v. *Iozia,* 13 F. R. D. 335, 338 (SDNY 1952), as to the required showing. Under this test, in order to require production prior to trial, the moving party must show: (1) that the documents are evidentiary[12] and relevant; (2) that they are not otherwise procurable reasonably in advance of trial by exercise of due dili-

---

[11] The Court quoted a statement of a member of the advisory committee that the purpose of the Rule was to bring documents into court "in advance of the time that they are offered in evidence, so that they may then be inspected in advance, for the purpose . . . of enabling the party to see whether he can use [them] or whether he wants to use [them]." 341 U. S., at 220 n. 5. The Manual for Complex and Multi-district Litigation published by the Administrative Office of the United States Courts recommends that Rule 17 (c) be encouraged in complex criminal cases in order that each party may be compelled to produce its documentary evidence well in advance of trial and in advance of the time it is to be offered. P. 142, CCH Ed.

[12] The District Court found here that it was faced with "the more unusual situation . . . where the subpoena, rather than being directed to the government by the defendants, issues to what, as a practical matter, is a third party." *United States* v. *Mitchell,* —— F. Supp. —— (D. C. 1974). The Special Prosecutor suggests that the evidentiary requirement of *Bowman Dairy Co.* and *Iozia* does not apply in its full vigor when the subpoena *duces tecum* is issued to third parties rather than to government prosecutors. Brief for the United States 128–129. We need not decide whether a lower standard exists because we are satisfied that the relevance and evidentiary nature of the subpoenaed tapes were sufficiently shown as a preliminary matter to warrant the District Court's refusal to quash the subpoena.

gence; (3) that the party cannot properly prepare for trial without such production and inspection in advance of trial and that the failure to obtain such inspection may tend unreasonably to delay the trial; (4) that the application is made in good faith and is not intended as a general "fishing expedition."

Against this background, the Special Prosecutor, in order to carry his burden, must clear three hurdles: (1) relevancy; (2) admissibility; (3) specificity. Our own review of the record necessarily affords a less comprehensive view of the total situation than was available to the trial judge and we are unwilling to conclude that the District Court erred in the evaluation of the Special Prosecutor's showing under Rule 17 (c). Our conclusion is based on the record before us, much of which is under seal. Of course, the contents of the subpoenaed tapes could not at that stage be described fully by the Special Prosecutor, but there was a sufficient likelihood that each of the tapes contains conversations relevant to the offenses charged in the indictment. *United States* v. *Gross,* 24 F. R. D. 138 (SDNY 1959). With respect to many of the tapes, the Special Prosecutor offered the sworn testimony or statements of one or more of the participants in the conversations as to what was said at the time. As for the remainder of the tapes, the identity of the participants and the time and place of the conversations, taken in their total context, permit a rational inference that at least part of the conversations relate to the offenses charged in the indictment.

We also conclude there was a sufficient preliminary showing that each of the subpoenaed tapes contains evidence admissible with respect to the offenses charged in the indictment. The most cogent objection to the admissibility of the taped conversations here at issue is that they are a collection of out-of-court statements by declarants who will not be subject to cross-examination and that the statements are therefore inadmissible hearsay. Here, however, most of the tapes apparently contain conversations to which one or more of the defendants named in the indictment were party. The hearsay rule does not automatically bar all out-of-court statements by a defendant in a criminal case.[13] Declarations by one defendant may also be admissible against other defendants upon a sufficient showing, by independent evidence,[14] of a conspiracy among one or more other defendants and the declarant and if the declarations at issue were in furtherance of that conspiracy. The same is true of declarations of coconspirators who are not defendants in the case on trial. *Dutton* v. *Evans,* 400 U. S. 74, 81 (1970). Recorded conversations may also be admissible for the limited purpose of impeaching the credibility of any defendant who testifies or any other coconspirator who testifies. Generally, the need for evidence to impeach witnesses is insufficient to require its production in advance of trial.

---

[13] Such statements are declarations by a party defendant that "would surmount all objections based on the hearsay rule . . ." and, at least as to the declarant himself "would be admissible for whatever inferences" might be reasonably drawn. *United States* v. *Matlock,* —— U. S. —— (1974). *On Lee* v. *United States,* 343 U. S. 747, 757 (1953). See also McCormick on Evidence, § 270, at 651–652 (1972 ed.).

[14] As a preliminary matter, there must be substantial, independent evidence of the conspiracy, at least enough to take the question to the jury. *United States* v. *Vaught,* 385 F. 2d 320, 323 (CA4 1973); *United States* v. *Hoffa,* 349 F. 2d 20, 41–42 (CA6 1965), aff'd on other grounds, 385 U. S. 293 (1966); *United States* v. *Santos,* 385 F. 2d 43, 45 (CA7 1967), cert. denied, 390 U. S. 954 (1968); *United States* v. *Morton,* 483 F. 2d 573, 576 (CA8 1973); *United States* v. *Spanos,* 462 F. 2d 1012, 1014 (CA9 1972); *Carbo* v. *United States,* 314 F. 2d 718, 737 (CA9 1963), cert. denied, 377 U. S. 953 (1964). Whether the standard has been satisfied is a question of admissibility of evidence to be decided by the trial judge.

See, *e. g., United States* v. *Carter,* 15 F. R. D. 367, 371 (D. D. C. 1954). Here, however, there are other valid potential evidentiary uses for the same material and the analysis and possible transcription of the tapes may take a significant period of time. Accordingly, we cannot say that the District Court erred in authorizing the issuance of the subpoena *duces tecum.*

Enforcement of a pretrial subpoena *duces tecum* must necessarily be committed to the sound discretion of the trial court since the necessity for the subpoena most often turns upon a determination of factual issues. Without a determination of arbitrariness or that the trial court finding was without record support, an appellate court will not ordinarily disturb a finding that the applicant for a subpoena complied with Rule 17 (c). See, *e. g., Sue* v. *Chicago Transit Authority,* 279 F. 2d 416, 419 (CA7 1960); *Shotkin* v. *Nelson,* 146 F. 2d 402 (CA10 1944).

In a case such as this, however, where a subpoena is directed to a President of the United States, appellate review, in deference to a coordinate branch of government, should be particularly meticulous to ensure that the standards of Rule 17 (c) have been correctly applied. *United States* v. *Burr,* 25 Fed. Cas. 30, 34 (No. 14,692d) (1807). From our examination of the materials submitted by the Special Prosecutor to the District Court in support of his motion for the subpoena, we are persuaded that the District Court's denial of the President's motion to quash the subpoena was consistent with Rule 17 (c). We also conclude that the Special Prosecutor has made a sufficient showing to justify a subpoena for production *before* trial. The subpoenaed materials are not available from any other source, and their examination and processing should not await trial in the circumstances shown. *Bowman Dairy Co., supra; United States* v. *Iozia, supra.*

IV

THE CLAIM OF PRIVILEGE

A

Having determined that the requirements of Rule 17 (c) were satisfied, we turn to the claim that the subpoena should be quashed because it demands "confidential conversations between a President and his close advisors that it would be inconsistent with the public interest to produce." App. 48a. The first contention is a broad claim that the separation of powers doctrine precludes judicial review of a President's claim of privilege. The second contention is that if he does not prevail on the claim of absolute privilege, the court should hold as a matter of constitutional law that the privilege prevails over the subpoena *duces tecum.*

In the performance of assigned constitutional duties each branch of the Government must initially interpret the Constitution, and the interpretation of its powers by any branch is due great respect from the others. The President's counsel, as we have noted, reads the Constitution as providing an absolute privilege of confidentiality for all presidential communications. Many decisions of this Court, however, have unequivocally reaffirmed the holding of *Marbury* v. *Madison,* 1 Cranch 137 (1803), that "it is emphatically the province and duty of the judicial department to say what the law is." *Id.,* at 177.

No holding of the Court has defined the scope of judicial power specifically relating to the enforcement of a subpoena for confidential presidential communications for use in a criminal prosecution, but other exercises of powers by the Executive Branch and the Legislative Branch have been found invalid as in conflict with the Constitution. *Powell* v. *McCormack, supra; Youngstown, supra.* In a series of cases, the Court interpreted the explicit immu-

nity conferred by express provisions of the Constitution
on Members of the House and Senate by the Speech or
Debate Clause, U. S. Const. Art. I, § 6. *Doe* v. *McMillan*, 412 U. S. 306 (1973); *Gravel* v. *United States*, 408
U. S. 606 (1973); *United States* v. *Brewster*, 408 U. S.
501 (1972); *United States* v. *Johnson*, 383 U. S. 169
(1966). Since this Court has consistently exercised the
power to construe and delineate claims arising under
express powers, it must follow that the Court has authority to interpret claims with respect to powers alleged to
derive from enumerated powers.

Our system of government "requires that federal courts
on occasion interpret the Constitution in a manner at
variance with the construction given the document by
another branch." *Powell* v. *McCormack, supra,* 549.
And in *Baker* v. *Carr,* 369 U. S., at 211, the Court stated:

> "Deciding whether a matter has in any measure
> been committed by the Constitution to another
> branch of government, or whether the action of that
> branch exceeds whatever authority has been committed, is itself a delicate exercise in constitutional
> interpretation, and is a responsibility of this Court
> as ultimate interpreter of the Constitution."

Notwithstanding the deference each branch must accord
the others, the "judicial power of the United States"
vested in the federal courts by Art. III, § 1 of the Constitution can no more be shared with the Executive
Branch than the Chief Executive, for example, can share
with the Judiciary the veto power, or the Congress share
with the Judiciary the power to override a presidential
veto. Any other conclusion would be contrary to the
basic concept of separation of powers and the checks and
balances that flow from the scheme of a tripartite government. The Federalist, No. 47, p. 313 (C. F. Mittel ed.
1938). We therefore reaffirm that it is "emphatically

the province and the duty" of this Court "to say what the law is" with respect to the claim of privilege presented in this case. *Marbury* v. *Madison, supra,* at 177.

B

In support of his claim of absolute privilege, the President's counsel urges two grounds one of which is common to all governments and one of which is peculiar to our system of separation of powers. The first ground is the valid need for protection of communications between high government officials and those who advise and assist them in the performance of their manifold duties; the importance of this confidentiality is too plain to require further discussion. Human experience teaches that those who expect public dissemination of their remarks may well temper candor with a concern for appearances and for their own interests to the detriment of the decisionmaking process.[15] Whatever the nature of the privilege of confidentiality of presidential communications in the exercise of Art. II powers the privilege can be said to derive from the supremacy of each branch within its own assigned area of constitutional duties. Certain powers and privileges flow from the nature of enumerated powers;[16] the protection of the confidentiality of

---

[15] There is nothing novel about governmental confidentiality. The meetings of the Constitutional Convention in 1787 were conducted in complete privacy. 1 Farrand, The Records of the Federal Convention of 1787, xi–xxv (1911). Moreover, all records of those meetings were sealed for more than 30 years after the Convention. See 3 U. S. Stat. At Large, 15th Cong. 1st Sess., Res. 8 (1818). Most of the Framers acknowledged that without secrecy no constitution of the kind that was developed could have been written. Warren, The Making of the Constitution, 134–139 (1937).

[16] The Special Prosecutor argues that there is no provision in the Constitution for a presidential privilege as to the President's communications corresponding to the privilege of Members of Congress

presidential communications has similar constitutional underpinnings.

The second ground asserted by the President's counsel in support of the claim of absolute privilege rests on the doctrine of separation of powers. Here it is argued that the independence of the Executive Branch within its own sphere, *Humphrey's Executor* v. *United States,* 295 U. S. 602, 629–630; *Kilbourn* v. *Thompson,* 103 U. S. 168, 190–191 (1880), insulates a president from a judicial subpoena in an ongoing criminal prosecution, and thereby protects confidential presidential communications.

However, neither the doctrine of separation of powers, nor the need for confidentiality of high level communications, without more, can sustain an absolute, unqualified presidential privilege of immunity from judicial process under all circumstances. The President's need for complete candor and objectivity from advisers calls for great deference from the courts. However, when the privilege depends solely on the broad, undifferentiated claim of public interest in the confidentiality of such conversations, a confrontation with other values arises. Absent a claim of need to protect military, diplomatic or sensitive national security secrets, we find it difficult to accept the argument that even the very important interest in confidentiality of presidential communications is significantly diminished by production of such material for *in camera* inspection with all the protection that a district court will be obliged to provide.

---

under the Speech or Debate Clause. But the silence of the Constitution on this score is not dispositive. "The rule of constitutional interpretation announced in *McCulloch* v. *Maryland,* 4 Wheat. 316, that that which was reasonably appropriate and relevant to the exercise of a granted power was considered as accompanying the grant, has been so universally applied that it suffices merely to state it." *Marshall* v. *Gordon,* 243 U. S. 521, 537 (1917).

The impediment that an absolute, unqualified privilege would place in the way of the primary constitutional duty of the Judicial Branch to do justice in criminal prosecutions would plainly conflict with the function of the courts under Art. III. In designing the structure of our Government and dividing and allocating the sovereign power among three coequal branches, the Framers of the Constitution sought to provide a comprehensive system, but the separate powers were not intended to operate with absolute independence.

> "While the Constitution diffuses power the better to secure liberty, it also contemplates that practice will integrate the dispersed powers into a workable government. It enjoins upon its branches separateness but interdependence, autonomy but reciprocity." *Youngstown Sheet & Tube Co.* v. *Sawyer*, 343 U. S. 579, 635 (1952) (Jackson, J., concurring).

To read the Art. II powers of the President as providing an absolute privilege as against a subpoena essential to enforcement of criminal statutes on no more than a generalized claim of the public interest in confidentiality of nonmilitary and nondiplomatic discussions would upset the constitutional balance of "a workable government" and gravely impair the role of the courts under Art. III.

C

Since we conclude that the legitimate needs of the judicial process may outweigh presidential privilege, it is necessary to resolve those competing interests in a manner that preserves the essential functions of each branch. The right and indeed the duty to resolve that question does not free the judiciary from according high respect to the representations made on behalf of the President. *United States* v. *Burr*, 25 Fed. Cas. 187, 190, 191–192 (No. 14,694) (1807).

The expectation of a President to the confidentiality of his conversations and correspondence, like the claim of confidentiality of judicial deliberations, for example, has all the values to which we accord deference for the privacy of all citizens and added to those values the necessity for protection of the public interest in candid, objective, and even blunt or harsh opinions in presidential decision-making. A President and those who assist him must be free to explore alternatives in the process of shaping policies and making decisions and to do so in a way many would be unwilling to express except privately. These are the considerations justifying a presumptive privilege for presidential communications. The privilege is fundamental to the operation of government and inextricably rooted in the separation of powers under the Constitution.[17] In *Nixon* v. *Sirica*, — U. S. App. D. C. —, 487 F. 2d 700 (1973), the Court of Appeals held that such presidential communications are "presumptively privileged," *id.*, at 717, and this position is accepted by both parties in the present litigation. We agree with Mr. Chief Justice Marshall's observation, therefore, that "in no case of this kind would a court be required to proceed against the President as against an ordinary individual." *United States* v. *Burr*, 25 Fed. Cas. 187, 191 (No. 14,694) (CCD Va. 1807).

But this presumptive privilege must be considered in light of our historic commitment to the rule of law. This

---

[17] "Freedom of communication vital to fulfillment of wholesome relationships is obtained only by removing the specter of compelled disclosure . . . [G]overnment . . . needs open but protected channels for the kind of plain talk that is essential to the quality of its functioning." *Carl Zeiss Stiftung* v. *V. E. B. Carl Zeiss, Jena*, 40 F. R. D. 318, 325 (D. C. 1966). See *Nixon* v. *Sirica*, — U. S. App. D. C. —, — 487 F. 2d 700, 713 (1973); *Kaiser Aluminum & Chem. Corp.* v. *United States*, 157 F. Supp. 939 (Ct. Cl. 1958) (*per* Reed, J.); The Federalist No. 64 (S. F. Mittel ed. 1938).

is nowhere more profoundly manifest than in our view that "the twofold aim [of criminal justice] is that guilt shall not escape or innocence suffer." *Berger* v. *United States*, 295 U. S. 78, 88 (1935). We have elected to employ an adversary system of criminal justice in which the parties contest all issues before a court of law. The need to develop all relevant facts in the adversary system is both fundamental and comprehensive. The ends of criminal justice would be defeated if judgments were to be founded on a partial or speculative presentation of the facts. The very integrity of the judicial system and public confidence in the system depend on full disclosure of all the facts, within the framework of the rules of evidence. To ensure that justice is done, it is imperative to the function of courts that compulsory process be available for the production of evidence needed either by the prosecution or by the defense.

Only recently the Court restated the ancient proposition of law, albeit in the context of a grand jury inquiry rather than a trial,

> " 'that the public . . . has a right to every man's evidence' except for those persons protected by a constitutional, common law, or statutory privilege, *United States* v. *Bryan*, 339 U. S., at 331 (1949); *Blackmer* v. *United States*, 284 U. S. 421, 438. . . ." *Branzburg* v. *United States*, 408 U. S. 665, 688 (1973).

The privileges referred to by the Court are designed to protect weighty and legitimate competing interests. Thus, the Fifth Amendment to the Constitution provides that no man "shall be compelled in any criminal case to be a witness against himself." And, generally, an attorney or a priest may not be required to disclose what has been revealed in professional confidence. These and other interests are recognized in law by privileges against forced disclosure, established in the Constitution, by statute, or at common law. Whatever their origins, these exceptions to the demand for every man's evidence are not lightly created nor expansively construed, for they are in derogation of the search for truth.[18]

In this case the President challenges a subpoena served on him as a third party requiring the production of materials for use in a criminal prosecution on the claim that he has a privilege against disclosure of confidential communications. He does not place his claim of privilege on the ground they are military or diplomatic secrets. As to these areas of Art. II duties the courts have traditionally shown the utmost deference to presidential responsibilities. In *C. & S. Air Lines* v. *Waterman Steamship Corp.*, 333 U. S. 103, 111 (1948), dealing with presidential authority involving foreign policy considerations, the Court said:

> "The President, both as Commander-in-Chief and as the Nation's organ for foreign affairs, has available intelligence services whose reports are not and ought not to be published to the world. It would be intolerable that courts, without the relevant information, should review and perhaps nullify actions of the Executive taken on information properly held secret." *Id.*, at 111.

In *United States* v. *Reynolds*, 345 U. S. 1 (1952), deal-

---

[18] Because of the key role of the testimony of witnesses in the judicial process, courts have historically been cautious about privileges. Justice Frankfurter, dissenting in *Elkins* v. *United States*, 364 U. S. 206, 234 (1960), said of this: "Limitations are properly placed upon the operation of this general principle only to the very limited extent that permitting a refusal to testify or excluding relevant evidence has a public good transcending the normally predominant principle of utilizing all rational means for ascertaining truth."

ing with a claimant's demand for evidence in a damage
case against the Government the Court said:

> "It may be possible to satisfy the court, from all
> the circumstances of the case, that there is a reason-
> able danger that compulsion of the evidence will
> expose military matters which, in the interest of
> national security, should not be divulged. When
> this is the case, the occasion for the privilege is ap-
> propriate, and the court should not jeopardize the
> security which the privilege is meant to protect by
> insisting upon an examination of the evidence, even
> by the judge alone, in chambers."

No case of the Court, however, has extended this high
degree of deference to a President's generalized interest
in confidentiality. Nowhere in the Constitution, as we
have noted earlier, is there any explicit reference to a
privilege of confidentiality, yet to the extent this interest
relates to the effective discharge of a President's powers,
it is constitutionally based.

The right to the production of all evidence at a criminal
trial similarly has constitutional dimensions. The Sixth
Amendment explicitly confers upon every defendant in
a criminal trial the right "to be confronted with the witnesses against him" and "to have compulsory process for
obtaining witnesses in his favor." Moreover, the Fifth
Amendment also guarantees that no person shall be deprived of liberty without due process of law. It is the
manifest duty of the courts to vindicate those guarantees
and to accomplish that it is essential that all relevant
and admissible evidence be produced.

In this case we must weigh the importance of the
general privilege of confidentiality of presidential communications in performance of his responsibilities against
the inroads of such a privilege on the fair administration

of criminal justice.[19] The interest in preserving confidentiality is weighty indeed and entitled to great respect. However we cannot conclude that advisers will be moved to temper the candor of their remarks by the infrequent occasions of disclosure because of the possibility that such conversations will be called for in the context of a criminal prosecution.[20]

On the other hand, the allowance of the privilege to withhold evidence that is demonstrably relevant in a criminal trial would cut deeply into the guarantee of due process of law and gravely impair the basic function of the courts. A President's acknowledged need for con-

---

[19] We are not here concerned with the balance between the President's generalized interest in confidentiality and the need for relevant evidence in civil litigation, nor with that between the confidentiality interest and congressional demands for information, nor with the President's interest in preserving state secrets. We address only the conflict between the President's assertion of a generalized privilege of confidentiality against the constitutional need for relevant evidence in criminal trials.

[20] Mr. Justice Cardozo made this point in an analogous context. Speaking for a unanimous Court in *Clark* v. *United States,* 289 U. S. 1 (1933), he emphasized the importance of maintaining the secrecy of the deliberations of a petit jury in a criminal case. "Freedom of debate might be stifled and independence of thought checked if jurors were made to feel that their arguments and ballots were to be freely published in the world." *Id.,* at 13. Nonetheless, the Court also recognized that isolated inroads on confidentiality designed to serve the paramount need of the criminal law would not vitiate the interests served by secrecy:

"A juror of integrity and reasonable firmness will not fear to speak his mind if the confidences of debate bar barred to the ears of mere impertinence or malice. He will not expect to be shielded against the disclosure of his conduct in the event that there is evidence reflecting upon his honor. The chance that now and then there may be found some timid soul who will take counsel of his fears and give way to their repressive power is too remote and shadowy to shape the course of justice." *Id.,* at 16.

fidentiality in the communications of his office is general in nature, whereas the constitutional need for production of relevant evidence in a criminal proceeding is specific and central to the fair adjudication of a particular criminal case in the administration of justice. Without access to specific facts a criminal prosecution may be totally frustrated. The President's broad interest in confidentiality of communications will not be vitiated by disclosure of a limited number of conversations preliminarily shown to have some bearing on the pending criminal cases.

We conclude that when the ground for asserting privilege as to subpoenaed materials sought for use in a criminal trial is based only on the generalized interest in confidentiality, it cannot prevail over the fundamental demands of due process of law in the fair administration of criminal justice. The generalized assertion of privilege must yield to the demonstrated, specific need for evidence in a pending criminal trial.

D

We have earlier determined that the District Court did not err in authorizing the issuance of the subpoena. If a President concludes that compliance with a subpoena would be injurious to the public interest he may properly, as was done here, invoke a claim of privilege on the return of the subpoena. Upon receiving a claim of privilege from the Chief Executive, it became the further duty of the District Court to treat the subpoenaed material as presumptively privileged and to require the Special Prosecutor to demonstrate that the presidential material was "essential to the justice of the [pending criminal] case." *United States* v. *Burr, supra,* at 192. Here the District Court treated the material as presumptively privileged, proceeded to find that the Special Prosecutor had made a sufficient showing to rebut the

presumption and ordered an *in camera* examination of
the subpoenaed material. On the basis of our examination of the record we are unable to conclude that the
District Court erred in ordering the inspection. Accordingly we affirm the order of the District Court that subpoenaed materials be transmitted to that court. We now
turn to the important question of the District Court's
responsibilities in conducting the *in camera* examination
of presidential materials or communications delivered
under the compulsion of the subpoena *duces tecum*.

E

Enforcement of the subpoena *duces tecum* was stayed
pending this Court's resolution of the issues raised by the
petitions for certiorari. Those issues now having been
disposed of, the matter of implementation will rest with
the District Court. "[T]he guard, furnished to [the
President] to protect him from being harassed by vexa-
tious and unnecessary subpoenas, is to be looked for in the
conduct of the [district] court after the subpoenas have
issued; not in any circumstances which is to precede their
being issued." *United States* v. *Burr, supra*, at 34. Statements that meet the test of admissibility and relevance
must be isolated; all other material must be excised. At
this stage the District Court is not limited to representations of the Special Prosecutor as to the evidence sought
by the subpoena; the material will be available to the
District Court. It is elementary that *in camera* inspection of evidence is always a procedure calling for scrupulous protection against any release or publication of
material not found by the court, at that stage, probably
admissible in evidence and relevant to the issues of the
trial for which it is sought. That being true of an ordinary situation, it is obvious that the District Court has
a very heavy responsibility to see to it that presidential

conversations, which are either not relevant or not admissible, are accorded that high degree of respect due the President of the United States. Mr. Chief Justice Marshall sitting as a trial judge in the *Burr* case, *supra,* was extraordinarily careful to point out that:

> "[I]n no case of this kind would a Court be required to proceed against the President as against an ordinary individual." *United States* v. *Burr,* 25 Fed. Cases 187, 191 (No. 14,694).

Marshall's statement cannot be read to mean in any sense that a President is above the law, but relates to the singularly unique role under Art. II of a President's communications and activities, related to the performance of duties under that Article. Moreover, a President's communications and activities encompass a vastly wider range of sensitive material than would be true of any "ordinary individual." It is therefore necessary [21] in the public interest to afford presidential confidentiality the greatest protection consistent with the fair administration of justice. The need for confidentiality even as to idle conversations with associates in which casual reference might be made concerning political leaders within the country or foreign statesmen is too obvious to call for further treatment. We have no doubt that the District Judge will at all times accord to presidential records that high degree of deference suggested in *United States* v. *Burr, supra,* and will discharge his responsibility to see to it that until released to the Special Prosecutor no *in camera* material is revealed to anyone. This burden

---

[21] When the subpoenaed material is delivered to the District Judge *in camera* questions may arise as to the excising of parts and it lies within the discretion of that court to seek the aid of the Special Prosecutor and the President's counsel for *in camera* consideration of the validity of particular excisions, whether the basis of excision is relevancy or admissibility or under such cases as *Reynolds, supra,* or *Waterman Steamship, supra.*

applies with even greater force to excised material; once the decision is made to excise, the material is restored to its privileged status and should be returned under seal to its lawful custodian.

Since this matter came before the Court during the pendency of a criminal prosecution, and on representations that time is of the essence, the mandate shall issue forthwith.

Affirmed.

MR. JUSTICE REHNQUIST took no part in the consideration or decision of these cases.

Appendix IX

PRESS RELEASES: THE CONGRESS

Members of the Senate and of the House normally issue press releases through their press aides. The subject is usually one that is relevant to the particular interests of the member or one that relates to a committee on which the member serves. Included here are examples of information released to the media by various members of the Congress.

News from the

Subcommittee on Communications

HOUSE INTERSTATE AND FOREIGN COMMERCE COMMITTEE

LIONEL VAN DEERLIN, Chairman

B-331 RAYBURN HOUSE OFFICE BUILDING
WASHINGTON, D.C. 20515   202—225-9304

FOR RELEASE: IMMEDIATE -- October 11, 1976

"BASEMENT TO ATTIC" REVAMPING OF COMMUNICATIONS ACT
ORDERED BY HOUSE SUBCOMMITTEE ON COMMUNICATIONS

A "basement to attic" revamping of the 1934 Federal
Communications Act -- statutory basis for the regulation of
most telecommunications systems including radio and television
-- has been ordered for consideration by the next Congress.

Chairman Lionel Van Deerlin, D-Calif., and Representative
Lou Frey, R-Fla., ranking minority member of the House
Subcommittee on Communications, joined in the decision to seek
the widest possible input of information and opinion in drafting
legislative options for the Subcommittee.

Van Deerlin called the original act out of date. When
it was written more than 40 years ago, he noted, radio provided
the only mass medium of electronic communication.

"Television was still in its infancy, and such new
technologies as coaxial cable, microwave, satellites and laser
beams were virtually unknown," he said.

Frey agreed, adding that the choice for a solution lay
between "the bandaid treatment" or a more fundamental revision
of the basic law.

The 1934 Act actually represented a joining of the Interstate Commerce Act of 1887 -- designed for the regulation of railroads -- and the Radio Act of 1927, which was drafted to systematize the licensing of radio stations.

It was the 1934 Act that established the Federal Communications Commission, with regulatory authority over broadcasting, the telephone industry and other early branches of communication. The law has remained virtually intact despite the technological revolution of recent years.

With legislation pending on cable rules, broadcast license renewal, First Amendment issues, pay TV and competition in the telephone industry, Van Deerlin and Frey said: "We view these as separate parts of our more central problem -- assuring American consumers the best and most efficient access to modern communications technology.

"We need to go back and take a look at the whole basis of regulation, and see where Congress could improve things by starting anew."

* * * * * *

senator charles h.
PERCY

ILLINOIS

FOR IMMEDIATE RELEASE

THURSDAY, DECEMBER 1, 1977

CONTACT: JOHN WALKER

(202) 224-7925

PERCY SAYS FDA WARNING ON LIQUID
PROTEIN IS INADEQUATE

WASHINGTON--- Senator Charles H. Percy (R-Ill.) said today that a proposed FDA warning label action issued today telling consumers that diet liquid protein may cause serious illness or death is inadequate and insufficient to protect the lives of liquid protein users.

"I consider the FDA announcement requiring warning labels on diet liquid protein a wholly inadequate response to a potentially lethal health problem," Percy said. "It is an affront to consumers to ask them to consult with a physician before using diet liquid protein when those <u>were</u> the precise instructions followed by at least 10 of the persons whose reported deaths may be linked to the liquid protein fast."

Percy said last week that the FDA should order diet liquid protein products off the shelves because of their possible link to deaths of liquid protein users.

"My office has now been notified by the Center for Disease Control (CDC), in Atlanta, of 31 deaths which may be associated with use of the liquid protein diet. The CDC reports that one was a 45-year-old Washington, D.C., man who died within the last several days after being on the diet for three months. That was five more deaths than we were aware of last week," Percy said.

"How many more people must die before the FDA orders the product off the market pending proof of its safety?"

Percy said six physicians who specialize in nutrition have expressed to him their concerns about the easy availability of diet liquid protein for quick weight loss.

"One doctor said that there are such significant risks in the liquid protein diet that he would never give it to an outpatient," Percy said.

The proposed FDA warning would read as follows:

> WARNING--Very low calorie protein diets may cause serious illness or death. DO NOT USE FOR WEIGHT REDUCTION OR MAINTENANCE WITHOUT MEDICAL SUPERVISION. Do not use for any purpose without medical advice if you are taking medication. Not for use by infants, children, or pregnant or nursing women.

#######

MUSKIE *News*

RUSSELL OFFICE BUILDING • WASHINGTON, D.C. 20510 • TELEPHONE (202) 224-5344

CONTACT: Bob Rose

For Immediate Release
June 28, 1977

GOVERNMENTAL AFFAIRS COMMITTEE APPROVES SUNSET BILL

The Senate Governmental Affairs Committee Tuesday approved and sent to the full Senate Sen. Edmund S. Muskie's "sunset" bill to force a comprehensive review of virtually every federal program within three terms of Congress.

Under sunset, virtually every federal program, agency and department would come up for review on a specified timetable. Exempted are retirement programs like social security and Medicare to which people contribute, expecting later payment. Programs with similar purposes would be reviewed together, with an eye toward eliminating duplication.

The "sunset" bill was so named because programs which did not pass a congressional review and receive specific reapproval would automatically go out of business.

"With more than 1,000 federal programs, the federal structure has become so large that no comprehensive list of federal programs even existed before we began work on this bill," Muskie said in a statement. "Sunset is designed to force Congress to take a comprehensive look at these programs, and decide which ones we can do without, which we can consolidate, and which we can make more effective. It is a good legislative complement to President Carter's zero-base budgeting, and I believe it is the only way to approach the massive job of making government less complex, more understandable, and more responsive to the needs and attitudes of the average taxpayer."

The bill approved by the Governmental Affairs Committee differs in several respects from sunset legislation approved late in the last session of Congress:

1) It sets a six-year timetable (rather than five years) for reviewing the federal establishment. The change allows the task to be approached within the context of two-year Congressional terms.

2) The bill adopts a new procedure for automatically ending unwanted programs, to assure that no substantive law is unintentionally repealed by the termination.

3) The bill contains new procedures for Congress to follow in determining which program areas should be studied most closely and comprehensively, thus allowing Congress to establish priorities for the review process.

4) Safeguards are included to ensure that programs are not terminated due to such problems as scheduling difficulties for a particular bill in Congress.

5) The Committee voted to exclude tax expenditures (losses to the Treasury as a result of various provisions of the tax code) from the "sunset" process.

6) A provision was included to assure the traditional independence of the Federal judiciary.

#   #   #

Appendix X

PRESS RELEASES: BRANCHES AND AGENCIES

Literally thousands of press releases are issued by the multiplicity of government departments, branches and agencies. Examples included here are from the Departments of Justice and Commerce and Health, Education and Welfare.

UNITED STATES DEPARTMENT OF
COMMERCE
NEWS
WASHINGTON, D.C. 20230

OFFICE
OF THE
SECRETARY

G 77-245

FOR RELEASE: WEDNESDAY,
DECEMBER 28, 1977

Denis Johnston
(202) 673-7953

COMMERCE DEPARTMENT RELEAS
A DETAILED LOOK AT AMERICA
QUALITY OF LIFE

A fresh, comprehensive look at the quality of American life was

presented today by the Department of Commerce with the release of Social

Indicators 1976.

"Publication of such a diverse group of important statistics reflects
our continuing concern for the broadly-defined well-being of Americans,
not just the economic facts which you hear about so often," said Secretary
of Commerce Juanita M. Kreps.

Social Indicators 1976 contains indicators of the quality of health,
education, housing, and family life as well as the more widely reported
income and population data. This compendium of government and privately
collected statistics contains breakdowns of many of these indicators by
income, race, and sex, and provides a look at their changes over time, as
well as international comparisons.

The new publication represents a continuation and expansion of Social
Indicators 1973, which was a landmark presentation of measures of social
change in a format similar to that used traditionally for economic indicators.

"Improving the quality of life in America, and individuals' satisfaction
with it, is a goal with which all Americans can identify," Secretary Kreps said
"This volume gives us another tool to help gauge our progress--or lack of it--
toward achieving that goal.

"The indicators of improvements in basic aspects of Americans' lives,
such as good health and long life, income sufficient to maintain a decent
standard of living, access to medical care, educational opportunity,
adequate housing, and the opportunity to work at a satisfying job, are in
many ways easier for the average person to appreciate than are the sometimes
mysterious movements of economic indicators to which we economists pay so
much attention," Mrs. Kreps continued.

"The release of <u>Social Indicators 1976</u> provides an opportunity for us to step back from the daily economic statistics and concentrate on some direct indicators of social conditions which really matter to the public."

<u>Social Indicators 1976</u> was prepared by the Commerce Department's Office of Federal Statistical Policy and Standards, with editorial and technical support provided by the Bureau of the Census. It is a product of the Federal Statistical System, with the bulk of the data supplied by an Interagency Committee on Social Indicators, chaired by Denis F. Johnston.

As part of a new social indicators program now in its early stages at the Census Bureau, similar data will continue to be published periodically. This new program also will attempt to analyze systematically some of the wealth of social data which are now scattered among various parts of the Federal government and other organizations. "The objective of this program," Secretary Kreps explained, "is to develop a more comprehensive and current socio-economic profile of American families and communities."

The volume contains a minimum of interpretation or analysis. It is basically a book of statistical charts and tables. It is designed primarily to depict trends over fairly long periods of time, but because of the length of time required for its preparation, the volume does not contain the latest data on all subjects.

Copies may be obtained for $7.00 each from the Superintendent of Documents, U.S. Government Printing Office, Washington, D.C. 20402, or from Department of Commerce District Offices in major U.S. cities.

UNITED STATES DEPARTMENT OF JUSTICE

Law Enforcement Assistance Administration

Public Information Office
Telephone (202) 376-3820

Washington, D.C. 20531

ADVANCE FOR RELEASE AT 6:30 P.M., EST
SUNDAY, DECEMBER 4, 1977

An LEAA News Feature

Women generally perform as well as men in police patrol work although there are some small differences, according to a report released today.

The seven-month study, financed by the Law Enforcement Assistance Administration (LEAA) and conducted in New York City, examined 82 patrol officers -- an equal number of men and women.

It noted that the performance of policewomen is more like that of policemen than it is different although the women made a better impression on the public.

Citizens who encountered the women officers said they were more competent, pleasant, and respectful than the men and "their performance seems to have created a better civilian regard" for the police department.

The study found that the women were less likely than men to join male partners in taking control of a situation or jointly making a decision. They were slightly less physically agile in such things as climbing ladders or steep stairs.

However, when the women patrolled with other women, their behavior differed: they were more active, assertive, and self-sufficient.

The report recommended assertiveness training and assigning new officers to work with more experienced women.

James M. H. Gregg, acting LEAA administrator, said the $155,000 study was conducted in 1975 and 1976 by the Vera Institut of Justice in cooperation with the New York City Police Department.

"This report is another important step forward in creating equal opportunities for women in law enforcement," Mr. Gregg said. "Today's police patrolwomen are pioneering in what has always been a man's world, and there are obstacles to be overcome. This report makes clear that they are being overcome."

The report said one of an officer's most important functions is taking control -- by explaining something to a citizen, or using eye contact, beckoning, or ordering, or by frisking, searching, or making an arrest.

The study indicated that skepticism by male officers may partly explain female officers' reluctance to take control of a situation with her male counterpart.

One woman officer told the researchers: "What am I supposed to do? When we respond to a job, my partner tells me to stand back and not get in the way because this is his sector and I don't know it anyway."

A male officer said: "The girls are okay on the service jobs, but when something heavy happens, I want her out of the way. Otherwise, I just have another person to worry about."

However, in the few incidents judged to present danger, men and women were equally likely to engage in efforts to gain control. In their choice of techniques, women were neither more nor less likely than the men to use force, display a weapon, or rely on a direct order.

The study said the patrolwomen took more sick leave than the patrolmen. This was consistent with earlier research showing that, in general, women are absent from work more frequently than men. The reasons, according to the report, were unclear -- women may be more prone to illness, may be sick longer, or may be more likely to stay away from work when family members become ill.

The report suggested that some differences in the styles of women officers may be attributed to low morale during the period of layoffs that decimated the ranks of New York City policewomen. Eight women officers assigned to a high-morale district -- Brooklyn's 77th Precinct -- performed more like men officers than the other women in the study. They made twice as many arrests as women studied in other precincts and issued more parking tickets than men in the study.

The report principally attributed the "small but consistent" differences to socially conditioned attitudes -- protectiveness or disdain by men and passivity by women. To counteract such behavior, the report recommended that law enforcement agencies train both supervisory personnel at precincts and patrolmen to develop a more accepting attitude toward women in patrol ranks.

"The results offer little support either to those who hold that women are unsuited to patrol or to those who argue that women do the job better than men. By and large, patrol performance of the women was more like that of the men than it was different," the study said.

The study was based on direct observation of 3,625 hours of patrol and 2,400 police-civilian encounters. It analyzed the types of action required of the officers, their style of patrol, their methods of gaining control, their initiative, physical strength, and the reactions of the public.

A limited number of copies of the report, "Women on Patrol: A Pilot Study of Police Performance in New York City," are available free from the LEAA's National Criminal Justice Reference Service, Box 6000, Rockville, Maryland 20850.

\# \# \# \#

UNITED STATES DEPARTMENT OF

COMMERCE

NEWS

WASHINGTON, D.C. 20230

OFFICE
OF THE
SECRETARY

THOUSANDS OF FACTS ABOUT AMERICAN LIFE IN THE 1970s CONTAINED

IN COMMERCE DEPARTMENT'S SOCIAL INDICATORS 1976

Here are highlights from each chapter of Social Indicators 1976, a new guide to the quality of life in the U.S., published today by the Department of Commerce:

1. POPULATION: If population growth continues at its recent rate of about 0.7 percent per year, the U.S. population would be 262 million by the year 2000. This assumes that American women on average would have 2.1 children.

o After years of decline following the "baby boom" years after World War II, the annual number of births in the U.S. in the 1980's is expected to increase slowly.

o The population is getting older. In 1940, only 7.1 percent of all Americans were 65 years of age or over. In 1970 that percentage had grown to 10.3 percent and by 2000 it is expected to be 12.2 percent. The proportion of the population under 20 years of age is expected to decline to 30 percent in 2000 from the 1970 level of 38 percent.

o The recent population growth rate in the United States of 0.7 percent compares with a worldwide average of 1.9 percent per year from 1970 to 1974.

2. THE FAMILY: The average size of the American family is declining. After reaching a peak of 3.7 persons about 1965, the average family size dropped to 3.4 persons in 1975 and is expected to reach 3.0 by 1990.

o The number of families headed by a woman has been increasing steadily. By 1975, about 36 percent of black families were headed by women, compared with almost 11 percent of white families.

o The growing number of divorces and annulments reflects increased family instability. Between 1953 and 1974, the annual number of divorces and annulments rose 250 percent and the number of children involved increased by 333 percent.

3. <u>HOUSING</u>: The proportion of housing units with all plumbing facilities has increased from 55.4 percent in 1940 to 96.8 percent in 1974.

o The percentage of households with one or more persons per room was 20.3 in 1940 compared with 5.3 in 1974.

o An overwhelming majority--82.1 percent-- of U.S. residents in 1974 believed their neighborhoods to be good or excellent places in which to live.

4. <u>SOCIAL SECURITY AND WELFARE</u>: Public and private expenditures for social programs (income maintenance, health, education, and welfare) increased from 13.4 percent of the gross national product (GNP) in 1950 to 27.3 percent in 1975.

o The growing importance of Social Security and social insurance benefits can be seen in the increase in the number of beneficiaries from 3.5 million in 1950 to 32.1 million in 1975, an increase from 2.3 percent of the population to 15 percent.

5. <u>HEALTH AND NUTRITION</u>: The gap between male and female life expectancy has continued to widen. An average female infant born in 1974 can be expected to live to age 76, almost 8 years longer than a male infant. In 1900, both had much lower life expectancies, but the difference was only 2 years.

o Per capita health care expenditures increased from $91 in 1955 to about $476 in 1975.

o Even though it has declined in recent years, the U.S. infant mortality rate is still higher than that of several other nations. The U.S. rate dropped from 24.7 per 1000 live births in 1965 to 16.7 per 1000 in 1974. The rate in Finland is about 12 per 1000, in Japan 11.3 and in Sweden 9.9.

o While the average American consumed 161 pounds of meat in 1960, this had risen to 187.5 pounds in 1974. However, per capita consumption of dairy products dropped from 430.2 pounds in 1960 to 345 pounds by 1974.

6. <u>PUBLIC SAFETY</u>: Between 1960 and 1975, the rate of violent crimes against persons tripled, while the much higher rate for property crimes went up 280 percent.

o In general, males are about twice as likely as females to become victims of violent crimes. About a third of all personal crimes of violence involve persons known to the victims.

o In comparison with other nations, the U. S. ranks among the lowest in the rate of deaths attributable to most kinds of accidents (falls, drowning, fire, etc.), but is by far the highest in the rate of death from homicide, and has an above-average rate from transportation accidents.

7. TRAINING AND EDUCATION: While the trend toward completing more years of schooling continues, information on actual achievemen as revealed by tests is less optimistic. A set of standardized tes taken by a sample of the adult population shows that nearly 20 percent demonstrated severely limited "functional competence" in a variety of fields, while 46 percent were judged to be proficient an a third were able to function with minimal adequacy.

o The number of high school dropouts recently has been higher than the average for the past few decades. Over one-fourth of the students entering the fifth grade in 1966 did not graduate from high school eight years later in 1974.

o Participation by adults in continuing educational programs and training courses reached a level of 17.1 million in 1975, compared with 15.8 million in 1972 and 13 million in 1969.

8. WORK: With more women entering the labor force and shifts in the age distribution of the population, the ratio of non-workers (all ages) to workers has dropped from a peak of 1.51 to one in 196 to 1.23 in 1975; the ratio is expected to fall further in the futur

o Female labor force participation had risen to 46 percen by 1975, and the rate for married women was nearly as high.

o The kinds of jobs people hold shifted between 1960 and 1975. Significant increases occurred in the proportion of workers employed in professional-technical, clerical-sales, and service occupations; corresponding declines were concentrated among semi-skilled and farm workers.

o The reasons cited by unemployed persons for their lack of a job vary somewhat by sex and also over time. About 75 percent of unemployed men had lost their last jobs, according to 1975 surveys, while 50 percent of the women had lost jobs and the other 50 percent had quit the previous job or were entering (or reentering the labor force. Reflecting the recession, the percent of all unemployed who had lost their previous jobs was higher in 1975 than at any time since the survey began in 1967. (This percentage has declined since 1975.)

o The average length of the expected working life for a 20 year old male dropped by 1.6 years between 1950 and 1970. The average expected length of his retirement went up during the same period from 5.8 to 8.1 years.

9. INCOME, WEALTH AND EXPENDITURES: The median income of all families, after adjustment for inflation, in the 1970s has been nearly double that of the late 1940s. For minority groups, it was nearly 2.4 times as large.

o In 1974, nearly half of low-income families were headed by women, compared with 23 percent in 1959.

o Government transfer payments, such as social insurance and various kinds of monetary welfare payments, significantly reduce the number of families and individuals considered to have incomes below poverty level, which in 1976 was defined as income below $5815 for a family of four. A Congressional study of poverty in fiscal 1976 showed that, without transfer payments, 25.5 percent of all families would fall below poverty income, while with the payments the total was 11.4 percent. (These figures were later revised to 27 percent and 13.5 percent, respectively.)

o The proportions of the average American's after-tax income spent on food and clothing dropped significantly between 1946 and 1974. Food expenditures totaled 32.3 percent of personal income in 1946 and only 21.2 percent in 1974; clothing took 15.3 percent in 1946 and 9.4 percent in 1974. In contrast, housing, the second largest expenditure category, rose from 21.7 percent to 27.8 percent of disposable income in the same period. Relative spending on transportation and medical care both rose even faster.

10. CULTURE, LEISURE, AND USE OF TIME: The amount of leisure time available to Americans went up 11 percent between 1965 and 1975, while the amount of time devoted to family care declined nearly 25 percent and time spent on "work for pay" changed little.

o Watching television is the favorite leisure activity of 46 percent of Americans, compared with 28 percent in 1960.

o Horseracing in 1974 remained the most-attended professional sport. From 1950 to 1974, attendance figures for professional baseball, football, horseracing, and greyhound racing rose from 95 million to 133 million or a 142 percent increase. In the same period, the U.S. population rose 39 percent.

11. SOCIAL MOBILITY AND PARTICIPATION: The pace of increases in adult men's educational attainment over that of their fathers' has slackened in recent years. Men born around 1900 had 2 more years of education than their fathers; those born around 1925 had 2.5 years more schooling than their fathers; and men born around 1950 attained 2.1 years more of education.

The peak year for participation by the voting age population in Federal elections was 1960 when 63 percent voted. That figure fell to 55 percent in 1972.

The number of people over 14 years old who reported doing volunteer work grew by 50 percent between 1965 and 1974--from 24.3 million to 36.8 million.

#

U.S. DEPARTMENT OF HEALTH, EDUCATION, AND WELFARE

FOR IMMEDIATE RELEASE
Tuesday, November 22, 1977

PARENT--(202) 245-6343

HEW Secretary Joseph A. Califano, Jr., has asked Social Security Commissioner James B. Cardwell to head a Departmental Task Force to "gather facts, views and ideas on the treatment of women under Social Security."

In a memorandum, dated November 17, Secretary Califano spelled out the areas of special concern that should be addressed by the Task Force. They include:

> --the treatment of married women who do not work in paid
> employment;
>
> --the treatment of single workers;
>
> --protection for divorced women;
>
> --effect of remarriage on widows' benefits; and
>
> --equity for individual workers versus protection for
> families.

In his memo, Secretary Califano noted that the roles of women and society's recognition of those roles have changed dramatically in recent years. "This is particularly evident in the increasing number of women who participate in the labor force and who bear the responsibilities, either alone or jointly, as heads of households," he said. "In light of these changes I want to be sure that women are treated fairly under the social security program."

A Task Force report must be ready for submission to the upcoming Advisory Council on Social Security no later than February 1, 1978. In addition the report will be made available to Members of Congress and concerned individuals and groups.

Members of the Task Force include: Nancy Amidei, Deputy Assistant Secretary for Welfare Legislation; Richard Beattie, Deputy General Counsel; Connie Downey, Director, Women's Action Program, Office of the Assistant Secretary for Planning and Evaluation; Sarah Juni, Director, Office of Intergovernmental Relations and Public Concerns, Social Security Administration; David Koitz, Office of the Assistant Secretary for Management and Budget; Laura Miller, Special Assistant to the Secretary; Virginia Reno, Office of Research and Statistics, Social Security Administration; and Lawrence Thompson, Office of the Assistant Secretary for Planning and Evaluation.

# # #

Index

353

THE
INFORMATION
ESTABLISHMENT